THE PEOPLE'S RACE INC.

Behind the Scenes at the Honolulu Marathon

Michael S. K. N. Tsai

A Latitude 20 Book
University of Hawai'i Press
Honolulu

21 20 19 18 17 16   6 5 4 3 2 1

Library of Congress Cataloging-in-Publication Data

Names: Tsai, Michael S. K. N., author.
Title: The people's race inc. : behind the scenes at the
Honolulu Marathon / Michael S.K.N. Tsai.
Description: Honolulu : University of Hawai'i Press, [2016] |
"A latitude 20 book." | Includes bibliographical references and index.
Identifiers: LCCN 2016022201 | ISBN 9780824866747
(pbk. ; alk. paper)
Subjects: LCSH: Honolulu Marathon—History.
Classification: LCC GV1065.22 .T73 2016 | DDC 796.42/520996931—
dc23 LC record available at https://lccn.loc.gov/2016022201

University of Hawai'i Press books are printed on acid-free
paper and meet the guidelines for permanence and
durability of the Council on Library Resources.

Contents

PART I

THE PEOPLE'S RACE

CHAPTER 1

A Good Day for a Marathon

The countdown to the 1992 Honolulu Marathon was hardly a countdown at all. Race organizers, having watched larger and larger fields of adrenaline-primed runners amassing behind the starting line each year, had long dispensed with the traditional 5–4–3–2–1, which only intensified the jostling amid runners once the starter's gun fired. Instead, an announcer simply called out the minutes—"Five minutes to start time. . . ." "Four minutes. . . ." "Three. . . ."

As usual, start-line coordinator Rick Taniguchi stood on the other side of the line, watching the crowd and clearing space for the dozen or so elite runners who would take their places at the front just before the starting gun. This time, however, Taniguchi was staring at the largest field in the race's then-twenty-year history. It was his job to ensure a safe start, a job he had always executed with fierce purpose. Once, a Japanese photographer set up a ladder near the start to get a better angle on the 100-yard herd of runners as they headed out. Taniguchi barked at him to move the ladder to the other side of the barricade, and then turned to other business. When he turned back, and saw the photographer and his ladder still in the same spot, Taniguchi cowed him with a glare, grabbed the ladder, and flung it over the barricade himself. Fearing he might be next, the photographer wisely departed. There was no such obvious transgression this year, but Taniguchi still stalked the starting area, eyes alert to the faintest hint of individual impulsiveness or crowd unruliness.

Thirty yards down the course, photographers and videographers reverse-straddled rumbling Harley-Davidsons, back to back with leather-clad volunteer drivers, trying to find a comfortable position for the 26.2-mile ride. Beyond them, Honolulu Marathon Association (HMA) president Jim Barahal sat in the bed of one of the pace trucks with road-race commentator Toni Reavis and reporters from both the two local daily newspapers and the Associated Press. In the other pace truck sat race director Jonathan Cross, Barahal's best friend and co-conspirator. In the six years since they had taken control of the marathon association, the race had enjoyed unprecedented success in raising participation numbers and recruiting up-and-coming African runners who were revolutionizing the sport. By embracing foreign sponsorship, and the prize money and appearance fees it made possible, the two friends had put the Honolulu Marathon in position to compete with the top marathons in the world. If this overall field, more than twice as large as the previous year's, could make it along the freshly redesigned course to the finish line without incident, and if one of the elite recruited athletes could approach or even break the course record, the vision Barahal and Cross began pursuing in the face of stern resistance years earlier would be realized.

The countdown that was not really a countdown ended with sixty seconds to go, as a human voice frayed to incomprehensibility by microphone distortion and loudspeaker crackle announced *"One minute. . . ."* An eager few in an already perspiring mass of already perspiring humanity started up a countdown of their own that fell into confused syncopation and then awkward silence. Finally, an unseen starter's pistol fired somewhere in the distance, and was met by a rising cheer from the thousands of spectators outside the barricades. The abruptly freed sea of runners shuffled slowly forward as the first round of fireworks exploded above the ocean.

With reliable microchip timing systems still a decade away, there was no telling exactly how many of the record 30,905 people who entered the 1992 Honolulu Marathon actually showed up on race day. But it took nearly fifteen minutes for those who had humbly self-seeded themselves at the back of the field to reach the starting line. By that time the lead runners—Simon Robert Naali of Tanzania, David Tsebe of South Africa, and Cosmas Ndeti, Zablon Miano, and Benson Masya of Kenya—had already sped through the downtown area, reversed course, and passed Honolulu Hale on the approach to the 5K mark. Conditions were characteristically warm and humid even at that early hour, but the leaders pushed the pace, soon rendering designated "rabbit" Mark Curp of Missouri unnecessary. Naali, Tsebe, and Miano broke from the pack early, reaching the 10K mark in just 30 minutes and 7 seconds—a minute faster than anyone had finished a

10K run in the state that year.[1] There was ample motivation: a $10,000 bonus for breaking the course record of 2:11:43 set six years earlier by Kenyan runner Ibrahim Hussein.

Led by the two pace trucks and attended by a phalanx of police escorts and volunteers on bicycles, the lead pack sped along Kapiʻolani Boulevard, continuing down Piʻikoi Avenue and turning on to Ala Moana Boulevard to reach Kalākaua Avenue, the main corridor through Waikīkī. As the leaders approached, hundreds of volunteers from high school athletic programs, civic clubs, and other community organizations snapped to attention, offering cups of water and sports drinks, wet sponges, and shouts of encouragement. Their cheers were almost drowned out by the cries of *"Gambatte!"* from the thousands of Japanese onlookers—some friends and family of the 18,286 entrants from Japan, some junior employees of the race's Japanese sponsors who had flown at their own expense to help with the race and make a good impression on their employers.

Naali pulled away after the eighth mile, at one point leading the pack by forty-five seconds. But as temperatures rose along the eleven punishing out-and-back miles of Kalanianaʻole Highway in East Honolulu, he couldn't keep his advantage. The sun was just rising when Masya, Ndeti, and Tsebe caught and passed the wilting Naali on the return trip down the highway, making it a three-way race as they turned onto Kealaʻolu Avenue in Kāhala for the final four-mile kick to the finish line at Kapiʻolani Park. Tsebe had the fastest marathon time of that year—a 2:08:07 finish in Berlin three months earlier—but he was next to fade, leaving Masya, the defending champion, in a race against the up-and-coming Ndeti, a gifted 20,000-meter runner attempting his first marathon. They ran stride for stride until Mile 24, when Ndeti finally fell back by a few seconds. Masya, who later revealed that he had been running with an injured knee, won the race in 2:14:19— too slow to earn the bonus for setting a record, but fast enough to secure the $10,000 winner's purse.[2] Ndeti arrived eight seconds later, earning $5,000 in prize money. Tsebe finished third at 2:16:35 and earned $2,500. On the women's side, Carla Beurskens (2:32:13) of the Netherlands won her sixth Honolulu Marathon at the age of forty, easily dispatching two-time Chicago winner Lisa Weidenbach (2:38:51).

Participants taking full advantage of the marathon's refusal to set a time limit for completing the race would cross the finish line for the next nine hours. The open-finish policy had been established early on, in keeping with founder Jack Scaff's desire to serve recreational runners of all levels. It had

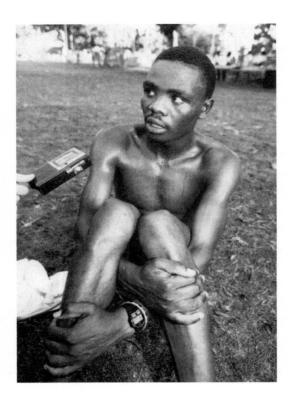

Benson Masya's 2:14:19 victory capped a day of vindication for Honolulu Marathon officials. Photo by Dennis Oda. Courtesy of the *Honolulu Star-Advertiser.*

continued through the most recent transfer of power, largely because it proved to be an attractive selling point to the skyrocketing number of Japanese participants, many of them first-time marathoners. With the largest field in history, the successful introduction of the redesigned course, and stirring defenses by the men's and women's champions against an elite set of challengers, all primed for greatness on the international racing stage, the Honolulu Marathon had good reason to celebrate its twentieth anniversary. For HMA president Barahal, race director Cross, and a coterie of behind-the-scenes marathon association stalwarts such as Taniguchi, Ronald and Jeanette Chun, and former Olympian Tommy Kono, the '92 race could well have been called the Great I-Told-You-So Marathon. Just eight years before, Barahal and Cross had staged a daring takeover, effectively driving out an old guard of volunteer directors who resisted the proliferation of corporate title sponsorship, prize money, and appearance fees that was transforming the modern marathon.

Under Barahal, the marathon had eagerly accepted sponsorship over-
tures from Japanese advertising giant ADK (formerly Asatsu) on behalf of
Japan Airlines that previous HMA boards had for years rejected. The part-
nership reaped immediate benefits, granting the marathon unique access to
a previously untapped Japanese market looking for events in a Japanese-
friendly environment, and thereby allowing a relatively small community
race, founded on the principles of health and community participation, to
survive and thrive in the age of the corporately backed Super Marathon.
The 1992 race marked the first time the Honolulu Marathon surpassed the
30,000-runner mark, more than doubling the previous record of 14,605
entrants set just a year before, and also making the marathon the second-
largest in the world. The dramatic increase was partially due to the burgeoning number of Japanese entrants (18,286, compared to 10,236 in
1991) brought in by Japan Airlines (JAL) and its subsidiary tour company
JALPAK, and partially due to a spike in local entries spurred by a $2 early-
entry promotion for Hawai‘i runners that itself was a response to JAL's requests for greater local participation for the twentieth anniversary. Over the
next five years, the Honolulu Marathon would average 32,253 entries, with
Japanese entrants (19,649 on average) accounting for 61 percent of the total. For a time, it was popular to note that the marathon attracted more
visitors to Hawai‘i than any of the large meetings for which the $200 mil-
lion Hawai‘i Convention Center had been constructed. The growth and
tilting demographics of the race did not pass unnoticed. The local morning
paper, the *Honolulu Advertiser,* wryly noted that the 259 entrants with the
Japanese surname Suzuki far exceeded the total number of entrants (162)
in the first Honolulu Marathon twenty years before.[3] In the years to come,
the editorial sections of both the *Advertiser* and the afternoon *Honolulu
Star-Bulletin* would highlight the economic benefit of attracting so many
Japanese visitors, while the letters section would print occasional complaints
from local runners offended by the marathon association's perceived indif-
ference to their participation. In fact, even the JALPAK officials were concerned that the marathon was "too Japanese" for Japanese runners lured by
the promise of Hawaiian hospitality and friendship.[4]

In 1992 and many times thereafter, the field of elite runners nearly
matched in quality what the overall field achieved in volume. While the prize
purse could not compete with those of larger races like the New York City
and Boston Marathons, Barahal and Cross had made good use of their

resources by identifying and recruiting promising African 10,000-meter runners whom they believed had the potential to be world-class marathoners. The strategy was first vindicated in 1985, when a then-unknown Kenyan runner named Ibrahim Hussein set a Honolulu Marathon course record with a 2:12:08 finish, and then went on to win the 1987 New York Marathon and the 1988, 1991, and 1992 Boston Marathons, ushering in the modern age of African marathon domination. By 1992, then, the Honolulu Marathon had established itself as a top launching point for the best athletes in the sport. The elite field that year was particularly stellar. Masya, whose troubled life ended in 2003, would win three Honolulu Marathons in all, as well as the 1992 World Half Marathon Championship and the 1997 Stockholm Marathon. Ndeti became one of the most dominant marathon runners of his generation, winning the Boston Marathon in 1995, 1996, and 1997. Simon Naali won two Honolulu Marathons as well as the 1990 Stockholm Marathon. He also represented Tanzania in the 1992 Olympic Games. Francis Naali would go on to take gold in the 2002 Commonwealth Games. Beurskens, the women's champion, would win an unprecedented eight Honolulu Marathons. Weidenbach (now Lisa Rainsberger) won the Twin Cities Marathon the following year; she had previously won the women's division of the 1985 Boston Marathon—the last American woman to win the race.

The '92 race was notable on other fronts. In response to the rapidly growing participation, race organizers altered the original marathon route, which had started at Aloha Tower and proceeded east down Ala Moana Boulevard. The new route began in front of Ala Moana Beach Park and then headed in the opposite direction toward the downtown area before circling back up Nuʻuanu Avenue, along King Street, Kapiʻolani Boulevard, and Piʻikoi Street, and then back to the original course on Ala Moana. The new route proved much better in accommodating the huge field, and it remains unchanged. The '92 race also marked the peaceful resolution of an ongoing dispute with wheelchair athletes, whom Barahal had initially barred from participating because of supposed safety concerns. Although popular with the other participants, the wheelchair athletes had over the years been subjected to shifting accommodation attempts, including having their own race the day before the marathon. Honolulu Mayor Frank Fasi finally mediated a solution: the wheelchair athletes would start fifteen minutes before the rest of the field. While disputes over prize money and other issues have arisen over the years, the wheelchair division remains a part of race day.

By almost every measure, then, in 1992 the Honolulu Marathon was in the best shape it had ever been. But it was also a very different race from the one founded twenty years earlier by an iconoclastic cardiologist, a maverick mayor, and a fringe group of dedicated long-distance runners, each chasing a personal vision of what a well-organized marathon could bring to an island state in the throes of extreme growth and development. Dr. Jack Scaff, the man most responsible for creating the Honolulu Marathon, was amid that throng of runners in 1992. He had participated in each of the previous nineteen marathons—from his days as medical director for the inaugural race, to his time as first president of the marathon association, and through his later estrangement from the organization. Through his Honolulu Marathon Clinic, Scaff had personally trained thousands of local runners in the race that day, each of them a testament to his once-revolutionary notions that a marathon could be an effective vehicle for promoting health, and that with proper training and motivation, just about anyone could complete one. Scaff had a well-established reputation as an outspoken advocate for the health benefits of long-distance running, and as a playful provocateur who delighted in upending lazily repeated assumptions about cardiac health. As a race promoter, he was also known for his outsize personality and ambitions. Like Barahal, Scaff wanted the race to fulfill Mayor Fasi's early mandate to become "the Boston Marathon of the Pacific." And yet, while the promoter in Scaff might have appreciated the record level of participation, the sight of hundreds of spent and miserable Japanese participants—many of whom had not trained at all—lying on the sidewalks in Hawaiʻi Kai or dragging themselves up Diamond Head Road did not sit well. Nor was Scaff satisfied by the yearly updates of how much money the race had contributed to the local economy, but with no mention of executive pay, or how the non-profit organization's gains were actually being used. These, however, were the new realities of the age of the Super Marathon.

Who could have foreseen?

CHAPTER 2

Birth of the Honolulu Marathon

The publication of Dr. Kenneth Cooper's *Aerobics* in 1968 is widely and rightly identified as the spark that ignited the American fitness movement of the late 1960s and '70s, which in turn created the necessary conditions for the so-called American Running Boom of the 1970s. While in the Air Force in the 1960s, Cooper developed a point system for physical activity in a variety of sports. He also developed a 1.5-mile and 12-minute mile test to measure aerobic capacity, which he identified as an indicator of good health.[1] He believed that walking three miles in less than forty-five minutes, five days a week, or running two miles in less than twenty minutes, four times a week, could help people achieve a level of aerobic fitness that would lead to a longer, healthier life.[2] Considered radical at first, Cooper's theories on exercise were eventually well received by an increasingly sedentary American populace dealing with obesity and heart disease at historic rates. In the decade following the publication of *Aerobics,* the number of Americans who regularly participated in running increased from 100,000 to 10 million.[3]

Cooper's argument that running and jogging were safe and viable means of improving health had substantial research support. In 1949, Scottish epidemiologist Jerry Morris conducted a study of some 31,000 men, age thirty-five to sixty-four, employed by the public transportation system. Though similar in class and lifestyle, those who worked as conductors were less likely than drivers to suffer heart attacks, and if they did, tended to have them later in life and were more likely to survive them. Morris identified the now-obvious difference that drivers were mostly sedentary, while conductors walked up and down the aisles and the stairs throughout their shift. A study comparing government clerks and postal workers produced similar findings.[4] Morris's publications on inactivity and cardiovascular disease became foundational to the study of lifestyle-related diseases.

Some years before, in 1963, University of Oregon track and field coach Bill Bowerman traveled to New Zealand to consult with renowned running coach Arthur Lydiard. While there, he witnessed a community fun run for "men, women and children, all ages and sizes."[5] He also started running himself, with Lydiard. Bowerman was in such good shape and spirits when he returned to Oregon that he enlisted local reporter Jerry Uhrhammer to help him establish what is believed to be the first jogging clinic in the United States.[6] Bowerman would later use a pamphlet written for this clinic as the basis for his best-selling book, *Jogging*. Of course, he would have an even greater influence on popularizing running and jogging as the co-founder of Nike and the designer of the first great recreational running shoe. He and Phil Knight initially ran their business, known first as Blue Ribbon Sports, as an import operation, bringing in Tiger running shoes from Japan. They began producing their own shoes in 1971, their legendary big break coming when Bowerman poured a rubber mixture onto his wife's waffle iron, and created the first "waffle" outsole—a significant upgrade from the thinner, less-forgiving soles in previous running shoes.[7] First introduced at the 1972 U.S. Olympic trials in Eugene, Oregon, the shoe was certainly a boon to competitive distance runners. It was also affordable enough to allow millions of novices to break into the sport without enduring the painful blisters and foot aggravations long assumed to be the price of membership in the running community.

By the summer of 1972, everything was in place for running to be embraced by the American public as a competitive sport and a healthful recreational activity. All it needed was the proper introduction, and that came via the 1972 Olympic Games in Munich, when Frank Shorter became the first American to win the Olympic Marathon since John Hayes sixty-four years earlier. A military brat, Shorter had been born in Munich and raised in New York. He ran for Yale University under coach Bob Giegengack, winning the NCAA 10,000-meter championship as a senior. Moving to Florida to attend law school, Shorter joined the Florida Track Club, where he ran alongside world-class distance runners Jack Bacheler and Jeff Galloway. Shorter arrived in Munich having won the 10,000-meter run and the marathon at the Pan American Games in 1971, and two of what would be four consecutive titles at the Fukuoka Marathon, the premier international marathon of the time. The Olympic marathon came just five days after Palestinian terrorists slaughtered eleven Israeli athletes who had been taken hostage a day earlier. This brutal incursion of real-world geo-political strife into the suspended reality of the Olympics cast a pall over the following events. Nevertheless, the performance by Shorter and his American teammates caused unbridled enthusiasm at home. The race itself lacked drama. Fueled by de-carbonated Coca-Cola, Shorter took the lead at the 15-kilometer mark and never relinquished it, winning in 2:12:19. Karel Lismont (2:14:31) of Belgium placed second, followed by defending champion Mamo Wolde (2:15:08) of Ethiopia. Fellow Americans Kenny Moore (2:15:39) and Bacheler (2:17:38) finished in fourth and tenth place, respectively—the best U.S. showing ever.

The event was televised by ABC, which captured not only Shorter's triumph over the European, Japanese, and African runners who had dominated the event over the last several Games cycles, but also the bizarre spectacle of imposter Norbert Sudhaus running into the stadium ahead of Shorter. Perhaps most significantly, Shorter's relatively early lead and all-but-guaranteed victory prompted ABC to keep its cameras on the marathon, providing the American viewing public much longer-than-normal exposure to the race and the informed commentary accompanying it. It was Marathon 101 for viewers whose previous awareness, if any, had been confined to the well-documented 26.2 miles from Hopkinton to Boston. The broadcast made a household name of Shorter. In the weeks and months following his win, millions of duly inspired Americans took their first tentative steps as recreational runners. Soon, stronger, healthier, and highly motivated newbie runners were looking for new ways to feed their passion, and small community races and fun runs that previously hosted only a few dozen participants were soon scrambling to accommodate thousand-deep fields. A half-dozen new running magazines hit newsstands, providing the niche publication *Runner's World,* itself only six or seven years old, with its first real competition. While running and jogging were undeniably going mainstream, the marathon was still seen as an extreme activity restricted to an endorphin-addled fringe. But with images of Shorter's victory fresh in the cultural memory, and signs of a running mania flooding the popular media, the fringe was starting to have a powerful allure. And nowhere was this more true than in a tropical island chain 2,000 miles west of the North American continent, where a boundary-pushing cardiologist in the mold of

Cooper, Morris, and Bowerman was preparing to take the sport—and American hearts—where they had never gone before.

Matters of the Heart

Among many other things, Jack Scaff is a master of the shaggy dog story. It's a quality noted (usually, but not always positively) in most written accounts of Scaff and his involvement in the founding of the Honolulu Marathon. He is certainly capable of providing a straight answer—his many scholarly articles on cardiac recovery are meticulously organized—but when talking about matters that excite his memory, Scaff becomes an unapologetic weaver of contextualizing webs. Thus, to learn how Scaff, a native New Yorker, came to live in Hawai'i, much less how and why he came to see the marathon as the perfect test of his ideas about cardiac recovery, you will first hear him explain how he pursued an internship in Africa, and how he made the acquaintance of a very young Maria Shriver.

Scaff was finishing his third year at Seton Hall College of Medicine and Dentistry (now the New Jersey Medical School) when his biochemistry teacher told him about a fellowship program offered by Smith Kline and French Laboratories that funded summer clerkships in foreign countries. Working through a family network of Scottish Presbyterian ministers and missionaries, Scaff wrote personal letters to prestigious hospitals around the world, including the Albert Schweitzer Hospital in Lambarene, Gabon, asking if they would be interested in his services. The strategy worked: "Before Smith Kline had heard about me, they were getting these letters from throughout the world."[8] On the advice of an uncle, Scaff elected to serve in the Philippines. On the way there, he had an experience common to generations of Americans who ended up relocating to Hawai'i: "When I got off the plane in 1960, in Honolulu, in the old airport, [there were] the greeters and the leis. [. . .] I could see Waikīkī and I could smell the plumeria, and I said, 'This is Heaven on Earth.'"[9] After medical school, Scaff followed the suggestion of scholar and author Lawrence Fuchs and pursued a position with the Peace Corps as a public health service officer. Scaff was interviewed by Sargent Shriver, founder and director of the Peace Corps. Present at the meeting was Shriver's young daughter Maria, the future first lady of California. Scaff spent three years as a lieutenant commander in the Philippines. As part of his duties, he visited Hawai'i twice a year to train Peace Corps volunteers. Finally, in 1969, after completing an internal medicine fellowship in cardiology at Long Beach Memorial Hospital, Scaff accepted a job as a full-time cardiologist with the Honolulu Medical Group, and moved to Hawai'i to stay.

While in California, Scaff had started running to alleviate a back condition. Undistinguished at short distances, he found that he could outlast most of his fellow runners over longer spans:

> We would go for a slow three-mile run. At the end of the three-mile run, the others were more tired than I was, and I learned about slow twitch/quick twitch fibers. I was a slow twitcher. I would go longer and longer, and finally I'd say, "Would you guys like to try six?" I was doing very, very well. At three, I couldn't keep up with them. At six, they couldn't keep up with me.[10]

He continued to run in Hawai'i and soon found a way to apply his new-found passion to his professional interest in improving the health of cardiac patients. In 1972, Scaff was working with cardiologist John Wagner. Over after-hours beers one day, Wagner expressed interest in using exercise to reduce cardiovascular risk factors. Scaff was intrigued, particularly with proving that exercise could help prevent arteriosclerotic heart disease—an idea that many in the medical profession considered unsound. The two men agreed that running was the right form of "habitual, steady state exercise" that could be done for a significant length of time several times per week.[11] But they weren't interested in treading over ground already staked out by Kenneth Cooper. They wanted to give people who had already suffered a heart attack, then considered a career-ending event, a significant goal that would motivate them to stick to a regimen of rehabilitative cardiovascular exercise. Even though neither man was quite sure at the time what that exact distance was, the marathon sounded like just the thing.

Scaff's strategy for selling his idea would be the one he would follow in a variety of road-race ventures over the next few decades: "First, we'll have to make it fun, and secondly, we'll have to make them think it's good for them."[12] He had been intrigued by the work of Dr. Thomas Bassler, a pathologist from Washington State who famously said that a person who did not smoke and who could complete a marathon in four hours or less was virtually assured of not suffering a heart attack within six years. Scaff was also aware of the Framingham Heart Study, a highly influential longitudinal project started in 1948 by the National Heart Institute (now the National

Heart, Blood, and Lung Institute) and Boston University to investigate the causes of cardiovascular disease. The results included evidence of a potentially protective effect of moderate exercise on heart health. The fact that such an ambitious extrapolation of as-yet unproven hypotheses brought with it the likelihood of alienating the conservative American Medical Association stoked Scaff's rogue tendencies. He'd show everyone.

In short order, Scaff and Wagner established the exercise-based Cardiac Rehabilitation Program at the Central YMCA, and soon they were escorting interested would-be runners on short jaunts around Kapiʻolani Park and Diamond Head. Scaff's ultimate goal was to enter his patients in a marathon, but before he did this, he wanted to experience the race himself. So in April of 1973, Scaff flew to Massachusetts to participate in the Boston Marathon and to attend the American Medical Joggers Association (AMJA) Conference, where he would speak on exercise testing, cardiac rehabilitation, and recreational long-distance running. At the conference, he ran into Bassler, and the two discussed Scaff's use of running as rehabilitative therapy for cardiac patients. Bassler encouraged Scaff to organize a "Honolulu Marathon," which would enable the AMJA to hold a conference in Hawaiʻi, and its members to run it as well. Also at the conference was Dr. Terry Kavanaugh, a kindred spirit from the Toronto Rehabilitation Centre, who was escorting eight cardiac patients to the Boston Marathon. Scaff told him about the proposed marathon, and Kavanaugh pledged to bring patients to Honolulu if Scaff could pull it off.

Despite competing on the hottest day in the race's history, Scaff survived his first marathon with his ambitions intact and returned to Honolulu eager to organize his first road race. He knew that a marathon had been staged in Honolulu two months earlier by Mid-Pacific Road Runners Club (MPRRC) members Jim and Leah Ferris. The Oʻahu Marathon had attracted sixty-five participants, making it the largest marathon ever run in Hawaiʻi. University of Hawaiʻi student Royden Koito won in a time of 2:55:50. Leah Ferris, the only woman in the field, placed twenty-sixth overall.[13] In an interview for the 1987 Honolulu Marathon broadcast on local NBC affiliate KHON, Jim Ferris recalled how Scaff approached him shortly after returning from Boston: "[He] wanted to take over, actually, and at the time I thought it was a blessing in disguise. [. . .] I couldn't imagine putting on a race bigger than seventy people."[14]

Scaff then met with MPRRC's Col. C. H. Greenley and Col. Tom Ferguson, and they agreed that the proposed marathon could replace a scheduled 50-mile race that December.[15] Greenley wrote to Honolulu Mayor Frank Fasi, introducing the club to him, informing him of the plans for the race, and asking for permission to use city streets. In a letter dated September 7, 1973, Fasi replied that "Having been born and raised in New England, I have long been impressed by the magnitude and success of the famous run in Boston. It seems to me that Honolulu could well host such an event, considering local interest and our location in the pacific area."

The Mayor Buys In

Like Scaff, the charismatic and combative Fasi was an East Coast transplant who saw opportunities in abundance in his adopted tropical home. The son of Sicilian immigrants, he grew up poor in East Hartford, Connecticut, but managed to graduate from Trinity College before serving in the Marines in the South Pacific during World War II. After the war, he abandoned plans to attend law school and settled in Honolulu, where he had spent many an enjoyable leave.[16] After a stint with the Army Corps of Engineers, he opened the Frank F. Fasi Supply Company, specializing in dismantling military buildings for lumber and selling surplus bamboo Quonset Huts—known locally as "kamaboko huts" because of their resemblance to the half-moon-shaped Japanese fish cake. Fasi not only made a small fortune, but also gained a measure of local prominence that he leveraged into a political career. Drawing on his bona fides as a second-generation American with a hardscrabble, working-class background, and as a proud WWII veteran, Fasi aligned himself with a Democratic Party that rose to power with the political coming of age of returned Japanese-American veterans educated under the G.I. Bill. The alignment was perfect for the ambitious Fasi, who served on the Democratic National Committee when the Democratic Revolution of 1954 effectively ended the Republican Party's dominance of the Hawai'i territorial legislature and, thanks to the gathering power of local labor unions, unseated those who ran the Big Five companies (Alexander & Baldwin, American Factors, Castle & Cooke, C. Brewer & Co., and Theo H. Davies) as de facto oligarchs of the territory. Fasi was elected to the territorial senate in 1958, a year before Hawai'i became the fiftieth state, but he was defeated by Republican Hiram Fong in a subsequent campaign for the U.S. Senate. Unsuccessful in his later bids for the U.S. House of Representatives and the governorship of Hawai'i, Fasi would nevertheless leave a large imprint on the landscape of Honolulu and forge a considerable political legacy during his five-and-a-half tumultuous terms as Honolulu mayor.[17]

Rapid economic growth resulting from statehood and high-volume, low-cost jet travel between Hawai'i and the continental United States made it possible for Fasi to act on his plans to build a modern Honolulu that rivaled in infrastructure and social sophistication the top U.S. cities. In 1959, tourism ranked far behind military spending and agriculture as key drivers of Hawai'i's economy. But within months of statehood, Pan American Airways, correctly anticipating a surge in tourist traffic, began Jet Clipper service to Hawai'i. Within two years, tourism was the new state's No. 1 industry, and between 1960 and 1970, annual visitor arrivals jumped from 296,000 to 1.7 million. Increasing jet travel in the 1960s further fueled the increase. In 1969, the Civil Aeronautics Board gave five more passenger airlines— Western, Continental, Braniff, TWA, and American—permission to offer service to Hawai'i. In 1970, Pan Am put the Boeing 747 jumbo jet, with a passenger capacity nearly double of other jets, into service for Hawai'i. These events produced an upward trajectory in arrivals that would span more than four decades, declining only once between 1960 and 1990.[18]

The tourism boom coincided with a surge in development produced by liberal lending policies set by local banks and a corresponding confidence on the part of Mainland investors. In 1960, the local building industry reported $164 million in building permits, an increase of 35 percent over 1959. For the 1961–1962 fiscal year, the state operating budget increased $10 million, to a record $104 million. According to University of Hawai'i economics professor James Mak, adding to this initial growth spurt was the local government's policy of laissez-faire with regard to the growing tourism sector, its active investment in building infrastructure on the neighbor islands, and its funding of the state university's travel-industry management program "for labor force training."[19] This transition to a service-based economy created a labor demand that produced a proportionately large increase in population, primarily on the island of O'ahu. In the 1960 U.S. Census, taken a year after statehood, the population of Honolulu had surged to 500,409— an increase of nearly 42 percent over the 1950 Census. Over the next twenty years, the city and county population would balloon to 762,565.[20]

Fasi's brash, get-'er-done attitude and his TV news-friendly theatricality were in sync with the Wild West feel of a Honolulu in radical transition. In 1971, Fasi thwarted a strike by employees of Honolulu Rapid Transit Co. (HRT), a privately owned company that provided O'ahu's only bus service, by flying to Dallas and purchasing sixty-seven new and used buses, then buying out HRT and starting the city and county-administered Mass

Transit Lines, Inc.[21] In grand Fasi style, he drove the first bus off the ship wearing a white cowboy hat.[22] To a degree unimaginable in the more litigious present, Fasi took a similarly imperious approach to many challenges of his day. Lacking any direct legal avenue to clear Hare Krishna T-shirt vendors from Waikīkī sidewalks, he had 400 huge cement planters installed along Kalākaua Avenue in the middle of the night. The next morning, the vendors no longer had any space to set up their tables. In 1976, Fasi decided to raze the parking lot adjacent to Honolulu Hale, the city and county headquarters, and replace it with grass. City council members agreed to the move but wanted to wait until they could secure alternative parking. But before Councilman Kekoa Kaapu could introduce a measure to delay the work, early on a weekend morning, Fasi mounted a bulldozer and demolished the lot himself.[23] Not surprisingly, Fasi's brash style and penchant for personal feuds earned him numerous detractors. But during his early years as mayor, he worked tirelessly to enhance civic life in Honolulu—an effort that endeared the self-proclaimed outsider and champion of the working man to his constituents, and kept the money flowing in the county. Fasi created satellite city halls, community gardens, and open markets. He improved city parks. He also threw his support behind new arts and culture programs, including Hawaiʻi's first ballet company, as important symbols of civic growth. A world-class marathon like the one that drew top international runners every year to Boston would therefore be yet another symbol of Honolulu's ascent.

With Fasi's blessing, the Department of Parks and Recreation got involved in the planning of Scaff's proposed marathon. In August an executive planning committee was convened, composed of co-chairs Greenley and Parks and Recreation director Young Suk Ko; Scaff, as the designated medical director; Ferguson; Jeanne Comer; Capt. Charles Hyder; and Sgt. John Trippany, an Army Rest & Recuperation specialist who would serve as the first race director. Sponsorship of the "Rim of the Pacific Run" was officially credited to the American Medical Joggers Association, the Mid-Pacific Road Runners Club, and the city and county of Honolulu. Though they did not serve on the committee, Parks and Recreation staffers Bill Pacheco and Tommy Kono, an Olympic weightlifting champion and coach, provided the most direct city and county support.

Race Preparations

Once the committee was formed, the organizers had roughly three months to plan the race. Because of its extensive road-race management expertise, the MPRRC took the lead in handling the logistics. The most critical task fell to Ferguson, who designed and measured the original marathon course. He headed a calibration team that included Hyder, Maj. Fred Barmore, Capt. Peter Johnson, and Lt. Edward Teague. To ensure that the course would qualify for the Amateur Athletic Union (AAU) certification, they first conducted a test at a one-mile course at Hickam Air Force Base, carefully calibrating the steel tapes, surveyor's wheels, and thermometers needed to measure temperature fluctuations that could potentially affect measurement. These would all be used to measure the actual 26.2-mile course. The course was laid out twice using different tapes, and then measured a dozen times with two different surveyor's wheels to arrive at an average measurement. As Ferguson told the *Honolulu Star-Bulletin* before the race, "We wanted as accurate a course as possible so time means something and a man can measure his progress. This is a runner's greatest reward."[24] Once sure that the instruments were calibrated, Ferguson, Hyder and high school volunteers Vernon Matsukawa and Ron Au spent every Saturday for three months painstakingly measuring the actual marathon course.[25]

The relatively few marathons held in the United States in 1973 fell into two very general categories. Those like the Oʻahu Marathon operated as small, no-frills community races for elite local runners. Those like the New York Marathon, established just the year before, modeled themselves after the standard-bearing Boston Marathon, and sought broader participation. Unsure what to expect in numbers, Scaff and the MPRRC decided not to mimic any other race, but to design their own from the ground up, with maximum safety and enjoyment as their guiding principles. The biggest divergence from the norm was their plan for aid stations. In previous Hawaiʻi marathons, runners got their snacks and water from people who offered them, or from caches they had set up on the course beforehand. At Boston and the other large marathons, aid stations were few and far between, placed only where the logistics seemed practical. For example, the initial aid station for Boston was at the six-mile mark for no reason other than proximity to shade and a water source. Aware of Honolulu's high heat and humidity even in December, and with the memory of his own sweltering first Boston marathon still fresh, Scaff arranged for aid stations every two to three miles to encourage proper hydration for both elite and recreational runners. Nearly every marathon has since adopted this standard. The organizers found that one issue couldn't be addressed to their satisfaction: oversight by the Hawaiʻi branch of the AAU, which was required for official certification of the course and for validation of the finishing times for elite runners seeking to qualify for the Boston Marathon. "Back in those days, you had to become a member of the AAU," Scaff recalled, "which was $2, and we charged a $2 entry fee. I thought it was criminal (that) you had to pay 100 percent more for an agency that wasn't doing anything."[26]

Aside from his official organizing duties, Scaff spent that fall and winter overseeing the training of two would-be marathoners who were perfect candidates to prove his theories on the rehabilitative effects of controlled long-distance running. Val Nolasco, a piano player at the old Tahitian Lanai, had suffered a heart attack two years earlier. He sought out Scaff after seeing him on a televised panel discussion of effective treatments of heart disease. Initially Scaff put him on a regimen of slow two-mile runs three times a week. After returning from Boston, Scaff told Nolasco that he would provide him with free medical care if Nolasco would consent to follow a supervised training program for a marathon. As Scaff explained to author Mark Osmun:

> I chose [Nolasco] basically because he was so frightened. He couldn't understand why [the heart attack] had happened to him, and since he couldn't, there was no reason to expect it wouldn't happen again. So he just figured he was going to die. But another reason I wanted him was that he wasn't really limited from a cardiovascular standpoint. His heart wasn't that strong—because of his poor exercise—but it could sustain a good amount of stress. And his heart attack had not been that big.[27]

Scaff made the same deal with Ray Thiele, an airline pilot who had suffered a heart attack in 1972. Thiele had lost his pilot's license because the Federal Aviation Administration ruled he was unfit to fly. Scaff and Thiele got the FAA to agree to reinstate Thiele if he could prove his full rehabilitation by completing a marathon.

Adopting the long slow distance (LSD) approach to training developed by German physician Ernst van Aaken and popularized by runner and author Joe Henderson, Scaff coached the two men through progressively longer runs at a slow-to-medium pace that would build cardiovascular fitness and muscular endurance without exposing them to oxygen debt. Local media coverage of their entry in the marathon's "cardiovascular division" gave Scaff an opportunity to share the first drafts of his gospel of long-distance running with a mass audience, and to promote the race not just as a sporting event, but a revolutionary first glimpse into the future of exercise as a key component of good health. "The cardiovascular division of the marathon is different from the rest," Scaff told the *Honolulu Advertiser:* "The men entered in it are interested only in finishing the race, and they will get no trophies—just the satisfaction that they have accomplished more than many of their peers who have not had heart attacks can do."[28] Though eager to prove that distance running could help cardiac patients achieve a full recovery, Scaff was also very aware of the potentially fatal consequences should he be mistaken. As medical director for the race, Scaff arranged to have health professionals at all fourteen aid stations; nurses on bicycles escorting Nolasco and Thiele; ambulances on call; and two-way radio communication, courtesy of Civil Defense Command, linking the aid stations and the race day headquarters at Kapi'olani Park.[29]

While Honolulu Parks and Recreation was only lightly involved in the operational planning, it provided funding and whatever ancillary support was needed. Tommy Kono drew on his network of personal and professional contacts to gather supplies and giveaways. He arranged for a donation of 200 blank T-shirts from local sporting goods store Honsport; then the executive board members, volunteers, and Kono himself hand-stenciled them, producing the first race finisher shirts. Parks and Recreation was most obvious on race day, when hundreds of city and county workers set up and took down course markers, staff registration tables and aid stations, and the start and finish areas. As Kono explained, the department's greatest value lay in the number of ready personnel it could provide: "Parks and Recreation people can take orders and give orders. They're very good at that kind of stuff because they deal with the public."[30] Government and community support was therefore far more significant that it had been for any previous road race. Interscholastic League of Honolulu officials volunteered to work the finish line alongside Parks and Recreation staffer Wally Nobriga, and dozens of police officers organized by MPRRC member and Honolulu Police Department official David Benson were ready to line the course. Seiko loaned the official timing clock, and Bob Meyer of the Nu'uanu YMCA secured the winners' trophies. By December, everything seemed to be in place. But no one really knew whether race day would prove to be the beginning of a grand tradition or a grim reckoning for outsized ambitions.

A Record-Breaking Debut

Though both newspapers reported the figure at 167, official Honolulu Marathon records state that 162 people entered the first Rim of the Pacific Run.

What is certain is that 151 people safely crossed the finish line—the largest field by far for a local marathon and, despite the distance, one of the larger road races of any distance ever staged in Hawaiʻi. It started in front of Aloha Tower at 6:30 a.m. and was a young man's race, with Fresno Pacific College student Donald Gregory aggressively staking an early lead, followed by the more conservative trio of UH's Koito (winner of the Oʻahu Marathon earlier that year), Army soldier Winfield Stanforth, and medical school student Duncan Macdonald. Gregory fell back after the first six miles, and Koito led Stanforth and Macdonald into Hawaiʻi Kai for the second half of the race. Fueled by an unconventional breakfast of Kix cereal and poi, Macdonald overtook Koito heading back along Kalanianaʻole Highway and built a lead over the final eight miles.[31] Macdonald, an elite middle-distance runner at Stanford before returning home to Hawaiʻi for medical school, set a Hawaiʻi marathon record with a finishing time 2:27:34.8, besting Harold Cole's ten-year-old standard of 2:27:47. Stanforth (2:34:26) placed second, followed by U.S. Navy sailor Gordon Haller (2:35:24), Koito (2:35:48), and Mid-Pacific Institute track coach Johnny Faerber (2:39:21). Also setting records that day were two precocious kids: Kristine Hilbe, 8, and Daven Chun, 9. The daughter of University of Hawaiʻi track and field coach Joe Hilbe, Kristine completed the race in 4:32:09, smashing the record for girls her age (admittedly a small pool) by more than an hour. Chun, the youngest of the so-called "Hunky Bunch," a local family of eight that became famous locally for their collective running exploits in the 1970s, broke the record for 9-year-old boys with a 3:19:01 finish, bettering the old mark by nine minutes.

In a testimony to the prevailing spirit of amateurism, Macdonald went home with nothing but the overall winner's trophy and a beer that someone handed him as he waited to take a urine test for a medical experiment he had agreed to participate in. As *Honolulu Advertiser* reporter Ben Kalb wryly noted, the only participants who earned any money were Myles Saulibio, a UH student who used the race to raise $300 in charitable pledges, and Hilo College student Johnny Notch, who found a dollar on the road in Hawaiʻi Kai.

The very last person to cross the finish line that day was perhaps the most elated—Val Nolasco. As he later told the *Honolulu Advertiser*, his game plan that morning was a bit less ambitious than the one set by Scaff: "I had a lot of doubt about finishing because I did not actually do 26 miles before. They say that when you run a marathon 60 percent of it is mental. So I said to myself if I made it to Hawai'i Kai, I'd be happy. But when I got there it turned out I turned around and finished."[32] Nolasco spent much of the morning trailing Thiele, but in the last mile Thiele could no longer endure the painful blisters on his feet, and he dropped out. Though both men would complete the Boston Marathon four months later, it was Nolasco who would earn the distinction that day of being the first American to complete a marathon after suffering a heart attack. And it was Nolasco who for the time being would serve as the sole vindicating proof for Scaff's controversial program.

For Scaff, that was plenty.

Onward

Plans for the second Honolulu Marathon began as soon as the last finisher's shirt was handed out. Within days, the organizing committee had a verbal commitment from a German track coach to bring runners for the next race. There was also hope that Olympians Frank Shorter and Kenny Moore and Boston Marathon winner John Anderson would participate. For his part, Scaff was intent on expanding the cardiovascular division. In addition to Nolasco, three of Kavanaugh's Canadian patients had finished the first Honolulu Marathon, bolstering Scaff's claims to an increasingly receptive public. This feat became the basis of University of California at Davis student Rudy Dressendorfer's PhD thesis; later, he, Scaff, Wagner, and James Gallop would collaborate on an article about the effects of marathon training on cardiac patients that appeared in the *Annals of the New York Academy of Sciences*. To an even greater degree than the first race, much of the advance reporting on the 1974 marathon featured the cardiovascular division and Scaff's repeated claim that distance running was a healthy endeavor for those recovering from heart attacks, or for those in danger of suffering one due to a sedentary lifestyle. By the time the second race came around, the cardiovascular division had grown to eighteen participants, including Nolasco, who had organized his own Hawai'i Kai Fun Runners group.[33]

But Scaff had greater ambitions for the race than simply boosting his sample size. Nolasco's successful finish, coupled with the widely covered accomplishments of youngsters Hilbe and Chun, convinced a curious local populace that running a marathon was not only possible but apparently safe. For Scaff and Wagner, the marathon had become the coveted tool they had envisioned, one that could motivate people to engage in "habitual, steady state exercise" that in turn would lower the incidence of cardiac disease in the

Jack Scaff, seen here at the finish of the 1978 Honolulu Marathon, spearheaded the effort to establish a world-class marathon in Honolulu. Photo by Alexis Higdon. Courtesy of the *Honolulu Star-Advertiser.*

community. The next step would be to develop a program for training these prospective runners safely and successfully to take on the Honolulu Marathon. The doctors also concluded that by attracting and grooming a steady flow of new runners, they could ensure the future of the race. Scaff and Wagner settled on a weekly clinic that would run for nine months leading up to the race in December. They would handle the instruction, but as with the race itself, they needed help from the city and county to secure a venue. They therefore turned to the person whose service to the Honolulu Marathon would continue long after every other person involved in the inaugural race had moved on: Tommy Kono.

Kono had assisted with the first marathon as the physical fitness specialist for Parks and Recreation, a position he had assumed a year earlier. While he accomplished a great deal in this role before retiring in 1997, this job may be the most mundane item on his long list of achievements. Of Japanese ancestry, Kono was born in Sacramento, California, in 1930. He spent a significant part of his teens in the Tule Lake internment camp, where his family had been forcibly relocated during World War II. This time brought two unexpected benefits. First, the arid, desert-like environment proved to be good for Kono, who suffered from severe asthma. Second, it was at Tule

Lake that he was introduced to weightlifting. "Originally, I started out in physique, not because I wanted to but because of my health," he recalled.

After the war, Kono returned home and graduated from Sacramento High School. He continued to lift weights, transforming his once sickly body into a sculpted physique of Charles Atlas proportions. He fulfilled his athletic potential as a weight lifter. In 1952, Kono won an Olympic gold medal in the lightweight division, setting a record (117.7 kg) for the snatch. This performance marked the beginning of a period of individual domination unmatched in U. S. weightlifting history. Between 1953 and 1959, Kono went undefeated in World and Olympic competition, winning six consecutive world titles and another Olympic gold medal in the 1956 Games in Melbourne, where he set new world marks in the clean and jerk (175 kg) and overall weight (447.5 kg) while competing in the light-heavyweight division. He would also earn a silver medal in the middleweight division at the 1960 Olympic Games in Rome. He won gold medals in three consecutive Pan American Games (1955, 1959, and 1963) as well as eleven AAU championships. He is the only athlete to set world records in four different weightlifting classes (lightweight, middleweight, light-heavyweight, and middle-heavyweight), and set twenty-seven world records over the course of his career.[34] Kono excelled as a bodybuilder as well, earning the title of AAU Mr. Universe three times (1954, 1955, and 1957)[35] and the Iron Man Mr. World title in 1954.[36] After his retirement from competition, Kono served as the Olympic weightlifting coach for Mexico (1968), West Germany (1972), and the United States (1976).

While his background was in weightlifting and bodybuilding, Kono was familiar with the marathon early on through his friendships with Dr. Richard You and Norman Tamanaha, whom You had given nutritional guidance. You had been one of the two physicians who accompanied the U.S. Olympic delegation to the 1952 Olympic Games in Helsinki. It was his persistent recruiting—"every year I saw him, and every year he would tell me that I belonged in Hawai'i"—that convinced Kono to move from Sacramento to Honolulu in 1955.[37] He soon met Tamanaha, who was in the midst of his run of impressive Boston Marathon appearances. "In '56, I went to the Olympics in Melbourne," Kono recalled: "Emil Zatopek— he was called the ironman in 1952, when he won the 10,000 and the marathon—he was there in '56 in Melbourne. He had written a book and was selling it at the Melbourne book store, so I bought it and brought it back to Norman." By observing European training regimens, Kono also knew about

Former Olympic gold medalist Tommy Kono helped organize the first Honolulu Marathon in 1973 and continued serving on the HMA board of directors until his death in 2016. Photo by Craig Kojima. Courtesy of the *Honolulu Star-Advertiser.*

using running to build overall conditioning. When Scaff and Wagner invited Kono to lunch to discuss their idea for a running clinic, Kono the Parks and Recreation physical fitness specialist was therefore all ears.

With a speed characteristic of those atypical times in Hawai'i government, Kono cleared the way for the two doctors to host the very first Honolulu Marathon Clinic at Kapi'olani Park in April 1974. Kono himself referred to the program as a jogging clinic. He felt using the Honolulu Marathon name would scare away potential participants. The clinic operated then as it does now. Scaff would start each session with basic instruction in pace, hydration, recovery, and other entry-level running essentials. Then volunteers led groups of would-be marathoners through nine months of progressively longer training runs. Participants self-selected novice, intermediate, or advanced training groups according to their ability and experience. Under Scaff's admonition for runners to carry on conversations to ensure they did not fall into oxygen debt, these groups made the Sunday "long" runs—the foundation of a weekly schedule of training runs at different distances and paces, and for different purposes—as much social events as regimented workouts.

Scaff's approach was at the forefront of a revolutionary movement that empowered recreational runners to complete a marathon without possessing extraordinary athletic prowess, and without being driven to conquer the dreaded distance apace. Finishing was the one and only goal. This approach directly contributed to dramatic increases in marathon participation—first in the early and mid-1970s, and less prominently but more significantly in the early 1990s. While many athletes who started running marathons via LSD training did develop into excellent runners capable of achieving the sub-3-hour finish considered by some to be the mark of the "true" marathoner, as a participatory event the marathon only found mainstream popularity when distance was separated from speed. And for better or worse, the Honolulu Marathon Clinic was a pioneering effort in cleaving the two.

In the decades to come, a philosophical debate would arise, pitting the so-called People's Race, which existed primarily for the pleasure and benefit of amateur runners, against races whose relevance was measured not just in large participation numbers but in the presence of elite professional athletes capable of setting record times. In 1974, the Honolulu Marathon was certainly a people's race, whose viability and growth was at least partially assured by the new Honolulu Marathon Clinic. But Scaff was not opposed to recruiting top marathoners. They could add to the prominence of the event and attract participants eager to share the road with the sport's highest-caliber athletes. To do this, however, marathon organizers had to find creative ways of dealing with the AAU's arcane guidelines for paying athletes. In Honolulu, the involvement of the American Medical Joggers Association would prove invaluable. Prior to the 1974 race, officers at the MPRRC learned that Frank Shorter, then the biggest name in the marathon world, was interested in running in Hawai'i. He would be competing in the Fukuoka Marathon just a week before, but was willing to race again despite the outrageously short turnaround. The problem was getting Shorter from Japan to Hawai'i. Under AAU rules, the Honolulu Marathon could not directly compensate Shorter without compromising his amateur status. Appearance fees and prize money routinely went to the AAU for redistribution. Scaff however figured out that although Shorter could not officially be compensated for running the race, the AAU could do nothing to prevent him from accepting a paid speaking engagement:

> AAU rules said that if an individual won prize money, they had to turn it in to the AAU and it would be dispensed. Or, if (the athlete) came out and they received appearance money, they had to turn it in, and then it might or might not get back to the person who it had been given to. [. . .] Frank Shorter had wanted to come to Hawai'i and of course he couldn't get around this. Well, I called him on the phone and said, "How much do you need?" And he said it was like $391. I said, "That's amazing! That's exactly the honorarium we offer our speakers at the American Medical Joggers Association." So he said "OK" and he came.[38]

In this way the Honolulu Marathon secured a prized appearance by Shorter, and his Olympic teammates Kenny Moore and Jeff Galloway as well. In only the race's second year, then, the top of the Honolulu Marathon field looked a lot more like Boston than anyone could have anticipated. Or as *Honolulu Advertiser* columnist Hal Wood quipped, "It's only the annual Rim of the Pacific Marathon that now has grown to the place where more than 260 of the world's finest runners mingle with some of the world's worst."[39]

Elite runners were secured, but Scaff wasn't done with sticking it to the AAU. As a sanctioned race, the Honolulu Marathon had to ensure that all participants were AAU members. That meant that in addition to the $2 entry fee, participants who were not already AAU members—essentially everyone but the most competitive runners—would have to pay an additional $2 for to join. AAU sanction was necessary for the top runners to qualify for the Boston Marathon, but it was of little use to the rest of the field. His solution was to offer two divisions: one for AAU runners and one for everyone else. It was widely known that some of the larger road races were quietly circumventing AAU regulations about paying athletes. But by eliminating the membership fee at the Honolulu Marathon, Scaff was mounting a shockingly transparent challenge to AAU authority. If the organization asked, he had his response already prepared: "Well, my goodness, by coincidence we're having two races on the same day, same time, same place."[40] The AAU never asked, and by the end of the decade, its hold over amateur road racing would crumble as athletes and race organizers openly revolted. In *Your First Marathon,* Scaff wrote that "In retrospect we helped inaugurate the demise of the AAU in long-distance, open-road events."

A largely unforeseen consequence of the emancipation of road races from AAU control would be the move by major international marathons to set aside their People's Race origins to become highly professionalized, revenue-generating mega-events headlined by highly compensated elite athletes. But that was still a decade away. In 1974, the Honolulu Marathon claimed success by nearly doubling its field, with 315 total entrants. Galloway set a new course record with a finish of 2:23:02, besting Moore, defending champion Macdonald, and Shorter. Cindy Dalrymple won the women's division in 3:01:59. In the following year, the field more than doubled again, hitting 782 entrants. A new course record would also be set, this time by New Zealander Jack Foster, who crossed the line in 2:17.24. Galloway came in second, followed by Tom Howard of British Columbia, and local school teacher Daniel Moynihan. Jackie Hansen, then the fastest female marathoner in the world, won the women's division with a course record 2:49:24.

Scaff's investigations into the health benefits of long-distance running remained one of the prevailing storylines through the first three Honolulu Marathons. But in addition to his success with the cardiac division runners, his Honolulu Marathon Clinic, though not officially affiliated with the race, was proving highly effective in preparing novice runners to complete the distance. In its first year, about fifty of the one hundred clinic participants entered the race. Nearly all of them finished. In 1975, 350 clinic participants entered the race and 98 percent of them finished, according to Scaff. Even the 1975 winner Foster found himself a guinea pig. Prior to the race, Scaff and fellow doctor Eric Banister accurately predicted that Foster would win the race, based on a series of tests that measured his oxygen consumption at different treadmill speeds. The results indicated that Foster could maintain a 12.5-mile-per-hour pace, which would set a course record. At the invitation of Terry Kavanaugh, then a member of the International Olympic Committee, Scaff and Banister presented these findings to an Olympic medical symposium at the 1976 Games in Montreal.[41]

Scaff was showing them.

CHAPTER 3

Rapid Growth Years

With ample evidence that the marathon would be a fixture on the local sports landscape, race organizers incorporated the Honolulu Marathon Association as a nonprofit organization in 1975. Already its public face, Scaff was elected the HMA's first president. Surrounding him was a revolving cast of colorful directors from the local running and recreation circles. Among the most prominent were Tommy Kono, former Royal Air Force pilot Willy Williamson, attorney Peter Searl, University of Hawaiʻi administrator Phil Olsen, and Honolulu Police Department Major David Benson. The mix of personalities could be volatile, but the ambition and impetuousness of the organization's early efforts at building the race matched the momentum with which running was entering the mainstream imagination.

By the mid-1970s, Americans were becoming familiar with the lexicon of running, from the "runner's high"—the term itself making the transition from the drug culture of the late 1960s to the fitness revolution of the 1970s—to the infamous "wall," which preserved some of the marathon's old association with danger. *Time* and *Newsweek* each devoted significant space to examining the so-called Running Revolution. By 1980, even *Mad* magazine (Issue #214) had joined in, using Edgar Allen Poe to mock the masochism of the long-distance runner: "Does your body ache," I asked, "each time that you perform this chore?" / Quoth the Jogger, "Ev'ry pore." In 1977, Jim Fixx's *The Complete Book of Running* hit bookstores, eventually selling more than one million copies. Even the politicians co-opted running. For supporters of Jimmy Carter, the president's jogging regimen recalled Teddy Roosevelt's idealization of the strenuous life at the same time that it provided of a new, more accessible image of the commander in chief. On the flip side, Carter's famous fall during a 1979 10K race in Maryland was openly mocked. More than thirty years after photographs of the tumble shot across wire services, the British newspaper the *Independent* chided: "Jogging has come to symbolise an American politician's resolve. His jaw is pugnaciously set and his eyes are focused on the bumpy road ahead. You can almost hear the image-consultants purring. At least until their man collapses into the arms of his secret servicemen, like Jimmy Carter. For Carter, jogging ended up as a potent symbol of his knackered presidency" (Viner).

With its year-round temperate weather and vibrant outdoor culture, Hawai'i was a natural place for the running craze to flourish. According to the National Running Data Center, in 1976 Hawai'i was the "runningest" state in the nation, with ten times more runners per capita than the national average. And even though the Honolulu Marathon was just a few years old, for many local runners it had become the highlight of an increasingly busy road-racing calendar. Attendance at Scaff and Wagner's Honolulu Marathon Clinic was so high that Tommy Kono, on behalf of Parks and Recreation, expanded the program to other locations on O'ahu.

> I noticed that there were a lot of people coming over from Kailua. I said, "That's a long way to Kapi'olani Park." So I looked into having another clinic. One on that side. We had some people coming over that knew about long-distance running. Both physical directors from Nu'uanu (YMCA) and Central (YMCA) also lived out there. So it was common sense to have it out there. I (was) going to try to promote it over there. So I got a volunteer and they took over there. I used to go there Sunday on that side then. Then they wanted it on the Leeward side in Central O'ahu, so I ended up going to Central O'ahu to do that. In the end, we had five clinics going on Sunday. I was never home on Sunday because I had to be at one of them. The worst one was Wai'anae because of the distance I had to travel. . . . Hawai'i (had) the most runners because every Sunday morning, everybody is running. That was a fad. With five clinics going on, naturally you're going to have everybody running all over the place.[1]

The dramatic increase in Honolulu Marathon entries through the first seven years reflected public enthusiasm for the race, even as declining finisher percentages pointed to the reality that not everyone who signed up in

Table 1   Honolulu Marathon Entries and Finish
Percentages, 1973–1979

Year	Entrants	Percent Finished
1973	162	93
1974	315	94
1975	782	90
1976	1,670	86
1977	3,500	83
1978	7,204	78
1979	8,500	77

(Honolulu Marathon Association, "Statistics 1973–2009")

spring and summer made it to the finish line—or even the start line—in December.

The rapidity of the growth didn't surprise Scaff and his volunteer executive board, but the growing scale of operations proved to be a challenge, especially as the original sources of support began shutting down. The American Medical Joggers Association ended its sponsorship early on but continued to hold an annual meeting in Honolulu, enabling the HMA to continue to circumvent AAU rules for paying athletes. A much greater concern arose when Parks and Recreation "started withdrawing because it started taking up too much manpower."[2] Supply and maintenance costs were becoming untenable. Because of a similar growing drain on their staffing and budgets, after the first four years the police and fire departments stopped volunteering their personnel. And when Eileen Anderson defeated marathon supporter Frank Fasi in the Honolulu mayoral race in 1980, the city and county of Honolulu withdrew even more. As Kono recalls, it was Anderson who "halted everything for city support because it cost them too much money." This decision proved costly for the HMA, which now had to pay for special-duty police to line the course—a budget item that has since grown from $14,000 to more than $200,000 per race. Kono and others in HMA have speculated that Anderson's husband, Honolulu Police Department (HPD) Major Clifford Anderson, then head of the Traffic Division, directly influenced the decision. Police assignments for race day had previously been secured by Honolulu Marathon race director David Benson, an HPD major who led the Juvenile Crime Prevention Division.

Race officials absorbed the losses by digging deep into a community of volunteers—some runners, many not—eager to be a part of the grand spectacle. On race days, thousands of volunteers from local businesses, schools, churches, and community groups manned aid stations, helped out along the course, and tended to operations at the start and finish. The HMA directors themselves remained intimately hands-on with all the preparations, from Scaff and his wife Donna stenciling race numbers by hand at the Palolo Chinese Home[3] to HMA director of administration Phil Olsen linking thousands of safety pins in groups of four so runners could attach the numbers to their shirts.[4] While tempers sometimes flared—Scaff's occasionally brusque manner and famously dark sense of humor did not always go over well with stressed-out volunteer directors—the shared labor and do-it-yourself spirit of those early years created a loyalty and sense of purpose in core volunteers. Some would devote decades of their lives to the organization, and it was during these early growth years that three of the stalwarts—Ron and Jeanette Chun and Rick Taniguchi—joined up.

Secret Weapons

A perpetually moving ball of nervous motherly energy, Jeanette Chun got her start in the marathon because of her dentist. A metabolic issue had caused Chun's weight to boomerang between 99 and 160 pounds. In an attempt to halt one of her weight-gaining cycles, Chun stopped eating regular food and subsisted on an improvised diet of lemon drop candies and water. Chun shed the extra weight but the sugary diet nearly ruined her teeth. Her dentist, Dr. Melvin Uyehara, suggested what by then was considered a far more reasonable weight-control option: Go check out Dr. Scaff's running clinic. "The clinic was on Sunday and he scheduled me for all Monday appointments, so I knew he'd ask me about it," Chun recalled. She completed her first marathon in 1978, dragging her wary but supportive husband Ron along for company. For Jeanette, who had quit her job as a teacher to raise a family, completing the 26.2-mile race was a transformative experience. "I was never a subservient person," Chun said. "But when you stay at home and your husband is the breadwinner, you can start to get like that. But after that first marathon, I'd fight back. I was liberated."[5]

The Chuns were so taken with the experience that as soon as the race was over, they told Scaff that they wanted to help in any way they could. It was an offer that in many ways secured the next four decades of the race. Jeanette started out simply, applying contact paper to recycled soda boxes for collecting entry forms. But Scaff had grand plans for expanding the marathon experience, and Jeanette happened to be in his sight lines when he decided that a premier marathon should host a carbo-loading party. "So (Scaff) gives me a list with (board member Kent) Davenport's name and whoever else and said that these people are going to help you," Chun recalled. "But they didn't know how to put on a party. I had to start from scratch."[6] Working with an undefined budget safely assumed to be quite lean, the Chuns relied on local-style goodwill to pull off the party, borrowing tables from the Liberty House department store, renting whatever else they needed on a handshake discount with a manager from AA Party Rentals, and calling on students from Maryknoll School, their son's alma mater, to set up and strike down. Held at Aloha Tower with tickets selling briskly at $10 apiece, the party was a huge success. At the next general meeting of the HMA, Chun addressed the board. "I just said, 'I want to thank you folks. I had a nice time.' And they said, 'Where are you going?' And I said, 'Home.'"[7]

Hardly. HMA's executive board urged Chun to remain an active part of the organization. Within a couple of years, she was the association's official secretary, and soon after its treasurer, since she was cutting all the checks anyway. But her contributions always went well beyond whatever her job title happened to be. As the marathon grew, Chun came to be involved in nearly every administrative aspect of the race, her Citron Street home slowly becoming the cluttered nerve center of the HMA. In the lead up to each race, Chun would work directly with government agencies, meet with sponsors, coordinate hotel reservations, and cut checks—as many as 1,200 a month as race day approached. Her sense of professionalism made her worry herself sick making sure that vendors and contractors were paid as promptly as possible. She knew when each post office made its last pick up, and if necessary she'd drive out to the airport to ensure her last drop made it out, often dropping a quarter in the mailbox to make sure it hadn't been emptied yet. One year, Chun cut 950 checks in a single month, but when she tried to balance the ledger, it was three cents off.

> It drove me crazy. (Ron) would read all the pages, all that small, little print. Then my mother would read. Then he would do it again. So I said, "Forget it. Too much. I'll reconcile it later." I was too tired. My eyes were tired, I guess. But later I found it. This is not my money so I have to reconcile it, even if it's three cents.[8]

Chun was also called on to deal with local residents inconvenienced by the annual traffic disruption. One year, a manager from Longs Drug Store in

Hawai'i Kai called to complain because staging for the race had blocked all the parking lot entrances, disrupting a planned promotion. There was no way to remedy the situation after the fact, so Chun asked him for his size so she could send him a shirt and some other race-day merchandise. The irate manager wanted nothing of it, but Chun persisted in her own unique way: "So I told him, 'You can spit on it.' And he said, 'O.K., give me a large one.'"[9]

The Chuns' marriage has survived their more-than-full-time commitment to the marathon in part because their responsibilities are cleanly divided. Whatever doesn't fall under Jeanette's purview generally falls under Ron's. Almost as soon as he volunteered his services, Ron, a Navy engineer, was put in charge of making race-day operations at Kapi'olani Park run more efficiently, and if possible, more economically. Chun excelled at both, redesigning procedures in the park and along the course, designing and building equipment to accommodate the race's growth, and assembling an army of loyal-'til-death (or retirement) volunteers ready to perform millions of dollars worth of labor in exchange for the Chuns' famous compensation package of "a T-shirt, a hat, maybe lunch." It didn't take long for Chun to put his imprint on the race, and to make clear how he, his volunteers, and the vendors he did business with were to be treated. After completing his first marathon, Chun alerted Scaff to the lack of organization at the finish area, where long lines of runners trying to pick up their finisher shirts backed up all the way into the corral near the finish line. In keeping with his leadership style, Scaff invited Chun to fix it. The next year, after remapping the finish area and having his volunteers set up the tents, risers, and other infrastructure, Chun crossed the finish line only to see people moving a stand erected the day before.

> They said they had changed their mind. I said, "Who?" They said, "The race director." I said, "No, no. We don't do work twice. Do it one time right and let it be. Next year, I'll make the plan with everything you want, but once it goes down, it stays. If they want to change it, they're doing it themselves. We don't treat volunteers like that. It's not right. It's not fair."[10]

Another year, Chun was asked to arrange post-race massages for the runners. He had no idea how to proceed, so he simply dialed his way through the Yellow Pages, eventually making contact with the head of the Aisen Shiatsu School. After a face-to-face meeting, the sensei spoke to his therapists about accommodating the projected 1,000 or so post-race clients. "(The therapists) rallied around him," Chun said. "They came out in force." With no budget to pay the therapists, Chun promised that he would provide lunch. But when the therapists went to the volunteer tent to pick up their food, they were told there was nothing left. Chun was livid. Still wobbly from completing his own run, he located Scaff in the crowd and lit into him.

> I told him, "You cannot do that. We promised them lunch! You knew what the deal was." He said, "I'm sorry." I said, "I'm sorry doesn't feed a hundred people." I was tired after the marathon. I didn't know people were looking at me. I went after Jack. I said, "No respect! Who's going to go cook a hundred hamburgers now?"[11]

Ultimately, Chun dug into his own wallet and bought lunch for the massage volunteers. The next day, at the traditional post-race assessment meeting, Chun went over his list of what went well and what needed to be improved. He didn't mention the massage therapists in front of the other directors, but after the meeting, he confronted Scaff again and "let him have it." It was not the last time Chun and Scaff would clash—once, after Scaff made a flippant remark that offended Jeanette, Ron Chun confronted the then-HMA president and threatened to "throw him in the [expletive] ocean"[12]—but it helped to create an organizational ethos that has helped the Chuns retain their core of volunteers, some for more than thirty-five years, and to maintain goodwill with scores of local vendors and volunteers—including the therapists from Aisen, who still provide post-race massages every year. For their part, Chun and Scaff have always remained on good terms.

In an organization largely led by affluent Mainland transplants with professional or military backgrounds, the Chuns represented the many local HMA staffers and volunteers of the early years. Hawai'i-born, service-oriented, working-class people, they were inspired by their own marathon experiences to put time and energy into a community event that touched the lives of thousands of people just like them—the type of people, in short, that kept the HMA from looking like the old, rich, white Boston Athletic Association of truthful stereotype. Jeanette was raised in the McCully-Mō'ili'ili area, then a largely Japanese-American community. She attended Maryknoll School and graduated with a degree in education from the University of Hawai'i. Ron grew up in the downtown area, where he sold strings of fish caught at nearby Waikahalulu Falls for spending money. He graduated from McKinley High School and then joined the Air National Guard and later the Navy. He met Jeanette at a high school football game, married her while still attending the University of California at Berkeley, and returned to Hawai'i with her to raise their family. In the military, Ron developed a fierce regard for organizational discipline, planning, and precise execution, as well as a hair-trigger sensitivity to disrespect, actual or perceived, that stemmed in part from the racist treatment he received at several stops as a career Navy electrical engineer.

Jeanette says the time they spent struggling as newlyweds with a young child while Ron was at school in California bonded them as a couple. They are also joined by the value they both place on fidelity to duty over all. It's what allowed Jeanette and her parents to find solace after her brother, Air Force First Lieutenant David Anthony Lum, disappeared after his plane crashed into the China Sea during the Vietnam War. Just twenty-six, Lum had flown 183 missions and had earned a Distinguished Flying Cross. He was supposed to have been reassigned to California as a flight instructor, but felt compelled to return for another tour because there was a shortage of pilots. The Chuns' sense of fidelity is also part of the unapologetic pride they take in their son David (named after his MIA uncle), who in 1999 was convicted of conspiracy, deprivation of rights, and conspiracy to obstruct justice after he and five other police officers beat a suspect and then covered up the incident. According to prosecutors, the officers beat prison guard Richard Doolin in a police cell block after he was arrested for violating a temporary restraining order against his wife, and then acted "unruly" while being processed. Doolin suffered broken ribs and other injuries in the assault. Chun pleaded guilty, but he refused to implicate his fellow officers because to "hurt people who I know and work with in order to save myself is to me inhuman and indecent and dishonorable."[13] Years after Chun was released—he was isolated from the general prison population due to his status as an ex-police officer—both Ron and Jeanette continued to express pride that their son did not betray his fellow officers.

The same year that the Chuns first got involved with the marathon, Edward Pei, then an assistant vice president at First Hawaiian Bank and treasurer for the HMA, recruited a young man he had been mentoring via the Honolulu Jaycees civic organization. Rick Taniguchi had recently completed a master's degree in finance at the University of Hawai'i and was getting started as a real estate analyst and project manager for Alexander and Baldwin. During his first year, he was one of several Jaycee volunteers who helped with race-day operations. By his second year, he was the finish-line chairman. To his own recollection, Taniguchi says he was "bright-eyed and bushy tailed," with "no clue what was involved." Like the Chuns, Taniguchi came from local stock. Both sets of grandparents immigrated to Hawai'i from Japan to work on the sugar plantations. His maternal grandfather arrived in the 1890s and worked as a boiler man at O'ahu Sugar; his maternal grandmother was a picture bride from Hiroshima. His paternal grandparents settled on the Big Island as farmers. Taniguchi spent his childhood in Kalihi, not far from where his parents operated a small mom-and-pop store on Nimitz Highway. The store lasted until a Government Employees Mutual discount department store arrived in the neighborhood. His father took a job with the state, and the family moved to Nu'uanu. The Taniguchi children made the most of their opportunities. Those surviving include a neurosurgeon, a retired Department of Education administrator, and an epidemiologist. Taniguchi himself carved a niche the early days of wireless phone service, and for most of his career he has worked for wireless communications companies.

Scaff took Taniguchi under his wing, and over many a beer drawn from Scaff's home tap, trained him to take charge of finish line operations, including the systems for processing runners as they completed the race. Bearing the acronym RATFINK (though no one remembers what it stood for), the system required multiple levels of recording, including physically removing and spindling a tag from each runner's bib, and using a Chronomix (a printer-timer device synched to the official clock) that allowed runners to be recorded with the push of a button. Periodic results were then printed on thermal paper and posted. Later, Taniguchi moved to the start line with other Jaycees, eventually taking full control of that operation as well. Just as Ronald Chun developed the protocols for the finisher's area through intuition and experimentation, Taniguchi proved adept at figuring out how to meet the increasingly complex demands of the starting area. Sometimes it required a handshake, sometimes sheer improvisation. When a lift was needed to elevate the race starter, city officials, and key sponsors above the start line, Taniguchi and the other race officials relied on the aloha of local businesses:

> When we were small, everybody was cooperative. The lifts and that sort
> of stuff, we used to get them over at Aloha Airlines. Nobody thought

anything of giving us a lift here, a lift there. Theo Davies, for example. They would just give us snorkel lifts and man lifts. If you've ever seen pictures of the start, where there usually is a starter or a JAL official or the mayor, they're up there on a lift. Those lifts were all provided literally at no charge.[14]

As the race numbers got larger, lining up the starting field according to projected finish times became more of a challenge. When the start was still at Aloha Tower and Pier 9, and could accommodate the entire field, Taniguchi would stage runners according to their anticipated pace. But without funding for elaborate custom signage, Taniguchi had to be creative about how to mark where each group should be. He tethered a softball to a long rope and had the best arm on his softball team heave it over a metal hook on the tower exterior. He then use this rope to hang signs—"Three Hours," "Four Hours," etc.—in ascending order across the pier. When the field was too large, the slowest group was staged upstairs.

Large and in Charge

As the race continued to grow, so did Scaff's prominence, both locally and nationally. In Hawai'i, he became the local media's go-to authority on long-distance running and cardiac health. Thanks to frequent visits by Olympic marathon runner turned journalist Kenny Moore, whom Scaff regularly hosted, he and the local running scene were also celebrated in the pages of *Sports Illustrated*. Indeed, many elements of the Scaff legend that would be invoked over the coming decades—the vision, the Falstaffian appetites, the "wry, abusive lines, all of which have the faint aroma of challenge"— were first described in a 5,600-word feature Moore wrote for the Feb. 27, 1978, edition of *Sports Illustrated*. The article identifies Scaff as "the catalyst" of Honolulu's burgeoning running scene: a quick-witted, bracingly honest champion of the running life who "is at his Napoleonic best when laying down the law on philosophy." His five essential rules for marathon training were listed, and there was also ample room for his theories about everything from pacing and hydration to the primitive origins of diarrhea, as well as the practical considerations of offering decarbonated Coke at aid stations. Scaff was also prominently featured in another article for *Sports Illustrated* that followed Moore, Scaff, and a group of hard-core distance runners through a 20-day, 500-kilometer ultramarathon organized by Scaff's wife Donna. Written with Moore's distinctive flair, the piece reads like a collision between Homer and Hunter Thompson (who himself would later contribute to the Honolulu Marathon's colorful archive of literature and lore).

Not surprisingly, some in the organization began to feel that their own efforts were being lost in Scaff's broad shadow. "They wanted to be me," Scaff says. By this time, the HMA Board of Directors had swelled to sixteen members, thanks to Willy Williamson's belief in the efficacy of delegation. Williamson was a former Royal Air Force Spitfire pilot who survived being shot down over Italy during World War II and who went on to be a stunt pilot in the films *Tora! Tora! Tora!* and *Those Magnificent Men in Their Flying Machines*.[15] He came to the organization via Scaff's Honolulu Marathon Clinic. In a by-now-familiar organizational pattern, he offered his help and Scaff promptly and without warning named him the vice president of race operations.[16] Not coincidentally, Williamson was vice president of operations at Aloha Airlines at the time, and he applied his own managerial style, recruiting new directors to oversee more than a dozen new committees formed to handle various aspects of the race. Like Scaff, Williamson had plenty of ideas on how to improve the marathon experience. As humorously depicted in Mark Osmun's 1979 book *The Honolulu Marathon*, it was Williamson who purchased the giant Zetachron that served for a time as the official timing clock, and it was Williamson who brought in the infamous Chronomix, much to the chagrin of fellow board member Peter Searl. Williamson also secured the first starter's pistol, which he himself used while perched atop a cherry picker. Never to be outdone, Scaff then came up with the idea of fireworks at the start.

By the turn of the decade, Williamson's desire to lead the organization had become increasingly apparent and divisive. In 1980, support for him was strong, but Scaff still prevailed in the annual election for HMA president. Williamson quit, prompting Scaff to look for a way to lure him back:

> We had written it up that we could have a CEO and then I could chair the meetings. So I became CEO. But I later found out that the CEO doesn't call the meetings, and doesn't need to be at all of them, so they quit asking me. They were running it independently.[17]

However primitive the Honolulu Marathon's organization and management practices may seem today, they were vastly more complicated than when Scaff worked with the MPRRC and the city to stage the first races. The annual doubling of the field for the first six years, and the withdrawal of Parks and Recreation support, demanded changes. By 1981, Scaff could declare himself the victor in his fight against traditional notions of cardiac recovery, and he had also fulfilled his and John Wagner's vision of using the marathon and the Marathon Clinic as vehicles for improving community health. Though his published prediction that the field would top 10,000 had not yet happened,[18] the Scaff who appeared in Moore's "The Rules of the Road" had been largely vindicated. There was still plenty that Scaff wanted to accomplish. Thirty-five years later, his head is still filled with ideas for increasing U.S. and non-Japanese participation, engaging local sponsors, and improving the race-day experience. But the HMA Board of Directors was clearly moving in a different direction, and Scaff was becoming concerned it was "tending more towards taking money out of the event or surviving on it rather than putting it back into the community."[19]

Rather than allow himself to be reduced to a figurehead in the organization he had helped to found, Scaff resigned.

CHAPTER 4

Transitional Times

James "Willy" Williamson was officially elected as president of the Honolulu Marathon Association in 1982, securing undisputed leadership at a transitional moment for the race and for the sport of marathon overall. With Honolulu Marathon entries now hovering around 8,000, the money flowing in and out of the association was becoming a topic of increasing interest. Under Williamson, race officials were more than willing to discuss the supposedly tenuous financial situation as a way to explain the conspicuous expansion of promotional activities. Between 1977 and 1981, HMA's operating budget skyrocketed from $50,000[1] to $250,000.[2] Annual expenditures included $19,000 for finisher shirts, $12,000 for park preparations, $12,000 for finishers' certificates, and thousands of dollars more for post-race food and beverages, the shell lei given to each runner at the finish line, and scores of other essentials and incidentals, not to mention the annual $2,000 post-race appreciation party for volunteers. To give Hawai'i residents a sense of the scale, HMA began its annual tradition of publicizing an itemized inventory of the necessary supplies. In 1981 the list included, among other things, 25,000 cups; 1,800 gallons of decarbonated, diluted cola; 6,000 sponges; and eighteen tons of ice.

HMA officials estimated that the race cost $3 to $5 more per runner than entry fees—$5 to $40, depending on when they were submitted—could cover. To make up the difference, the HMA began selling its own line of T-shirts, visors, tote bags, medallions, and other items emblazoned with the image of the marathon's mascot, the King's Runner, as well as a souvenir results book and a half-hour video recap of the race. As then-HMA vice president Gary Murfin later recalled:

We began to recognize that there was big demand for anything that had "Honolulu Marathon" on it. John Kelleher,[3] who was an entrepreneur at heart and an advertising retail guy, really recognized the opportunity to help develop the commercial side of the event relative to T-shirts and running gear and branding the marathon.[4]

Individual and corporate donations (roughly $43,000 in 1980), the HMA-sponsored Hawai'i Festival of Running ($16,929), personalized photos ($12,000), and the carbo-load party ($8,600) generated further revenue.[5]

With Hawai'i residents at this time still making up three-fourths of the overall field, the marathon was the state's largest recreational sporting event by a wide margin, and one of the most anticipated sporting events of the year. Finisher shirts were a coveted status symbol, not just of athletic achievement but also of pop culture cachet. Radio station KKUA broadcast the event live from several points along the course, and the local CBS affiliate KGMB-TV produced an annual one-hour special of race highlights. Several affiliated events held in the week leading up to the race heightened the anticipation and added to the sense of the race as a major event. In 1981, race week began with the Asian Pacific Congress and American Medical Joggers Association Medical Marathoners Symposium, and the annual Conference on Race Administration, which featured Atlanta Track Club executive director Royce Hodge, London Marathon co-founder Christopher Brasher, and Katherine Switzer, the first woman to officially run the Boston Marathon.[6] The HMA's carbo-loading party was held at Aloha Tower, an affiliated pasta party was held at the La Mancha restaurant in Waikīkī, and an early version of the Honolulu Marathon Expo took place in Kapi'olani Park.

Growing Pains

Williamson took over leadership of the HMA just in time to prepare for the historic tenth running of the Honolulu Marathon. He was determined to reverse two years of declining participation, and to reach Scaff's goal of 10,000 entrants. He would achieve far more than that. At his direction, the association capped the entry fee at $10, despite protests from the treasurer that it was "too low and (would) result in a severe strain on our resources."[7] The discounted entry, a specially embroidered finisher's shirt, and the anniversary itself led to a record 12,275 entrants. In an interview with the *Honolulu Advertiser's* Mike Tymn, Williamson said that the race was straining

Willy Williamson succeeded Jack Scaff as president of the Honolulu Marathon Association. Photo courtesy of Dr. Jack Scaff.

its capacities given the congestion along Kalaniana'ole Highway, but that this was a non-issue, since "I personally think that we have reached our peak this special year."[8]

By the end of the decade, of course, marathon participation would swell well beyond 12,000 runners. What Williamson was forced to consider during the brief years of his presidency would however have far-reaching implications in the boom years to come. In his interview with Tymn, Williamson talked about the financial hardships resulting from the city and county's new policy of requiring the marathon to pay for police services, and from the city's insistence that wheelchair athletes, who had been banned the previous year, had to be accommodated. The issue of accommodating wheelchair athletes in foot races had been troubling race directors for several years. In 1974, Boston became the first marathon to have a wheelchair division, and most other races soon included disabled participants. Some offered separate but affiliated events; others had wheelchair racers start ahead of the field. But as the number of disabled athletes swelled in the late 1970s and early 1980s—spurred by the emerging disability rights movement, by legislation like the Architectural Barriers Act of 1968 and the Rehabilitation Act of 1973, and by improved wheelchair design and technology—the demands by these athletes to compete in road races created a simmering controversy. Opponents argued that wheelchairs, and especially so-called hand-crank racing chairs equipped with gears similar to bicycles, were not analogous to running. Instead, they argued, such athletes should compete in cycling races. Some race directors sidestepped the ethical and legal arguments by saying they opposed mixing runners with faster-moving wheelchair athletes because it compromised safety for everyone.

The HMA's decision to ban wheelchairs in 1981 occurred in the midst of a contentious, high-profile battle on the East Coast. In 1977, Bob Hall, winner of the first wheelchair marathon in Toledo, Ohio, in 1974, and the first wheelchair athlete to compete officially in the Boston Marathon,[9] registered for but was denied entry into the New York City Marathon. Hall sued, and was granted an injunction allowing him to participate. But the New York City Road Runners Club (NYCRRC) continued to argue its case in the courts, and in 1982, the New York State Court of Appeals affirmed the club's right to bar "vehicles" from its foot race.[10] Wheelchair athletes would continue to participate in the marathon, but were ineligible for separate recognition or prize money, and were frequently delayed along the course in favor of able-bodied competitors. Finally, in 1999, nine members of the Achilles Track Club successfully filed a suit against the NYCRRC, claiming that wheelchair athletes were being discriminated against, in violation of the Americans with Disabilities act of 1990. The NYCRRC then introduced a new wheelchair and handcycle division, with prize money for top finishers.

Like the NYCRRC, the HMA cited safety concerns as its reason for restricting wheelchair athletes from competing—an argument undermined by lack of evidence of injuries or disruption at the Boston Marathon or any other road race already open to wheelchair competition. This issue was a point of contention between the HMA and the city of Honolulu for much of the next decade, but the tenor of negotiations was clear from Williamson's comments to Tymn:

> When the city advised us that a permit would not be issued for the
> Honolulu Marathon unless wheelchair athletes were permitted to

Elite wheelchair athletes Jim Knaub and Kenny Carnes helped to promote the wheelchair division despite inconsistent treatment from Honolulu Marathon organizers. Photo by Carl Viti. Courtesy of the *Honolulu Star-Advertiser.*

participate, the marathon association found itself in the untenable situation of having only three choices. One, to cancel the race because of the degradation of acceptable safety standards; two, take the city and county to court; or three, to allow limited integration this year. Reluctantly, after considerable deliberation, we decided on the third alternative. We did, however, insist that the City and County of Honolulu assume liability for any accidents or injuries as a result of allowing wheelchairs on the course.[11]

The Amateur Athlete Revolt

An even larger issue brewing in the marathon world soon challenged the principles on which the Honolulu Marathon was founded. During the early boom period of the 1970s, many larger marathons adopted thinly veiled methods for circumventing the AAU's restrictions on athletes accepting money, such as Scaff's arrangement with the American Medical Joggers Association. But in 1980, the *Washington Post* reported that the New York City Marathon had paid some $50,000 in prize money to its top finishers the previous year—a direct violation of amateurism rules. Winner Bill Rodgers confirmed that although he did not directly receive any prize money, he "had an arrangement before the race to get a certain amount in expenses."[12] What he received was about $10,000 in guaranteed income—the amount believed to have been reserved for the first-place finisher. Another runner claimed that he had received a check from Perrier, one of the race sponsors. NYCRRC president Fred LeBow denied paying prize money to the top finishers, but remarked that "in athletics, track and sports, there has always been some kind of payment in some form under the table."[13]

By the early 1980s, top American runners were chafing against the fraudulence of the situation, and calling for systemic reform. The athletes wanted to accept directly the prize money that the big races and their growing roster of sponsors were willing to pay for top performances. But The Athletics Congress (TAC),[14] which had effectively replaced the AAU as the direct authority over amateur road racing in the United States, held firm. Athletes who competed for prize money were no longer amateurs under International Association of Athletic Federations (IAAF) rules, and were therefore ineligible for international competition, including the Olympics—still considered the pinnacle of marathon competition. The athletes' frustration reached a new level when the United States boycotted the 1980 Olympic Games in Moscow in response to the Soviet Union's invasion of Afghanistan. For a group of elite distance runners in the prime of their abilities, the incentive for maintaining the charade of amateurism had disappeared. As Don Kardong, who finished fourth in the 1976 Olympics in Montreal and won the 1978 Honolulu Marathon, recalled some thirty years later:

> It made you feel like a drug dealer if you took (under-the-table payments). And you were afraid that you might get suspended for taking it. It was just an awful system. The thing that kept the system together was saying, "Well, if you want to be in the Olympics, you've got to keep your amateur eligibility." Then there was the boycott and people were furious.[15]

The first major challenge to the TAC came from Jordache, the designer jeans company and an early supporter of road racing in the United States. The company offered to sponsor the New York City Marathon if the NYCRRC would pay its proposed $250,000 prize purse directly to the top finishers. LeBow, then working with the TAC on an alternative prize distribution system, balked at the proposal, and Jordache contracted a sports promotion firm to stage its own race in Atlantic City. Despite some $50,000 in guaranteed prize money, the race did not attract an elite field. With the exception of Tom Fleming, a 2:12 marathoner, top runners avoided the event, fearing that while the TAC might turn a blind eye to under-the-table payments, it would make good on its threat to revoke the amateur status of any runner who participated in the Jordache event. Happily and without apology, unheralded runner Ron Nabors of San Francisco took home the $15,000 top prize.[16]

The TAC addressed the crisis by proposing a Grand Prix circuit of running events. Prize money would be paid to the top finishers' clubs, which in turn would use the funds to defray the runners' "training expenses." TAC executive director Ollan Cassell, a 1964 Olympic gold medalist in the 4x400 relay, told *Sports Illustrated* at the time, "The IAAF needs some kind of experience before diving into dark waters. They want to know where the rocks are."[17] Though a step forward, this proposal did not go far enough for an increasingly unified front of top runners. A year earlier, Rodgers, Herb Lindsay, and Greg Meyers had organized the Association of Road Racing Athletes (ARRA)—a de facto union for elite runners. At a meeting in Chicago, the ARRA discussed the TAC proposal, and decided not only to boycott the series but to set up its own circuit of prize-money races. As ARRA president, Kardong envisioned a professional tour like those for golf and tennis that would ensure a viable living for top runners. With the biggest names in American road racing, including the top female competitors Joan Benoit Samuelson, Mary Decker Slaney, and Patti Catalano Dillon all on board, the ARRA vote doomed the TAC Grand Prix. What remained to be seen was how the TAC would respond to the runners' intention to flout amateurism and its guidelines by openly competing for prize purses.

The answer came at the 1981 Cascade Run Off, a 15-kilometer race in Portland, Oregon, with a $50,000 prize purse provided by Nike and earmarked for direct payment to the top finishers. In race director Chuck Galford, who also served as legal counsel for the ARRA, the athletes had a well-connected ally. He understood the interests of corporate sponsors in elevating the profile of distance running through large prize purses and promoting elite-level athletes. He also wasn't afraid of a showdown with track and field's ruling body. More than 6,000 runners competed. Meyer won in 43:18; Olympic hero Frank Shorter, who favored a less confrontational approach, attended but did not participate. Both Meyer and New

Zealander Anne Audain, the first-place woman, received $10,000. Lindsay accepted a second-place check for $6,000 but immediately gave it to Rich Castro, manager of the Frank Shorter Racing Team, who deposited it into an escrow account, pending the TAC response.[18]

The TAC suspended Meyer, Catalano Dillon, Cindy Dalrymple, Benji Durden, John Glidewell, Ed Mendoza, Pete Pfitzinger, and Ric Rojas for participating, and declared that any amateur athletes who raced against them in subsequent ARRA events would risk losing their amateur status, and therefore their eligibility for the Olympics and other IAAF-sanctioned international events. Other national federations also moved against runners under their jurisdiction who ran in the Portland race, most notably the New Zealand Amateur Athletic Association (NZAAA), which suspended Audain, Allison Roe,[19] and Lorraine Moller. But the athletes were generally undeterred. Audain and Moller scored an important victory by effectively forcing the NZAAA to back down from enforcing amateur provisions relating to prize money. As Audain told noted race commentator Toni Reavis:

> We threatened that if the federation didn't stand by us in this matter we wouldn't run for New Zealand ever again. Remember that the Commonwealth Games were scheduled for Brisbane, Australia in 1982. We told the NZAAA that if they didn't reinstate us for domestic competition, we would go to the track and run the necessary qualifying times for the Games in front of all the media. Then if they didn't put us on the team they would look like a bunch of fools because we were by far the best women runners in the country with the best chance for medals, and the public was very much behind us. It was basically a bluff, but within ten minutes they did reinstate us for New Zealand competitions, and that forced the IAAF eventually to reinstate us as well.[20]

The banned athletes found stronger support at the Bobby Crim 10-miler in Flint, Michigan. A lifelong Democrat, Crim was then state Speaker of the House. The race was a fund-raiser for Special Olympics, and seeing the TAC-ARRA standoff as a labor issue, Crim sided with athletes by ignoring the TAC's "contamination" rule and allowing banned runners to compete.[21]

With the tide turning toward the athletes, the IAAF gave Cassell and the TAC leeway to quell the open rebellion. The resolution would come from Shorter, who had always favored a measured approach to introducing prize money into open competition. Drawing on his legal training from the University of Florida, he studied the International Olympic Committee by-laws and discovered that the rules allowed trusts to be established for athletes to cover training expenses. Shorter, Lindsay, and attorney Bob Stone approached Cassell with the discovery, and he successfully got the IAAF's approval.[22] He then hired attorney Alvin Chriss to establish the TAC trust at the Bank of Boulder (Colorado), where Bolder Boulder 10K race director Steve Bosley served as president. Chriss designed a trust model that would provide cost-of-living payments to athletes based on the Consumer Price Index of different cities, ensuring that athletes would get 25 percent of the average cost-of-living, then about $6,000.[23] Once the trust system was set up, the TAC reinstated the eight suspended athletes.

More of a half-step than a quantum leap in the sport's move from supposedly pure amateurism to professionalism, the trust plan was a compromise, but a necessary one for carrying out the transition. First, it opened the floodgates for corporate sponsorship money. Now the very best runners in the world would not just subsist but thrive financially on the returns of their hard work and abilities. It also created competition among the prestige marathons to attract the top athletes, who much like prize fighters only competed two or three times a year due to the physical demands of the sport. But to raise the sort of money required to secure a competitive field of elite runners who could break course and world records, and thereby offer a return on investment in the form of media coverage and positive publicity, races would need a critical mass of entrants, a generous corporate sponsorship, or most likely, both.

Standing on Tradition

In the 1982 interview, Williamson happily embraced the characterization of the Honolulu Marathon as a "people's race."[24] Like other race organizers across the country, Williamson and the HMA directors faced an existential dilemma: stand on tradition and risk failing in the open market for elite competition, or embrace the new reality of prize purses and appearance money, and with that, accept a more corporate approach to race promotion. Under Williamson, the Honolulu Marathon continued to identify with its volunteer roots. The directors believed that the race could not compete with Boston or New York. As HMA personnel director Michael Coad told the *Honolulu Advertiser*'s Ann Miller:

We absolutely do not give prize money. We don't have it to give. We're probably the last major marathon still done by a volunteer group. That's not to say we don't need a lot of help. But we're still very strongly dedicated to a strictly amateur run. We've never even considered giving prize money.[25]

In the same piece, HMA board member Jim Moberly speculated about what it would cost to bring three-time New York City Marathon winner Alberto Salazar, then considered the top male marathoner in the world, to Honolulu. "A lot of money," Moberly concluded: "I don't think there's any question. Alberto has never been secretive about that at all. Our philosophy has always been not to pay any kind of prize money. We never have. We've subsisted on our location and we put on a nice race." Salazar would in fact come to Honolulu the following year, along with Allison Roe and other running luminaries—but not to race. Unwilling to offer compensation beyond flight, hotel accommodations, and a nominal per diem, Honolulu race officials had to watch Salazar and the other elite runners make public appearances on behalf of their sponsors at events in and around the marathon.

Even though the HMA officials stood fast against prize money, or significantly raising entry fees, the costs of staging even a so-called people's race forced the board to seize merchandising opportunities, and to establish various levels of corporate sponsorship. In 1979, the race finished $30,000 in the red, a deficit covered only after board members solicited donations from the *Honolulu Advertiser* (several editors had connections to the Mid-Pacific Road Runners Club) and the Liberty House department store. Individual board members had long been leveraging their personal and professional connections with airlines and local businesses for financial support and in-kind donations. The most significant backing, however, came from Nike, which had gotten an early jump on attaching its name to prominent road races across the country. Nike covered the cost of finisher shirts—$50,000 by the early 1980s, according to then HMA treasurer John Fitzgibbon[26]—and in some years brought in winners of other Nike-sponsored races to compete.

Because entry fees couldn't cover race expenses alone, the growing numbers of participants put even more financial pressure on the HMA. According to Murfin:

The entry fee was actually lower, as I recall, than New York, Chicago, or L.A. It didn't go a long way. As we began to draw more (and) have a greater need for more support from the City and County, particularly with regard to traffic and all that police control—we had no resources to draw upon unless we created them ourselves.[27]

Murfin turned to working out a sponsorship agreement with Dole Food Company, still a strong presence in islands dating back to its days as one of the world's largest pineapple distributors. For an organization trying to hold on to its purist philosophy, the negotiations were a painful awakening for the HMA. Murfin described the situation:

Of course, they had strong demands with regard to promotion and advertising. At that point in time, nobody wanted to give up our independence. That was a battle because Dole helped bring in some of the elite runners through their coffers, not through ours. Everything was a negotiation. Where did their name go? Where would we put them? How would they appear on the finisher shirt? These were all sacred things to the people who had been running the organization and devoting their blood, sweat, and tears, so to speak, to creating the event and moving it along.[28]

When Murfin succeeded Williamson as HMA president following the 1983 race, he found himself hard pressed to balance the desire to remain a people's race with the challenge of keeping the race viable in the face of growing professionalization of the athletes and the influx of corporate money and influence.

Murfin had come to Hawai'i in 1970 as a PhD student in political science at the University of Hawai'i at Mānoa. He had a master's degree in intelligence research from American University School of International Service, and had spent time in Vietnam as a researcher for the Secretary of Defense Advanced Research Projects agency, and later as an Army intelligence officer. Soon after arriving in Hawai'i, Murfin took up running and joined Jack Scaff's Honolulu Marathon Clinic, completing his first marathon on the Big Island in 1975. Along with another political science student, Murfin approached Scaff about conducting a study linking physical and psychological health among clinic participants. In 1977, Scaff recruited Murfin to fill the newly created position of HMA research director. The study itself yielded a few interesting results, but then in the early '80s, Murfin turned his attention to the race's economic impact. In a 1982 study, he determined that approximately 40 percent of the field came from out of state, spending between $90 and $175 per day for an average of 10.3 days. Murfin concluded that the marathon brought nearly $9 million to the state each December.[29] In subsequent years, race officials would use economic impact to argue that the state should provide subsidies and in-kind contributions to the Honolulu Marathon, as it did for events like the NFL Pro Bowl and the PGA Sony Open. The HMA also used economic impact to fend off criticism about the marathon's race day effect on traffic, and to justify its heavy emphasis on Japanese participation.

Murfin served as HMA president for less than two years, and while his time is often overlooked in retrospectives on the race, like Williamson, he was among the first to confront emerging issues in the sport and seek avenues of growth that helped set the Honolulu Marathon's course toward becoming a premier destination event, and one of the largest and most influential races in the world. It was during Murfin's presidency that the question of how to secure a competitive field despite limited resources divided the board of directors, and ultimately set the race on a radical new course. The HMA had long recognized the value of attracting top talent to compete, dating all the way back to Scaff's sidestepping of AAU amateurism rules to secure Frank Shorter for the 1974 marathon. The board had already allotted a small portion of money for bringing in elite runners, whose appearance would raise the race profile, thereby luring potential sponsors and attracting more participants. The job of recruiting these athletes fell to the so-called elite athlete coordinator. Local orthopedic surgeon Kent Davenport held the post in the early 1980s, overseeing an annual budget ranging between $10,000 and $30,000, most earmarked for travel through an agreement with PanAmerican World Airways. Before the AAU amateurism rules were relaxed, Honolulu had done admirably in putting together a competitive field of local, national, and international runners each year. But with the introduction of official prize purses and guaranteed appearance money, the promise of a free trip to Hawai'i, free accommodations, and the chance to win a prize ribbon and a commemorative koa bowl was not as alluring as it had once been. In the short term, the HMA needed some creative thinkers who could somehow turn modest resources into elite-level competition. In the long term, it needed to resolve the question of whether to remain a people's race and abandon for good the idea of competing with larger, better-funded races, or to embrace a new set of values and find a niche within the hardening landscape of the new, big-money, high-participation marathon. In 1983, Davenport decided to take a sabbatical from his position as elite athlete coordinator. As his replacements, he asked a couple of new friends, recently arrived from Michigan.

Dr. James Barahal and Dr. Jonathan Cross were only too happy to accept.

PART II

TURNING POINTS

CHAPTER 5

The Marathon from Myth to Modernity

The marathon of mass participation and massive economic import is a modern beast with DNA drawn not just from its obvious lineage to ancient Greece, but from running traditions in societies as far away as the South Pacific.

The origin of the marathon is commonly linked to the apocryphal tale of a Greek *hemerodromoi* (messenger) who ran twenty-five miles from the Plain of Marathon to the city of Athens, announced the victory of out-manned Athenian forces over Persian invaders, and then promptly died. More than 550 years after the supposed event, and burnished by centuries of retelling, the earliest written version appears in Latin in the Greek historian Plutarch's essay "On the Fame of Athens." This tale contains all the elements of a classic sport narrative: martial conflict, a superhuman feat of strength and endurance, and a noble death.

As understood by scholars today, the actual story is even more incredible—if not quite as romantic. In 460 BC, Persian forces numbering anywhere from 25,000 to 60,000 landed in a bay near Marathon, intent on exacting revenge on the people of Athens for their intervention in the Ionian Revolt decades earlier. According to Michael Clark, professor of Defense Studies at King's College London, the Persians' plan was to draw Athenian forces into battle at Marathon, then to sail around Cape Sounion to attack the city from the undefended south.[1] Athenian forces numbered between 9,000 and 10,000, augmented by about 1,000 soldiers from Plataea. According to *The Histories* by Herodotus, the Athenians also dispatched a professional runner named Pheidippides to Sparta to solicit help against the Persians. He covered the rugged 140-mile distance in a single day, only to be told that Spartan forces could not be sent until after the end of a lunar festival, several days later. Pheidippides then ran the 140 miles back to Athens to deliver the bad news. Undeterred, the Athenians and Plataeans marched to the Plain of Marathon, and despite being significantly outmanned, turned back the Persians in a pair of pitched battles on the plain and at the port. Following the battle, another messenger was dispatched to Athens ahead of the returning army to inform leaders of the victory and to warn them of the Persians' impending arrival from the south.[2] Drawn from sources long since lost, Plutarch's first-century account narrows the identity of this messenger to two likely candidates: "Heraclides of Pontus records that it was Thersippus of Eroedae. . . . The majority of the sources, however, tell us it was Eucles."[3]

The Modern Sport

Differing accounts of the Battle of Marathon and of the heroic treks of Pheidippides and Thersippus/Eucles appeared over the next two millennia, eventually finding a more permanent if historically inaccurate home in Robert Browning's 1879 poem "Pheidippides," which credits the titular messenger with the run to and from Sparta, *and* from Marathon to Athens. Browning also replaces Pheidippides's supposed dying words, recorded in various histories as "Nike" ("victory"), "Nenikikamen" ("We have won"), or "Chairete, nikomen" ("Hail, we are the winners") with the more exultant English "Rejoice, we conquer!"—a phrase that has worked its way into many a modern marathon narrative.

> So when Persia was dust, all cried "To Akropolis!
> Run, Pheidippides, one race more! The meed is thy due!
> 'Athens is saved, thank Pan,' go shout!" He flung down his shield
> Ran like fire once more: and the space 'twixt the Fennel-field
> And Athens was stubble again, a field which a fire runs through
> Till in he broke: "Rejoice, we conquer!" Like wine thro' clay,
> Joy in his blood bursting his heart, he died—the bliss![4]

With its romantic depiction of service to country, courage, and self-sacrifice, "Pheidippides" resonated deeply with Victorian-era audiences already fascinated with the ancient Greek world. The poem was certainly well known by the time Pierre de Coubertin prevailed in his quest to resurrect the Olympic Games as a grand demonstration of the ennobling, morally instructive nature of competitive sport. De Coubertin was a French aristocrat and educator whose interest in athletics and educational reform was rooted in a sense of shame over the defeat of his home country in the Franco-Prussian war—a defeat he attributed to a fundamental weakness in the contemporary French character. He was heavily influenced by the Muscular Christianity movement that took root in England in the mid-1800s. This movement, which emphasized the positive role of athletics in promoting Christian morality, physical fitness, and the sort of masculine character believed necessary to keep the Anglican church vital, led directly to the foundation of the Young Men's Christian Association (YMCA) and the widespread introduction of physical education programs in English schools.[5] Though less interested in its religious aims, de Coubertin embraced Muscular Christianity's assumption that sport and the physical fitness it required were essential components of individual development—an assumption he saw as rooted in ancient Greek ideals of balance and self-control—and by extension, national vitality.

Victorian fascination with ancient Greek culture took various forms in the 1880s, including the staging of local athletic festivals that invoked the name and spirit of the original Olympic Games, held quadrennially from 776 BC to 394 AD. In 1894, at an international conference on athletics at the Sorbonne, de Coubertin successfully argued for an international Olympic Games. And at the suggestion of his close friend, the noted philologist Michel Breal, de Coubertin included in the inaugural games a 25-mile race from Marathon to Athens commemorating Pheidippides' legendary feat.

Held in Greece in 1896, the first modern Olympic Games drew widespread international attention. The more than 70,000 spectators crowding Panathinaikon Stadium celebrated as the hometown favorite, Greek water carrier Spiridon Louis, won the world's first marathon competition in a time of 2:58:50. Having survived the race, and having won a donkey-drawn carriage from Greek King George I as his bounty, Louis promptly retreated to his home in Marousi, never to race again. His stirring victory was celebrated across Greece, but it was the race itself that captured the imagination of sporting enthusiasts around the globe. A new athletic frontier had been discovered, one that could be approached only by athletes of rare fortitude, and even then only at the risk of fatal exhaustion. Two months later, another twenty-five mile race was staged in Paris, with a cash prize awarded to winner Len Hurst of England. Another marathon-style race was held in New York later that year, with a distance just exceeding twenty-five miles.

Only ten of the thirty competitors made it to the finish line.[6] The next year, the newly founded Boston Athletic Association held its first Boston Marathon. Fifteen runners started the race; ten finished, led by New Yorker John J. McDermott in a time of 2:55:10.

Over the coming decades, the marathon became an irregular but enthusiastically promoted event for local athletic clubs and road-race promoters. Typically staged as head-to-head battles between top runners, or open-field competitions for adventurous runners seeking to test their mettle, the marathon was incorporated into a well-established tradition of running and pedestrian ("heel-to-toe") competitions whose own roots extended to the heyday of Caledonian clubs in America in the 1860s and 1870s. Initially held as a means of perpetuating and celebrating Scottish culture in America, these events proved so popular that the Caledonian clubs quickly opened them to athletes of all ethnicities and nationalities, which in turn attracted larger and larger crowds of paid spectators.[7] Promoters sold tickets for the finish line, offered relatively large purses for the top runners, and appealed to ethnic or regional loyalties when publicizing the races. These practices soon brought them into conflict with high school and collegiate athletic organizations, which embraced amateurism as an athletic ideal, and with high-society athletic clubs in the Northeast United States, for whom amateurism helped keep working-class athletes, who lacked the means to train fulltime without prize money, from compromising the "integrity" of gentleman sports.

For the first dozen years after the 1896 Olympic Games, the distance of a marathon as a competitive sporting event varied between twenty-four and twenty-five miles. That changed at the 1908 Olympics in London, when the current standard of twenty-six miles, 385 yards was adopted to accommodate the British Queen Alexandra and Mary, then-Princess of Wales. (Rome had been originally chosen to host the 1908 games, but withdrew after the 1906 eruption of Mt. Vesuvius.) Originally designed to start and end at the newly constructed White City Stadium, the marathon was remapped to begin on the Grounds of Windsor Castle so that Mary and her children could watch the start from the nursery on the east terrace. The 26-mile mark was just inside the stadium, near an entry tunnel opposite the royal viewing box. The course was extended an additional 385 yards so that the race would finish in front of Queen Alexandra.[8]

The race itself was a thrilling spectacle that also reinforced the danger of the distance in the popular imagination. Hot, humid conditions wore

heavily on the field of fifty-five competitors. In the final mile, Italian runner Dorando Pietri held a shaky lead over South Africa's Charles Hefferon
and American John Hayes. Entering White City Stadium, Pietri made an
errant right turn, corrected himself, and then fell to the cinder track from
exhaustion. With a rapt crowd of 90,000 looking on, Pietri rose, then stum-
bled and fell four times, as he attempted to will himself through the final
385 yards. As Martin and Gynn note, medical personnel were "bewildered
as to how to proceed. They did not want to provide assistance that would
disqualify Pietri, yet they felt obliged to do something lest Pietri experience
dire consequences in the presence of the queen and a full stadium."[9] After
his third fall, at the insistence of an on-site physician, Pietri was assisted
by race organizer Jack Andrew, and managed to cross the finish line first,
ahead of Hayes and Hefferon. But the Americans protested his win, claiming
that Andrew's intervention gave Pietri an unfair advantage. He was then
disqualified, bringing to a head months of tension between the U.S. Olympic contingent and its British hosts. The Americans were already angry that
their flag was not displayed above the stadium along with those of the other
competing nations, and during the opening festivities they retaliated by
refusing to dip their flag in ceremonial deference to King-Emperor Edward
VII as they paraded around the track. The Americans had also accused
British judges of rigging a 400-meter race in favor of an English runner.
Thus, by the time Pietri crossed the marathon finish line, American coaches
were convinced that the British organizers would do anything to prevent an
American from winning.[10]

While Hayes was recognized as the official winner, it was Pietri who
endeared himself to the public through his courageous effort. In the *Daily
Mail,* Sherlock Holmes creator Sir Arthur Conan Doyle wrote about watching Pietri from within the stadium:

> Thank God, he is on his feet again—the little red legs going incoher-
> ently, but drumming hard, driven by a supreme will within. There is a
> groan as he falls once more, and a cheer as he staggers again to his feet.
> It is horrible, and yet fascinating, this struggle between a set purpose
> and an utterly exhausted frame.[11]

Queen Alexandra arranged for the Italian to receive a special commemorative trophy for his performance. British fans even raised money to help
him open a bakery back in Italy. They needn't have bothered. Buoyed by

his instant celebrity, Pietri enjoyed a profitable second career as a professional runner. Just two months after losing the gold medal, he defeated Hayes in a widely hyped rematch in front of 20,000 people in New York.[12] The combination of Hayes' victory for the United States and the story of the plucky Italian who drove himself to physical collapse in his quest for glory led to a boom in popularity for marathons—a craze that would be felt thousands of miles away, in the Territory of Hawai'i.

Early Marathons in Hawai'i

On March 21, 1909, nine months after Pietri's dramatic performance in London, Nigel Jackson, a Honolulu resident originally from New Zealand, won what is considered to be the first marathon ever staged in Hawai'i. Some forty-six impetuous runners began the 29-mile race from A'ala Park in downtown Honolulu to the Haleiwa Hotel on O'ahu's North Shore. Thirty-one made it to the finish line. The event was big news, with the local papers providing daily updates on who was in and out of the field. For weeks leading up to the race, the *Hawaiian Star* promoted a contest, asking readers who would win and what the time would be. Top prize for guessing the correct order of finishers was $10; the prize for guessing the winning time was $5. The paper ran daily updates on the voting. Community interest was so keen that thousands of spectators bought tickets for a special Oahu Railway and Land Co. train ride to transport them to the finish line.[13] Honolulu Mayor Joseph Fern fired the starting pistol at 7:30 a.m., sending the runners northward in the already rising heat. Troopers from the Fifth Cavalry lined the route, and a fleet of about 100 automobiles supplied water and liniment to the runners.[14] Jackson, thirty-six years old, took the lead around the 20-mile mark, but was nearly knocked out of the race—literally—when an automobile startled a horse ridden by a cavalry escort. The frightened horse reared up and kicked Jackson in the leg. In pain but undeterred, Jackson limped the last two miles to the finish line, where he was greeted by about 2,000 spectators.[15] He completed the non-standard course in 4:50:33, followed by Harry Gorman and Wilson Feagler.

The race was so successful that arrangements for another marathon began immediately. As the *Pacific Commercial Advertiser* reported, "Sunday's big event has augmented the present Marathon craze to such an extent that many of the contestants and their friends visited this office and literally demanded another race, so that they would have an opportunity to show that their recent experience taught them how they could beat anybody else on the Islands."[16] Set at the new 26.2 Olympic distance, and with a field of runners eager to challenge Jackson, this race was held just a month later, and promised to be a moneymaker. Participants paid a $1 fee to enter, and spectators were charged admission to the track. Betting was an important ingredient in the excitement—even for the runners. Dal Fahy, who had competed in the previous marathon, publicly wagered $100 that he would beat Jackson. But Jackson prevailed again, in a time of 3:48. His prize purse was $100.

The Territory's passion for long-distance running made it a popular destination for prize-chasing runners. Jackson, who was managed by Irish running great Paddy Walsh, participated in at least two more marathons that year, besting Japanese rival Tsukamoto on October 3rd, and placing third in another race in November. In Hawai'i, race promoters and reporters focused on ethnic and social distinctions. Newspapers meticulously listed the participants' ethnicities, employment, military service, and residency. In that first marathon of March 1909, it was reported that "of the starters 23 were Anglo-Saxon, 4 were Germans, 5 were Portuguese, 3 were Porto [*sic*] Ricans, 6 were Hawaiians, one was French and 1 was Chinese. An Australian won, an American was second, and a German third."[17] One of most popular runners of the era was C. K. Charlie, a milkman from the Kaimukī district frequently referred to in the local media as Charlie the Chinaman. "Like St. Yves," the *Pacific Commercial Advertiser* reported, "his legs are hardly long enough to reach from his body to the ground but how they did keep going." The local Japanese community rallied around a plantation worker from Hilo named Tsukamoto, who like many road racers of the day competed in everything from sprint events to full-scale marathons. Tsukamoto's appearance in a 1909 10-mile race in Honolulu was a ballyhooed event, measured by the amount of money circulating around the race. The *Pacific Commercial Advertiser* reported that Tsukamoto was given $500 upon his arrival to cover training expenses and lodging, and that a local Japanese merchant had collected $2,500 ($62,500 in 2014 dollars) from local Japanese to wager on a Tsukamoto victory. The Japanese community was excited:

> Never before have the local Japs been so worked up over a contest here. They are perfectly sure that Tsukamoto can win and they are getting their money together to back their confidence. It is not likely that much wagering will be done on the race but that is not the fault of the Japanese. They do not see how their man can lose. They say that a man who comes from a family of rikshaw men, who has been used to trotting mile

after mile with a heavy load tagging behind him, can easily outrun any haole.[18]

Charlie and Tsukamoto were key attractions because of their appeal to Hawai'i's large Chinese and Japanese populations. As sports historian Benjamin Rader explains, the rising popularity of competitive sports from the mid-1800s to the early twentieth century allowed athletes from newer immigrant populations to cross cultural and social boundaries due to their prowess, serving as a source of pride for the ethnic groups they represented.[19] This dynamic was perhaps most pronounced in the world of boxing, itself a highly popular sporting culture that ran counter to Victorian values. But while the emergence of ethnic minority athletes on the U.S. Mainland also led to the promotion of champions from the dominant culture (i.e., the Great White Hope), in Hawai'i, with its mix of indigenous Hawaiians, American and European Caucasians, and its waves of Chinese, Japanese, Korean, Portuguese, and other settler groups brought to work on the sugar plantations, the situation was quite different. In Honolulu in particular, "local"-ness was celebrated, and traveling athletes from the U.S. Mainland and Asia, even when represented positively, were still presented as threats to a local honor that homegrown athletes needed to defend.

Perhaps the most revered local runner in those early marathon days was Antone Kao'o. Nicknamed the "Waialua Horse," he had been a messenger for King Kalākaua and Queen Kapi'olani, and served in the Royal Guard at 'Iolani Barracks prior to the overthrow of the Hawaiian monarchy in 1893. He was also a renowned kumu hula, and the composer of the well-known Hawaiian chant "E Liliu E," written in honor of Queen Lili'uokalani, Hawai'i's last reigning monarch. Kao'o took up competitive long-distance running relatively late in life, becoming a champion marathoner and long-distance race walker well into his late forties. Although his exact age remains in dispute, he was reported to be forty-seven when he placed third in the 1909 A'ala Park-to-Hale'iwa marathon.

Kao'o's history as a royal messenger made him not just an important link to Hawai'i's recent past as a sovereign nation, but also a living reminder of Hawai'i's own running traditions. Like the *hemerodromoi* of ancient Greece, the kūkini of ancient Hawai'i were runners of legendary prowess, trained from childhood to deliver messages swiftly over great distances for their chiefs. As Martha Beckwith notes, "Chiefs looked doubtfully upon the first horses introduced upon the islands; their runners were swift of foot and could easily run down goats on the mountain."[20] The kūkini were sometimes called on to fetch fish from distant ponds, leading to several legends involving extraordinary conquests of distance over time. In one such tale, Makoa of Kaʻū is dispatched from Kailua to Hilo—76.6 miles one way—to get mullet for Kamehameha. Makoa completes the rugged trek, which would take a normal man four days, so swiftly that he returns to Kailua with the fish "still quivering."[21] Hawaiian historian David Malo tells the story of Ulunui of Oʻahu, who could supposedly carry a fish from Kaʻelepulu fishpond in Kailua through Waialua and into Waikīkī before it expired.[22] In still another variation, Kaohele, son of the king of Molokaʻi, was said to be fast enough to run from Kaluaʻaha to Hālawa and return "before a fish put on the fire at the time of his starting had been roasted."[23] Betting on footraces was also well established in ancient Hawaiʻi. According to Malo, organizers would pit two of the fastest kūkini against each other in long- or short-distance races:

> When people had made their bets, the experts came to judge by physical examination which of the two runners was likely to win, after which they made their bets. One man, after staking all of his property, pledged his wife and his own body (*pili hihia*), another man bet property he had borrowed from another (*pili kaua*). When all the pledges had been deposited (*kieke*, literally bagged), the betting was at an end.[24]

Like his legendary forebears, Kaoʻo was supremely confident of his abilities. He also leveraged his reputation, popularity, and willingness to take on all comers into guaranteed purses, training fees, and backing for wagers in a series of high-profile races against Jackson, British runner Jimmy Fitzgerald, and American serviceman "Soldier" King. In the lead-up to a one-on-one 15-mile race against King in October 1910, the *Evening Bulletin* reported, "If offers to wager fabulous amounts on Kaoo are any criterion, there are many Honolulu people who consider that the old Waialua Horse has a great show against Soldier King. The Hawaiians will be with Kaoo to a man, and they will not listen to any suggestion that he might be defeated. [. . .] The race should be a beauty, and all Hawaii will pin their faith on Kaoo."[25] The *Hawaiian Gazette* reported that as much as $10,000 ($250,000 in 2014 dollars) was wagered on the day of the race: "Individual Hawaiians, who were not classed as millionaires, flashed fifties and hundreds to show their faith in their favorite, and the King backers were flabbergasted at the amounts.

[. . .] A good many army officers relieved the Hawaiians of their gold, according to reports, and King got his orders to beat it or the military forces would go broke."[26] King ultimately defeated Kaoʻo, who at one point complained that King had struck his heel in violation of the rules. Still, these were highly profitable times for elite local racers like Kaoʻo. In a tune-up for the race against King, Kaoʻo agreed to a head-to-head match-up against Nigel Jackson over fifteen miles, with each runner putting up $150 ($3,730 in 2014). A year later, Kaoʻo raced Fitzgerald with a guarantee of $300 in appearance money and 60 percent of the net receipts.

The first marathon craze in Honolulu lasted just a few short years. In the following decades, interest would revive periodically after a particularly stirring or noteworthy marathon performance in the Olympic Games. In the 1940s and 1950s, marathons in Hawaiʻi were staged under the sanction of the AAU. Shaking off the early associations with gambling, these events took on the appearance of more formal amateur track and field events. The most prominent was the Hawaiian AAU Marathon, first run in 1943 as the Hawaiian Marathon, and then revived a decade later. The '43 race marked the debut of accomplished Hawaiʻi distance runner Norman Tamanaha. He finished the race in 3:03:00, the fiftieth-fastest marathon time in the world that year. Starting at high noon, the race stretched from the old Honolulu Stadium in Mōʻiliʻili to Makapuʻu Point and back. Despite his strong performance, the thirty-six-year-old Tamanaha found the experience so miserable that he vowed never to run another marathon.[27] The vow held until 1947, when Tamanaha and Felix Castilliano—two of four runners sponsored by the Hawaiʻi AAU—became the first local runners to complete the Boston Marathon. Tamanaha finished in 3:09.00, placing forty-sixth out of a field of 157.

Tamanaha had started running seriously in 1933. In an attempt to improve his health after a serious sinus condition, he trained for a five-mile run around Diamond Head sponsored by the YMCA.[28] Competing in races from two-milers to half-marathons, Tamanaha was the most dominant local runner of his generation. But like Kaoʻo, his best long-distance running and highest acclaim came in middle age. In November 1951, at the age of forty-five, Tamanaha began training under U. S. Olympic Games team physician Dr. Richard You, a fellow Hawaiʻi resident. To supplement a rigorous training regimen, You put Tamanaha on a 5,000-calorie-per-day diet that included heavy doses of protein, vitamin A, vitamin C, and thiamine.[29] Five months later, Tamanaha returned to Boston, placing fifth overall with a stunning 2:51:35 performance.

Three months after this breakthrough run, Czech runner Emil Zatopek captured the world's attention with an unprecedented performance in the 1952 Olympics in Helsinki. Zatopek set Olympic records in the 5,000- and 10,000-meter events before smashing the Olympic marathon record of 2:29:19, set in the 1936 Berlin Games by Kitei Son, by more than six minutes. (Zatopek's wife Dana Zatopkova won a gold medal in the javelin at the same games). This performance, made all the more dramatic by his seemingly agonized running style that legendary sportswriter Red Smith once called "the most frightful horror spectacle since Frankenstein," ignited renewed fascination with the marathon. The local AAU, headed by You, took advantage of the interest to revive the Hawaiian AAU Marathon. Once again, Tamanaha proved to be the ablest runner in the Territory, conquering the roughly 26-mile course from downtown Honolulu to Red Hill and back in 2:51:35, a time he might have bettered had he not had to walk the final 300 yards due to cramps. The win earned him a return trip to the Boston Marathon, scheduled for just three weeks later. Undaunted by the quick turnaround, Tamanaha turned in a personal best performance in the much more competitive race, finishing tenth overall in 2:38:36. He would continue his age-defying streak over the next three years. He won the Hawaiian AAU Marathon in 1954 (3:36:36), 1955 (3:36:31), and 1956 (3:16:04). He also continued to build his national reputation with impressively high-level performances at Boston: 2:45:45 (13th), 2:38:30 (15th), and 2:38:40 (25th).

Tamanaha was forty-nine when he "retired" after the 1956 Boston Marathon. While he would never return to Boston, he was a prominent competitor in open- and masters-division races well into his sixties, and a mentor and coach for a new generation of Hawai'i distance runners who would profoundly influence the local running scene over the next two decades. And yet, for all of Tamanaha's accomplishments, after the occasional excitement of the Olympic marathon faded, long-distance running remained largely an afterthought for the public. The year after Tamanaha's retirement, Joe Palacat broke the Hawaiian AAU Marathon record with a time of 3:16:2, beating Adam Travens, eighteen-year-old Waipahu student Kokichi Uyehara (the first "amateur" to complete the race), and a handful of other competitors. As was customary, there were no aid stations, and only a token police presence to keep traffic at bay. As the *Honolulu Record* noted, the spectators amounted to something less than a crowd: "There [*sic*] numbers were comparatively few—nothing like the thousands who follow the rivalry of the senior league, or even the vaudeville of professional wrestling. The appreciation of Honolulu's sports-minded hasn't extended far enough to include one of the most grueling tests."

Rise of the Mid-Pacific Road Runners Club

In 1962, Harold "Ky" Cole and Harold Kuha gathered a group of fellow local runners including Jim Ferris, Horace Itoku, Peter McDonald, and Johnny Faerber to found the Mid-Pacific Road Runners Club, an affiliate of the national Road Runners Club of America.[30] Over the next decade, the club would become the pre-eminent sponsor of local road races on Oʻahu, providing a year-round slate of events, many originating at Kapiʻolani Park, for the island's small but devoted community of middle- and long-distance runners. The group assumed responsibility for the Hawaiian AAU Marathon—an event that Kuha himself would win three consecutive times in the mid-1960s—eventually moving it to Maui in 1971, and renaming it the Norman K. Tamanaha Marathon, in honor of Hawaiʻi's most famous racing champion.[31]

The Mid-Pacific Road Runners Club's grassroots races attracted local participants from different athletic backgrounds, providing competition for the growing tide of runners arriving from the Mainland, including many retired military. Others were like E. Walker "Happy" Chapman, a local all-around athlete who excelled in basketball, baseball, tennis, and golf. Despite having never run competitively, Chapman joined the University of Hawaiʻi men's track team under legendary coach Moses Ome. After graduating, Chapman worked at Pan American Airlines and served as a volunteer track coach for Damien Memorial School, a small Catholic private school in Kalihi, eventually becoming its first physical education teacher. Chapman later served as track and cross country coach at Mid-Pacific Institute, and eventually cross country coach for Hawaiʻi Pacific University, where he helped develop NACC Div. II All-American runners Darlene Mota, Tara Mac-Donald, Mary Baumgarten, and Sylvia Fisher. But compared to the other MPRRC members, Chapman was a relative hobbyist. He entered his first marathon having never run more than six miles previously, but he still finished in tenth place. And he didn't own real running shoes until Johnny Faerber sold him a pair out the trunk of his car for fifteen dollars. According to Chapman, the main MPRRC members "were a hardcore bunch of guys and they were basically crazy in some ways. I wouldn't consider myself a hardcore runner. I like sports so I do a lot of sports. The runners (in the club), especially in the early days, that was their life. They lived and ate and breathed running."[32]

Mike Tymn, a former Marine, arrived in Hawai'i in 1971. He had been an accomplished road racer for the Santa Clara Valley Youth Village in the 1950s, and he quickly tapped into a discrete Hawai'i subculture that appreciated his gifts as a runner: "There were 50 or 60 road runners. The only marathon was held on Maui and only the insane went over to take part in it."[33] Tymn was an important figure in the local running community for the next thirty years, not only establishing himself as a top Master's Division runner, but also chronicling the rise of the marathon in Hawai'i as a regular contributor to the *Honolulu Advertiser*. In Tymn, the local marathon scene had an advocate who could explain the history, culture, and science to a skeptical mass audience. As the sport found mainstream popularity, Tymn provided more nuanced insight, expertly explaining controversies over sponsorship, mass participation, and professionalism. In a 1988 column, he recalled how little most runners thought of the marathon in the early days of the sport:

> Distances of four, five, and six miles were considered the true tests of one's mettle. You ran the marathon only if you were too slow to do well at the shorter distances. As a group, distance runners were pretty much second-class "athletes," although they weren't called athletes then, as they are now. The real athletes were sprinters. With the attention given to the pursuit of the four-minute mile, middle-distance runners began gaining some degree of respect during the '50s. But long-distance runners were strictly weirdos.[34]

Tymn certainly was familiar with these attitudes when growing up in Northern California, and he may have encountered some of them after arriving in Hawai'i. But the American Running Boom had largely rendered such sentiments antiquated, quaint. By the mid-1980s, the eccentric fringe had been sucked whole into the mainstream thanks to the American Running Revolution and the proliferation of large-scale marathons. For the Honolulu Marathon, the revolution was just beginning.

CHAPTER 6

The Michigan Guys

Jon Cross and Jim Barahal first crossed paths in 1975 at the University of Michigan in Ann Arbor. One of the best milers the state had ever produced, Cross had been a member of the school's famed 1974 Big Ten championship cross country team under Ron Warhurst, but was preparing to skip the 1975 season to accept an early entry to dental school. Barahal, a stand-out multisport athlete in high school, was in medical school, and had recently taken up running to stay in shape.

As part of Warhurst's prescribed personal training regimen, Cross had just completed a brisk 10-mile run, and he arrived at the track to do a series of wind sprints. There he spotted Barahal. He had seen him around campus before, often running with Cross's former teammate Kim Hildebrand. Barahal introduced himself and asked if he could join Cross in his sprints. It was a bold request—Barahal surely knew of Cross's elite pedigree. As a high school senior, Cross had set state prep records in the one-mile (4:21) and two-mile (9:19) events. Choosing the Wolverines over the University of Tennessee, Cross set the school record for the six-mile as a freshman, and then a new one as a sophomore. Undiagnosed hypoglycemia had disrupted Cross's performance during the previous season, but he had still been a key member of a national powerhouse that included future Boston Marathon winner Greg Meyer. Happy for the company, Cross said "sure" and the two set off on a set of spirited, hold-nothing-back sprints. As Cross recalled: "He beat me by ten yards on every sprint. I said, 'You're as fast as Greg Meyer'— because Greg beat me by ten yards in a sprint. He goes, 'Oh, I just started running.'"[1] Afterward, Cross went to the locker room, retrieved his indoor track spikes, and gave them to Barahal. He then introduced him to Warhurst, who agreed to let Barahal work out with the team.

It was a full year before they saw each other again. Cross went to dental school classmate Earl Bogrow's apartment to work on a project, and "It turned out Earl was Jim's roommate. Barahal is sitting there playing Dan Fogelberg on the guitar with long hair and stuff."[2] Acquaintance renewed, the two began training together, first on their own and later with the full cross country team, which Cross rejoined for its third consecutive Big Ten title campaign in 1976. After graduating, Barahal moved out and Cross took his place as Bogrow's roommate, with Barahal frequently crashing on their couch. In 1978, Barahal visited Hawai'i to interview for an internship, and just for fun, he ran the Honolulu Marathon. He returned to Michigan smitten with the islands, and determined to talk his friends into joining him there. Bogrow bit first, moving to Honolulu after accepting a job with the state. Cross would take a bit more convincing.

Within months of his arrival, Barahal established himself as one of the state's top competitive road racers, at a time when weekend 5K and 10K races were attracting thousands of participants. Barahal saw that a high-level runner could be top dog in this up-and-coming, running-mad town, and if he himself didn't have quite the ability to do it, he certainly knew who did. Cross had kept in touch with Barahal and Bogrow, but managed to sidestep politely their invitations to join in the fun. During one call, however, his two friends—double-teaming him from separate lines in their Makiki apartment—refused to give up, cajoling him for the better part of an hour. Actually, Cross was ready for a change. He had just spent an uninspiring year practicing dentistry in an area of the Detroit suburbs largely populated by auto workers. "They called me up and they said, 'You've got to get out of Michigan,'" Cross recalled. "They just hammered me so I said OK and I went and told my parents, 'I'm moving to Hawaii.'"[3]

Barahal's vision for Cross was quickly but briefly realized. After joining the already dominant Tantalus Gold running team, Cross contributed to a streak of relay race victories, and set individual course records for the Norman Tamanaka 15K, the four-mile Honolulu Symphony Fun Run, and the Wahiawa Pineapple 10K. But injuries, including a torn calf muscle suffered in a relay race, began to take their toll, and the arrival of more elite talent like Marine Corps Marathon winner Farley Simon hastened a slide from the top. Not that Cross minded terribly. During his record-setting

Jim Barahal brought a more business-minded approach to running the Honolulu Marathon Association. Photo by Dean Sensui. Courtesy of the *Honolulu Star-Advertiser.*

finishes, Cross had been largely unchallenged. With the arrival of Simon, the return home of three-time Honolulu Marathon winner and former Olympian Duncan Macdonald, and the emergence of local runner Jonathan Lyau, Cross had a cohort of truly elite runners with whom he could train and socialize. And as Simon and Macdonald and others sped past him, Cross found himself at another important junction.

> I realized that I wasn't really running for the right reasons. . . . Once I matured and realized that I was running because I was just trying to prove myself as an athlete, then my drive kind of diminished. A lot of athletes are like that, though. They are trying to prove something. Once I realized, I had to kind of adjust to running because I love to run rather than because I was trying to prove myself as an athlete. I was very highly driven in high school and college because of being bullied and stuff growing up.[4]

Former Michigan State runner and Barahal friend Jonathan Cross dominated the Honolulu running scene upon his arrival. Photo by David Yamada. Courtesy of the *Honolulu Star-Advertiser.*

During this period of reflection, Kent Davenport invited Barahal to take over as HMA's elite athlete coordinator. Barahal told Davenport he would only accept the offer if Cross could join him. Oddly eager to get the deal done, Davenport agreed.

African Investment

Whatever long-terms goals, if any, Barahal and Cross might have had when they joined the HMA, it became immediately apparent to them that the organization was not being managed as efficiently, and perhaps not as ethically, as they had believed. As the two-man Invited Runners Committee, Barahal and Cross were supposed to secure the best available talent with little more than free flights to Hawai'i as an incentive—and even that turned out to be in question. As Cross recalls, board member David Benson, a major in the Honolulu Police Department, had secured a commitment of $30,000 in flight vouchers from Pan American Airways for recruiting elite athletes. But when Barahal and Cross checked, there was only $10,000 left, and not a single commitment from an elite runner to compete. Board members had apparently used the flights for something other than recruiting athletes. "It turned out that Pan American didn't like that arrangement so that was the last year they did that," Cross said.[5] For HMA's two newest members, it was an early hint that the unpaid directors were getting compensated in other ways—a conclusion that the organization's departed president Jack Scaff would later echo.

The immediate challenge was to assemble a competitive field using what was left of the travel vouchers and a few neighbor island hotel rooms that Barahal secured through his own connections. The friends were almost uniquely suited for the task. In the time before the Internet, searchable databases, and real-time race updates, Barahal and Cross pored over cheaply printed running newsletters, keeping track of new and emerging amateur, collegiate, and international runners with the nerdy passion of fantasy football enthusiasts a generation later. That first year, they managed to broker an agreement with a talented if somewhat overlooked Puerto Rican Olympian: Jorge "Peco" Gonzales, winner of the 1982 Central American and Caribbean Games and 1983 Pan American Games marathons. They also confirmed defending champion Kevin Ryan, former Honolulu Marathon record-holder Dean Matthews, Belgian runner Frederik Vandervennet, and Kjell-Erik Stahl of Sweden. But their real genius as talent evaluators could be seen in Cross's risky, and not immediately successful, investment in a crop of unproven African runners.

About a month before the 1984 marathon, local high school track coach and longtime Honolulu Marathon volunteer Dennis Swart asked Cross for help in picking up runners flying in for the Dr. Scholl's Pro Comfort 10K Championship. The race brought together the winners of a national series of 5K races to compete for a share of $100,000 in prize money. Swart knew that Cross kept close tabs on elite runners at all distances, and would jump at the chance to spend time with the top cross country athletes in the country. It was a stellar field by any measure. The favorites were U.S. Olympians Pat Porter and Paul Cummings, and Mark Nenow, then the world 10k world record holder. There was also a strong African contingent made up of current and former members of the University of Texas-El Paso's (UTEP) powerhouse cross country team, including 1984 Los Angeles Olympic 10,000-meter bronze medalist Michael Musyoki, fellow Kenyan Gabriel Kamau, and Zack Barie of Tanzania. Other All-American runners from Africa included Simeon Kigen (Kenya) of Mississippi State University, Ashley Johnson (South Africa) of Western University, and former University of Richmond standout Sosthenes Bitok (Kenya). Cross agreed to help, but made one request: "I want the Africans."

Cross's interest was partly professional, but mostly personal. The son of an itinerant Presbyterian minister, Cross was born in Corning, New York, but spent much of his childhood moving from state to state until his family finally settled in Michigan, where both his parents were raised. As a child, he had something of an inferiority complex. As Cross recalled, "If you couldn't play American baseball, you were shunned by all of the kids and kind of bullied. I don't know if I was awkward or if no one gave me any lessons, but I was just a terrible baseball player and so I was kind of ostracized." And yet, while hopeless with a bat and glove, Cross had raw athletic ability. In the seventh grade, he finished first in a 600-yard run in gym class and was encouraged to try out for track. He started out as a 440 runner in eighth grade, but lost his spot for missing practice during spring break: "They said, 'OK, Cross, you're not a 440 guy anymore, you're going to have to run the mile.' I said OK. So then I beat the seniors. They told me right away that if I kept going, I could be the best runner that high school ever had."

Cross drew early inspiration from a pair of 1960s Ethiopian sports heroes—Abebe Bikila and Mamo Wolde. Bikila was a young private in the Imperial Bodyguard when he caught the eye of Onni Niskanen, a Swedish sports trainer and director of physical education for Ethiopia's Ministry of Education. Bikila, who enjoyed soccer, volleyball, and basketball, had taken to running from a hilly area known as Sululta to Addis Ababa and back— more than twenty-one miles—almost every day. Niskanen was quickly convinced that Bikila could be a world-class distance runner, and under his training, Bikila won the National Armed Forces Championships marathon in 2:39:50, defeating Wami Biratu, then considered the nation's top marathoner. Weeks later, Bikila improved his time by an astounding eighteen minutes to earn one of the two spots for the 1960 Rome Olympics.[6] At the Games, Bikila and countryman Abebe Wakjira, who had both grown up running barefoot, were worried that competing without shoes would reflect badly on their country. They took a test run in shoes, but the experiment was a mistake, as they both developed blisters. They would run barefoot.

Bikila's stunning victory in Rome is one of the most famous stories of the modern Olympics. Lightly regarded in a field that included favorite Sergei Popov, who had set a world record (2:15:17) in the 1958 European Championships, Boston Marathon winner Paavo Kotila, and Moroccan Rhadi ben Abdesselem, who had placed first in the International Cross Country Championships earlier that year, Bikila was largely unnoticed as he kept pace with the lead pack through the first half of the race. At the 22-kilometer mark, as the course climbed up the Raccordo Anulare, Bikila and Rhadi pulled away, opening a one-minute lead over Popov and New Zealander Barrington Magee.[7] With 500 meters left and Rhadi still at his side, Bikila spotted the Obelisco di Axum, a fourth-century Abyssinian obelisk that had been stolen during the Second Italo-Ethiopian War of 1935. Bikila and Niskanen had earlier set this landmark as Bikila's signal to begin his final push toward the finish. He followed the stratagem to perfection, surging ahead of Rhadi for the win. Bikila's time was 2:15:16.2, bettering Popov's world record by 0.8 of a second, and shattering Emil Zatopek's Olympic record of 2:23:03.2. In fact, all top five finishers—Bikila, Rhadi (2:15:41.6), Magee (2:17:18.2), and Russians Konstantin Vorobiev (2:19:09.6) and Popov (2:19:18.8)—broke the 2:20 barrier. With the victory, Bikila became the first black African to win an Olympic gold medal. He dominated the sport over the next half-decade, winning nine of the next ten marathons he entered, his only stumble a fifth-place finish at the Boston Marathon in 1963. Despite an appendicitis scare two weeks earlier, Bikila was at the peak of his powers at the 1964 Olympics in Tokyo, where he set another world record (2:12:11.2) and became the first marathoner to win consecutive Olympic gold medals.

An injury foiled Bikila's bid for a third gold medal. Unknown to race officials, he began the marathon at the 1968 Games in Mexico City with a fracture in his left fibula; he lasted seventeen kilometers before dropping out. But before he fell back from the lead pack, Bikila had a word with his fellow Ethiopian competitor Degaga "Mamo" Wolde. Many years later, American Olympic runner Kenny Moore, who had witnessed but could not understand the exchange, learned what had been said:

> "Lieutenant Wolde."
> "Captain Bikila."

"I'm not finishing this race."

"Sorry, Sir."

"But Lieutenant, you will win this race."

"Sir, yes sir."

"Don't let me down."[8]

Wolde had served in the Imperial Bodyguard with Bikila, and had also undergone specialized training with Niskanen. He had competed with little success in the 800 meters, 1,500 meters, and 4x400 relays in the 1956 Games in Melbourne, and in the 10,000 meters and marathon at Tokyo. But he flourished in the high altitude of Mexico City, taking the silver medal in the 10,000 meters, and qualifying for the 5,000 meters, though he dropped out to save himself for the marathon. He ran a relatively conservative first half, patiently following leader Naftali Temu of Kenya, who had beaten him in the 10,000 meters five days before. Wolde finally took the lead at the 30-kilometer mark, and steadily pulled away from the pack for a convincing victory, finishing in 2:20:26.4, followed by Kenji Kimihara of Japan (2:23:31.0) and Michael Ryan of New Zealand (2:23:45.0). Wolde later settled for a bronze medal in the 1972 Olympic Games in Munich, African domination giving way for the moment to Frank Shorter's American running renaissance.

The impact that these two Ethiopians had on young Jon Cross in Ypsilanti, Michigan, is incalculable. To this day, he drops their names into casual conversation the way a Boston Celtics fan turns to Bill Russell and Larry Bird as eternal points of reference. When Swart offered Cross the chance to spend some time with the inheritors of Bikila and Wolde's great legacy, Cross the fan was excited, and Cross the elite athlete recruiter was intrigued. When the athletes arrived for the Pro Comfort Series event, Cross craftily turned what should have been a fifteen-minute ride from Honolulu International Airport to Waikīkī into an all-day social outing.

> I picked them up and I said, "Do you want to go to Waikīkī and go to your hotel or do you want to go to a beautiful lookout and see some scenery?" "We want to go to the lookout!" I took them to Pali Lookout and then I drove them around and I said, "Do you want to go back to your hotel or do you want to go see some beautiful women on the beach?" "We want to go to the beach!" So I took them to the beach.[9]

Musyoki won the highly competitive 10K, setting a new state record with his 28:13.8 finish. Kigen finished second, followed by Johnson and Bitok. The performances were impressive, and Cross knew from Wolde's example that 10,000 meter specialists could make the jump to 26.2 miles.

Before the UTEP runners left, Cross asked them to help him find a promising Kenyan runner who would be willing to compete in the Honolulu Marathon in exchange for a round-trip ticket to Kenya. The runners put Cross in touch with legendary Tanzanian middle-distance runner Filbert Bayi, who was training and coaching in New Mexico. Through Bayi, Cross secured a commitment from James Munyala, a Kenyan steeplechase specialist who won three straight NCAA Championships (1975–1977) while attending UTEP. Cross and Barahal also worked through regional Adidas manager Ernie Severn to get Ibrahim Kivina, who represented Tanzania in the 10,000 at the 1984 Olympic Games in Los Angeles. Neither runner had ever attempted a marathon, but Cross was sure they could be competitive. Recent examples encouraged him. Portugal's Carlos Lopes, a 10,000-meter runner, won the gold in Los Angeles despite having run only two marathons before, and British runner Steve Jones, a 5,000-and 10,000-meter specialist, set a world record of 2:08:05 in that year's Chicago Marathon, having dropped out of his only previous marathon a year before.

The trend did not continue in Honolulu that year. Both Munyala and Kivina dropped out during the race, which Gonzalez won in a very respectable 2:16:25. Afterward, HMA president Gary Murfin collared Cross, and gave him a not-so-gentle rebuke:

> (Murfin) had gone to watch the San Francisco Marathon and the Africans had dropped out of the race that year. He came to me and he said, "Jon, you know you're wasting your time with the Africans. They can't run that far. They are good at the 10,000 and six-mile but they're not capable of running that distance." I kind of bit my tongue and thought to myself, "Yeah, well I'll show you later."[10]

While Munyala and Kivina did not perform as hoped, the Invited Runners Committee had succeeded in attracting a competitive field. More importantly, they had made connections within the ex-pat African running community that would serve them well in the years to come. And there was this: In the lead up to the marathon, Cross and Barahal had befriended a Kenyan runner named Ibrahim Hussein, who had won a free trip to Honolulu for winning the 1984 Duke City Marathon in New Mexico. While competing for the University of New Mexico, where he earned a degree in economics, Hussein had been the Western Athletic Conference champion in the mile, 1,500 meters, and 3,000-meter steeplechase events. He had planned to run the Honolulu Marathon, but was advised against it because of poor weather conditions. Barahal and Cross made it a point to stay in touch; their African experiment had not produced the desired results in 1984, but 1985 was a whole new year.

Scaff Reappears

Shortly after the 1984 Honolulu Marathon, former HMA president Jack Scaff and popular local entertainer Carole Kai announced an ambitious new entry into the already crowded field of Honolulu fun runs. The Great Aloha Run would span an unconventional 7.5 miles from Aloha Tower, along Honolulu Harbor in Downtown Honolulu, to Aloha Stadium in the Hālawa area (the course was later lengthened to 8.15 miles). As usual, Scaff was not modest in his ambitions for the race, which he claimed would one day join the Lilac Bloomsday Run in Spokane, Washington, the Bay-to-Breakers in San Francisco, California, and the Atlanta Peachtree 10K in Georgia as one of America's premier open road races. The idea for the race came from Buck Buchwach, renowned publicist and executive editor of the *Honolulu Advertiser*. Buchwach first came to Hawai'i during World War II as a reporter for the *Pacific Stars & Stripes,* and after the war, and a brief stint as a military reporter for the *Advertiser,* he became a publicist, working for the likes of Frank Sinatra and a vacationing Harry Truman. One of Buchwach's biggest claims to fame came in 1954, when he came up with the idea of a Statehood Honor Roll, a massive scroll—a one-block long section was unfurled along Bishop Street in the Downtown area—that 120,000 residents signed, petitioning Congress to approve the Territory of Hawai'i's bid for statehood. Thirty years as an *Advertiser* editor had not diminished Buchwach's promotional impulses, so when a bored, mission-less Scaff strolled into his office in 1984 to toss around ideas for new road race, Buchwach was already two steps ahead of him.

Scaff found an ideal partner in Kai, who had previously sponsored a charity "bed race," in which groups pushed wheeled bedframes, complete with box spring, mattress, and designated rider, along a course. The race drew much media attention but only modest returns, and as more road races competed for weekend venues, and especially in Kapiʻolani Park, Kai found herself on the wrong side of Tommy Kono, who recalled:

> I criticized her and said, "You know your bed race is like Good Friday—we don't know when it's going to fall on. You keep moving it around. You've got to pick a date." We had so many runs and races, I made a calendar. I gathered all the promoters together and I said, "O.K., we're going to promote races this way so there's no conflict and not all of them are going to be held in the Waikīkī area. We've got to disperse it. [. . .] I said yours is always moving around. By the way, your race is lousy. She's a smart businesswoman and said, "Maybe you could help me." I said, "No, but I can direct you to somebody who can . . . Jack Scaff."

The Great Aloha Run was a remarkable success from the get-go. The first one attracted 11,592 runners and walkers, setting a world record for participation in an inaugural running event, and supporting Scaff's boast that the race could potentially attract upwards of 12,000 participants. It has since established itself as the second-largest annual road race in Hawaiʻi after the Honolulu Marathon, attracting about 20,000 walkers and runners each year, most of them local residents. The race is also known for its massive health and fitness expo, which doubles as the packet pick-up site. The race donates roughly $400,000 to charitable organizations each year, relies almost exclusively on locally-based sponsors, spends 97 percent of its overhead costs at local businesses, and sponsors many community programs throughout the year—all qualities of what Scaff considers a high-level people's race. Only nominal cash prizes are provided for the top three male and female finishers in the open and military divisions. From 1985 on, then, the Great Aloha Run has provided a useful reference point for mapping out the very different path the Honolulu Marathon would follow over the next thirty years.

A Record Performance, A Secret Revealed

By 1985, generous prizes and guaranteed appearance fees were standard practice for the upper echelon of big-city marathons, making it even more difficult for second-tier races like the Honolulu Marathon to attract elite athletes. Both the New York City and Chicago marathons were offering prize purses in excess of $270,000. Even the Boston Athletic Association (BAA) found their principled stand against paying athletes no match for the changing times. Strong-armed by the local government into accepting a sponsorship, the BAA was already planning to offer some $250,000 in prize money, with $30,000 and a new car going to the men's and women's division winners, for the marathon the following year. Lacking the resources to compete for the biggest names in the sport, Barahal and Cross doubled-down on their strategy of looking for emerging talents, lesser-known but competitive veterans, and above all, elite African middle-distance runners with the potential to jump to marathon distance.

Early reporting on the 1985 Honolulu Marathon failed to recognize that entry numbers had dropped for the third consecutive year, dipping below 10,000 for the first time since 1981. Instead, writers focused on Barahal and Cross's success in attracting an impressive field of elite runners, supposedly with nothing more to offer than flights, hotel, and per diem. A month before the race, Tymn quoted Cross as saying, "It's not easy getting them to accept. The first thing they ask is how much appearance fee we pay. Then they ask about the prize money. I get a little embarrassed when I have to tell them we don't have the funds for either." But then Tymn began to wonder about other, less visible benefits:

> Cross and Barahal have little ways of skirting the rules and enticing world-class competitors to come here. For example, in inviting a top African runner to compete, they might offer round-trip fares from the runner's home country. There are other things such as generous per diem allowances or plane fares for coaches, spouses and companions, which are within the amateur rules and race guidelines. But Cross and Barahal are a little guarded when pressed for other ways they add to the package.[11]

In a November 29 article by *Honolulu Star-Bulletin* freelancer Jack Wyatt, race commentator Toni Reavis sidestepped the issue of paying athletes by comparing the HMA's reliance on Hawai'i's attractiveness as a destination favorably to the Boston Marathon's mistaken assumption that its "hallowed tradition" would also be enough to attract a top field.[12] Two days later, Wyatt quoted Cross as forcefully declaring "No way can we compete with marathons that give money."[13]

But a day before the race, the evening edition of the *Honolulu Star-Bulletin* published a surprising revelation. In a sidebar article by Pat Bigold, Barahal admitted that the HMA was indeed paying appearance

Eight-time winner Carla Beurskens and Ibrahim Hussein, a three-time winner, join Honolulu mayor Frank Fasi. Photo courtesy of the *Honolulu Star-Advertiser*.

money to top athletes—"but it's not much."[14] Bigold also reported that prize money would be awarded to the top two male finishers and the top female finisher. This information appeared in two brief paragraphs—surprisingly minimal play, given the attention paid to the issue in previous stories. In fact, the lead story on the race that day, written by Cindy Luis, still contained the paragraph: "No prize money over the table will be given to elite runners but there's still the 'atmosphere of Hawaii,' as former world-record miler Jim Ryun calls it, that lures name runners who will have good showings.' "[15]

Regardless of how they did it, Cross and Barahal had indeed lured a remarkable field. Gonzales would defend his championship. Also returning were 1979 winner Dean Matthews, Doug Kurtis, Kjell-Erick Stahl, and Frederik Vandervennet. Two runners Cross met through the Dr. Scholl's Pro Comfort Championships—Simeon Kigen and Zack Barie—were in field, as was Filbert Bayi himself. The women's division, though lighter on talent, boasted Carla Beurskens, who was dominating the competition in her native

Netherlands but had yet to break through in the United States. And then there was Ibrahim Hussein, whose jump from middle distance to the marathon had reached the point that only three months earlier he had actually placed higher than Gonzales at the New York City Marathon. Hussein flew in to Honolulu two weeks early, to get used to the heat and humidity. In a pre-race interview, he boldly predicted that given the quality of the field, a time of 2:13—the course record was 2:15:30, set by Dave Gordon in 1982—was possible. Hussein's read proved too conservative. Competing against perhaps the best overall field in the race's history, he himself obliterated Gordon's record with a 2:12:08 finish, becoming the first African to win the Honolulu Marathon. Bill Reifsnyder of Pennsylvania matched Hussein stride for stride for the first twenty miles, and finished in 2:14:41, also breaking the course record. Beurskens dominated the women's race, finishing in 2:35:49.

The pay issue resurfaced in the post-race coverage. Bigold reported that "The Marathon Association had originally wanted to keep the new practice of using money to bring in running talent secret. But Cross, who was primarily responsible for negotiating with top athletes, disclosed yesterday that even last year the association had paid per diem expenses of $50 to some runners."[16] Hussein was awarded $2,000 for his first place finish, plus another $1,500 for setting the record. Reifsnyder, whose agent said would never have run the race without appearance money, won $1,000 for coming in second and $1,500 for breaking the previous record as well. Beurskens was awarded $1,000 for her women's division win. In the same article, Barahal said that Hussein's record finish and "a little more financial incentive" would attract even more elite athletes. The result will be a race "that can stand up to any of the big-budget marathons." Barahal also said that despite the prize money and appearance fees, the Honolulu Marathon would keep the atmosphere of a "people's race."

Before long, that claim would be discarded as well.

CHAPTER 7

The Coup

Whatever ambitions Jim Barahal and Jon Cross may have had when taking on the task of recruiting elite runners for the Honolulu Marathon in 1984, they surely had broadened in scope and audacity by January 1986. Criticized by others in the organization as they built a competitive field of elite runners by soliciting sponsorships and offering prize money and appearance fees for the first time in the race's history, the two were ecstatic about Ibrahim Hussein's record-shattering performance. His successful transition from middle-distance runner to champion marathoner vindicated Barahal and Cross's much-questioned investment in African runners. Their success in getting the Honolulu Marathon Association board to approve using a portion of a Japan Airlines sponsorship for appearance and prize money was publicly credited with producing arguably the most competitive field in the race's history. The path forward seemed obvious: more sponsorship, richer purses, bigger and better fields. In their eyes, the only thing standing in their way was a board of directors bloated to the point of paralysis, and therefore lacking the will to embrace inevitable change. While Willy Williamson had once championed the expansion of the board as a means of expanding capacity and responsibility to meet the demands of a growing race, continued growth of that board had seemingly occurred with no specific purpose, to the point that there were now in excess of thirty so-called directors, each with his or her own well-defined area of responsibility, who aligned in competing blocks and effectively cancelled each others votes. Frequent Honolulu Marathon guest Frank Shorter recognized it. After the 1985 marathon, he remarked that HMA would have more than enough money to compete with other top marathons if it streamlined its operations.[1] The estranged

Scaff was typically more blunt, telling *Honolulu Advertiser* columnist John Christensen, "If (the organizers) would quit paying themselves per diems, there would be plenty of money available."[2]

Even as Barahal and Cross were basking in the glow of Hussein's victory, a plan was well underway not just to leverage their newfound clout to affect board policy on sponsorship and athlete pay, but to gain control of the organization itself. Some important groundwork was in place. They had positive relationships with African runners, their agents, and Ernie Severn of Adidas. They were working directly and exclusively with new sponsors obtained through Barahal's Waikīkī connections. They had also set themselves up as the go-to HMA contacts for the local reporters who covered the marathon: the *Honolulu Advertiser*'s Mike Tymn, with whom Barahal sometimes trained, and the *Honolulu Star-Bulletin*'s Pat Bigold, whose goodwill they had earned by giving him the exclusive scoop about the HMA providing appearance fees and prize money in the 1985 race.

The pair had been paying close attention as well to recent turmoil within the Boston Athletic Association (BAA). Its leadership had been steadfast in opposing corporate sponsorship, appearance fees, or prize money. But thanks to the Association of Road Racing Athletes rebellion, and to the resulting loosening of restrictions on athletes accepting appearance and prize money, the Boston Marathon had seen its previously unchallenged reputation as the world's top race fall apart, as the growing roster of high-paying marathons decimated its elite field. The 1985 race showed how bad things had become. Cramps forced defending champion Geoff Smith of Britain to walk to the finish line, yet he still won by five minutes. A credible champion, Smith had also won the 1984 race by more than four minutes, pointing out the relative weakness of the "elite" field. Even Bill Rodgers, a four-time Boston Marathon winner, decided to skip it, choosing to compete instead in the New Jersey Waterfront Marathon, which offered guaranteed appearance money.[3] The actual and perceived decline of Boston's elite ranks rippled through the overall field, which dropped in participation to 5,594 from 6,924 the previous year. Fearing the economic fallout from the race's decline, newly elected Boston Mayor Ray Flynn strong-armed BAA officials into accepting sponsorship money by privately threatening to withhold the permits that allowed the race to pass through the individual municipalities along its famous Hopkinton-to-Boston course. The organizers capitulated, and signed a ten-year title sponsor agreement with John Hancock Financial Services.

Cross and Barahal decided that something similar might work in Honolulu. As Cross recalled:

> Jim went to this one hotel guy that he was close with and he was explaining to him the situation and he said, "Well, you give me some negative press, I'll go to the mayor and maybe we can force something to happen."[4]

Barahal knew exactly who to call. In Pat Bigold, he had a knowledgeable and highly motivated ally in the media. Bigold had been frustrated by the HMA leadership's secrecy and lack of access, and he was grateful for Barahal's apparent willingness to be open about the state of the organization and the challenges it faced.

> [Barahal] did strike me as a guy that I wanted to know because he seemed to me like he was a good source. As a reporter, I found his stuff was reliable. He was someone I could talk to. He seemed to have accurate information and he was a newsmaker. That's what every reporter wants: a guy who is a newsmaker. A guy who is quotable. And he was quotable. He was really quotable.[5]

While not much of a runner himself—"I was a 400-meter runner, the highlight of whose career was running a guy off the track at the Boston Armory because I crossed the lanes illegally. The poor guy went off the track. I was disqualified. That might have been the end of my track career, I'm not sure."[6]—Bigold knew about the sport because he had covered several Boston Marathons as a reporter for the *Lawrence Eagle Tribune* in Massachusetts. In an off-the-record conversation with Barahal prior to the 1985 Honolulu Marathon, Bigold remarked that he wished "you guys would be more like Boston." According to Bigold, Barahal replied, "Yes, it's going to change."[7]

Shortly into the new year, Barahal contacted Bigold with a prime scoop. An anonymous sponsor was ready to put up the money for a $100,000 prize purse, but only if there was a "radical change" in HMA leadership. Barahal claimed this was necessary because of board mismanagement. Race director John Kelleher and board member David Benson had both used the flight vouchers reserved for recruiting elite runners for unrelated trips to the U.S. Mainland and Europe. There was a lack of transparency about the HMA's operating budget, and deep divisions were paralyzing the executive board.

Barahal further suggested that the board members didn't understand running, and had exiled more knowledgeable figures like Scaff. "The marathon belongs to the running community," Barahal told Bigold: "But the association believes it belongs to them. That is an insensitive and arrogant attitude."[8]

The resulting article for the *Honolulu Star-Bulletin*, "Marathon Threatened by Infighting," ran on January 3, 1986. It included less-than-convincing HMA defenses by Kelleher and John Maughan, who became the interim president when Gary Murfin moved back to the Mainland. The two men claimed they had been working on a prize structure similar to Barahal's, and that the board had tried to keep the previous year's payments to athletes secret because of how embarrassingly small the amounts were. Kelleher also said that his trip to the New York City Marathon was in keeping with his duties as race director. Without citing a source, Bigold also revealed the amounts of appearance money given to top runners in the 1985 race, incentives in some cases augmented by funds provided by Adidas. In addition to his reported prize winnings, Hussein for instance had been paid a $3,000 appearance fee and an additional $2,000 from Adidas. Reifsnyder received $2,000 (not $1,000 as previously reported) for his second-place finish as well as $1,000 in appearance money. Guaranteed money had also been given to Simeon Kigen ($3,000), Dean Matthews ($2,500), Jorge Gonzales ($2,000 plus $2,000 from Adidas), Steve Ortiz ($2,500 plus $1,000 from Adidas), Doug Kurtis ($1,500 plus $500 from Adidas), Erik Stahl ($2,000), Filbert Bayi ($1,000), and Zack Barie ($1,000). Women's winner Carla Beurskens received $1,000 plus per diem for eighteen days. The article was exactly the sort of fire that Barahal's contact had advised him to start. The only question was whether Barahal and Cross could survive the flames long enough for help to come.

Reckoning

Barahal and Cross mounted the narrow stairwell leading up to the Honolulu Marathon Association's second-floor office fully prepared to catch hell. In the wake of Bigold's article, the HMA executive board had called an emergency meeting to discuss the public airing of grievances, and to demand an explanation. The two were late in arriving, and several board members had already taken the floor to condemn the perceived betrayal. When Cross and Barahal entered the room, someone had just finished speaking and people were clapping. Defiantly unflappable and a reflexive smart aleck, Barahal raised his hands in mock humility, thanking the room for the applause. No one laughed. The tiny conference room was packed with thirty or so people, so Cross sat on a table as the executive committee invited the rest of the board members to share their accounts of how the article had negatively impacted their lives. Barahal and Cross remained silent as members spoke of their embarrassment at being asked about the accusations and their indignation at having their volunteer efforts tarnished in such a public forum. Then head of the Aid Station Committee, Dewey Millar, recalled the intensity of the scene:

> There was a lot of upset because [Cross and Barahal] had gone to the newspapers and printed some rather critical comments about the operation of the marathon. That upset a lot of us at the time because they hadn't come and said any of that to us. They just went straight to the newspaper. [. . .] We were all volunteers trying to do our best and this kind of criticism cut deeply. There was a lot of discussion about whether it was really appropriate for them to continue on the board if that was the way they wanted to conduct business.[9]

The executive board had intended to put Barahal and Cross's future in the organization up to a vote. But before the motion could be introduced, board member Jeanette Chun stood up and addressed the meeting.

By this point, Jeanette and her husband Ron were widely recognized as the two indispensible figures in the HMA, due to their control over the race's administrative and operational functions. So when Jeanette rose to speak, the audience was all ears. She told the board members that Barahal and Cross reminded her of her own sons, and that she was inclined to forgive them for their "mistake." Few welcomed her comments. "Everybody gave her stink eye," Ron Chun recalled. But few were willing to contradict her. Barahal and Cross were grateful for her support, but remained defiant. When asked if he would promise not to criticize the organization in public again, Barahal flatly refused. The board then posed the same question to Cross.

> I said, "Look, you guys do what you've got to do, but if you think that you can kick us out and this shit isn't going to hit the fan . [. . .] (If) you don't think there is going to be a lot of repercussions in the running community if you kick us out, you've got another thing coming. But do what you've got to do. If you want to kick us out, kick us out."

The board decided to shelve the vote for a later date that never came. In purely practical terms, Jeanette Chun's support meant that Barahal and Cross could go about their business for the foreseeable future—and without apology.

In truth, while Bigold's article did further sell the notion of Barahal and Cross as the white hats arriving just in time to save the marathon association from itself, the original idea of causing a stir in order to justify outside intervention that would force a change in leadership proved largely unnecessary. Independent of Barahal and Cross's sagitation, the HMA executive board was already on shaky ground with rival factions—one aligned with race director Kelleher and another with former race director David Benson—vying for control of the board. The conflict came to a head when Benson, in an attempt to regain his old post, challenged Kelleher. According to Cross, the vote split 3–3, with HMA president Maughan then casting the deciding vote for Kelleher:

> I remember we walked down the stairs at the marathon office and Benson says, "That's it. I quit. I've had it. If Kelleher is going to be race director, I quit." After that, almost all the people that were aligned with (Benson), they quit, too. So it almost cut the board in half. All of a sudden, now we just had the John Kelleher side of it.

Barahal had already been using his authority as co-chair of the Invited Runners Committee to position himself as the direct contact for AT&T, Japan Airlines, and other sponsors secured for funding the financial incentives for elite athletes. As the go-between for this new money, Barahal had made it virtually impossible for the HMA leadership to get rid of him, and his and Cross's influence was steadily expanding. In short, it was only a matter of time before Barahal would take full control over of the HMA, and he and Cross were not above accelerating the process through some targeted provocation. Both were certain that Kelleher could not remain race director, in part because of Kelleher's not-so-secret substance abuse issues. So they sat down one night and made a detailed list of the duties carried out by Kelleher and the directors who supported him. They then used this list to badger their targets. As Cross recalled: "We decided that we would just make life miserable for people . [. . .] That's how we kind of weeded out some people. Jim's philosophy was, you know, it's a volunteer organization and if this is how people want to spend their volunteer time, dealing with us, they can stay." So for example, one day Cross peppered Kelleher with questions about ambulance arrangements and other race day concerns, prompting an irritated Kelleher to curse at him in front of HMA staffers.

Among those who stayed was Dewey Millar, who succeeded the interim Maughan as HMA president. A native of Vancouver, Canada, Millar had moved to Hawai'i in 1968 to earn an MBA at the University of Hawai'i, and then went into real estate development. He was another Honolulu Marathon Clinic alumnus who joined the association in the late 1970s as a volunteer with the Aid Station Committee. During the initial growth phase, Millar worked with the Outrigger Canoe Club, Hawaiian Airlines, the Honolulu Club, and other organizations to provide volunteer staffing at the aid stations on the course. He was not opposed to Barahal and Cross's efforts to increase payments to elite athletes, but he was clearly devoted to the race's history as an event that promoted a healthy lifestyle and was committed to the enjoyment of the entire field. Millar took over the leadership of the HMA at a point when the first American running revolution was reaching exhaustion and road-race participation nationwide was static or declining. In Honolulu, the number of local entries fell but was offset by U.S. Mainland and international entries, and most notably, a steady increase in runners from Japan. Millar focused his attention on enhancing the experience for all runners—everything from toilet facilities to musical entertainment to finisher certificates—and on dealing with unresolved insurance issues and a mini-controversy that arose when the scheduled race day fell on the anniversary of the bombing of Pearl Harbor.[10] Busy with these concerns, Millar chose to keep a polite distance from Barahal and Cross, leaving all matters of elite athlete competition and compensation to the Invited Runners Committee.

Barahal Ascending

Though they hadn't immediately succeeded in provoking a "radical change" in the HMA leadership, Barahal and Cross enjoyed pursuing their vision of a professionalized, world-class marathon without have to worry about board restrictions or criticism. The result in 1986 was a sizable increase in prize money and the strongest elite field in the race's history, with eight sub-2:12 marathoners. In a race-week article highlighting this success, the *Honolulu Advertiser*'s Tymn compared Barahal and Cross to other "dynamic duos," including legendary West Point gridiron stars Doc Blanchard and Glenn Davis, the Dallas Cowboys' Hershel Walker and Tony Dorsett, and the circus impresarios P. T. Barnum and James Anthony Bailey.[11]

The race itself did nothing to dispel the sense that the Honolulu Marathon was moving forward. Thanks to "grants" from JAL and AT&T, the race offered a $40,000 prize purse, with guaranteed payments of $10,000 for both the men's and women's winners, and a $10,000 bonus for anyone who beat Hussein's year-old course record. While not enough to compete with the huge purses now offered by New York, Boston, or other Fortune 500-backed races, these incentives were enough to get a maximum effort from a rising generation of young marathoners eager to make names for themselves. Under near-ideal conditions—59 degrees with low humidity—the race got off to a brisk start.[12] Defending champion Hussein set the early pace for a lead pack of Bayi, Gidamis Shahanga of Tanzania, and Jose Gomez of Mexico. A few seconds back were Reifsnyder, Kenyan Peter Koech, and 10K specialist Tom Wysocki, recruited as a pace setter for the first mile. Bayi fell back as Hussein continued to push the pace, reaching the 10K mark at Diamond Head Road in 29:54—faster than the winning time for eight of the nine Hawaii Diet Pepsi 10K races up to that time. Hussein reached 15K in 44:58, bettering Duncan Macdonald's state record by 1 minute and 18 seconds. His record-blitzing pace continued as he hit the halfway mark at 1:03:24, nearly four minutes ahead of Farley Simon's state record for the half-marathon. By twenty miles, Hussein held a 3:30 lead over his nearest competitor, Nyambui, with little sign of tiring. The only uncertainty was whether he could break his own course record. And indeed, despite what he described as a loss of concentration down the stretch, Hussein did set a new standard with a 2:11:43 finish. Suleiman Nyambui held on for second place and a $5,000 prize, followed by Shahanga ($2,500) and Bayi ($1,500). Barahal and Cross's early investment in Beurskens also proved prescient, as the defending women's champion also turned in a record-setting performance, her 2:31:01 besting Patti Catalano's previous record of 2:33:24, set five years earlier. On top of her own $10,000 first place prize, Beurskens took home the $5,000 bonus for setting a new women's division record. Arriving nearly five minutes behind Beurskens, Lisa Weidenbach earned $1,000 for her second-place finish.

If the 1985 race proved the viability of Barahal's vision, the even greater success of the 1986 marathon—two course records and a 1,000-entry rebound in overall participation—sent a clear signal inside and outside of the HMA that he represented not just the race's future, but now its present. In the immediately following weeks, Barahal and Cross would be depicted in the editorial pages of the dailies as the saviors of the Honolulu Marathon, and initially at least, community discussion of the merits of its entry into the professional arena yielded mostly positive responses. The only public dissent to this heroic narrative came from within the HMA. In a letter to the *Honolulu Star-Bulletin* responding to an editorial declaring that Barahal and Cross had "rescued" the marathon, Millar disputed several of the claims about the supposedly troubled state of the HMA, and took sharp issue with the praise lavished on the two doctors.

> The suggestion that the Honolulu Marathon needed "pulling back from the brink" is clearly not supported by the facts. Further, to single out Barahal and Cross as being somehow responsible for a "rescue" is to ignore the contribution made by twenty other association board members whose collective efforts are critically necessary to the success of every year's marathon.[13]

It didn't matter. A few weeks later, Barahal was elected the new president of the HMA, and Millar and his remaining supporters left soon after.

Barahal was just thirty-four when he took control over the HMA, but he combined supreme confidence with practical business acumen. The son of a psychologist, he had started Doctors on Call, a mobile medical service catering to tourists. As Barahal told Stanley Bronstein for the self-help book *A.IQ (Achievement I.Q.) Moments,* in the Hawaiʻi medical community, "There was an attitude that no one wanted to stoop low enough to serve the visitors."[14] With no such reservations, Barahal built his practice from the ground up. Operating out of a small office in the Hyatt Regency, he became a familiar sight, buzzing through Waikīkī's congested streets on a moped to make his appointments. The business took off quickly, and by DOC's fifth year, a string of hotel-based clinics was serving 35,000 patients. In a savvy move, executed at roughly the same time he and Cross were making their move to take over the HMA, Barahal began directing all of his referrals to Straub Clinic and Hospital, as a way of showing how much his practice was worth. These free samples led to Straub proposing a merger.[15] Barahal became a millionaire, but through Doctors on Call he had also made important Waikīkī contacts. He was also on hand to witness the beginning of the Japanese tourism boom.

However prepared Barahal might have felt for his new position at HMA, he could not have foreseen the difficulties lying ahead. The new year kicked off with a loaded column by the *Honolulu Advertiser's* Tymn, who for a month or so had been publicly speculating that as local entries continued to drop, the Honolulu Marathon field would eventually contract to a much smaller but more realistic 5,000 participants. In this new column, Tymn compared the growing success of the Great Aloha Run (GAR) with the uncertainties surrounding the Honolulu Marathon, and suggested that the GAR's lottery door prizes were a strong incentive for many local participants. GAR co-founder and former Honolulu Marathon Association president Jack Scaff responded, and Tymn aired Scaff's thoughts in a column titled "What the Marathon Lacks Is Marketing, Promotion." The relationship between the two men had been prickly during Scaff's years at the HMA. Scaff took issue with some of Tymn's public observations, and Tymn, a top master's runner, poked fun at Scaff's attempts to prove himself a "real marathoner" by breaking the 3:30 line. In Tymn's column, Scaff said the GAR's popularity arose from the quality of the race and course, and the local perception that "it is the thing to do." But he didn't stop there. Continuing Tymn's comparison, Scaff claimed that the problem with the current Honolulu Marathon was its lack of marketing and promotion to local participants. Scaff suggested that cross-promoting the race with his own Honolulu Marathon Clinic would help. Tymn then quoted former HMA member Bob Meyer regarding the HMA's focus on out-of-state runners and elite competitors:

> My feeling is that the race was designed for the local people, not for all these big-name runners that you have to pay for. It was designed as a family affair, that was the whole thing. People used to be able to see themselves on television. Now all they see is the lead runner and that's about it.

The rest of Tymn's column gave the HMA's Jim Moberly the chance to say that declining local participation would be offset by greater numbers of Japanese, Australians, and New Zealanders, and quoted Honolulu Marathon aid station volunteer and running coach Happy Chapman, who said that including elite runners in the marathon inspired the rest of the field. But it was the comments by Scaff that initiated what would become decades of unflinching critique from the man still most associated with the race, and whose contact information many reporters still kept in their Rolodexes under "Honolulu Marathon." The article also offered an early hint of the blowback to come, as the marathon established itself as a "destination" race, that is, one focused upon and populated by runners from outside its host community.

The same issues re-emerged in the weeklong lead-up to the 1987 marathon, but they paled in comparison to two largely unforeseeable calamities that let Barahal show his leadership abilities were not limited to recognizing and taking advantage of opportunities. On Saturday, December 12, a powerful storm led to the cancellation of the Honolulu Marathon's separate wheelchair event, the latest in a string of attempts to accommodate wheelchair athletes without actually putting them on the course with the runners. The unstable weather also threatened to disrupt the main race, scheduled for the next day. Barahal announced that the final decision on whether to hold the race would not be made until several hours before the planned start. Cancellation would have been a disaster, since there was no practical way to reschedule the race before the out-of-state participants—roughly half of the registered 8,793 runners—returned home. Publicly, Barahal stressed that safety was his only concern: "We want to take the attitude that the race will go on. But we're not going to do anything to jeopardize the safety of the participants and the volunteers. If there are flash flood warnings, we'll have to evaluate carefully."[16]

Thankfully, the weather cleared sufficiently. But while the storm was washing out the wheelchair race, another tempest was roiling in the guts of hundreds of participants, including at least one elite athlete, who had attended the marathon's carbo-load party on December 11. Because of Doctors on Call, Barahal was among the first to respond to a wave of patients suffering from symptoms of food poisoning. He reported the outbreak to the state Department of Health (DOH), which launched an investigation. Between 150 and 200 cases were initially reported, a number later revised to 370, although DOH official Steven Terrell-Perica later speculated that the actual figure might have been as high as 1,000, with most of the stricken opting not to seek medical assistance.[17] The DOH identified the cause as salmonella poisoning, and traced it back to the carbo-load party. It is not known how many participants dropped out due to the poisoning. Swedish runner Kjell-Erik Stahl later complained that he was "never so sick running a race."[18] Because he was not directly responsible for the party, Barahal emerged from the weekend largely unscathed; in fact, the *Honolulu Star-Bulletin*'s Pat Bigold wrote a lengthy article that painted with heroic strokes Barahal's efforts to deal with the twin crises. Hero or not, he handled these negative situations in a poised manner, displaying an openness and accessibility in the face of potential disaster that was at odds with the cool superiority he fronts in less demanding situations. He would draw frequently on his talent for directness as he shepherded the HMA along a path strewn with as many uncertainties as possibilities.

CHAPTER 8

A Japanese Marriage

In 1976, a person whose name, age, and gender have been lost—if not to history, then at least within the dusty archives of the HMA office—became the first Japanese national to run the Honolulu Marathon. In the official tracking of Japanese participation, Runner X accounted for 0.1 percent of the 1,670 people who submitted entries for that year's race. Twelve years later, Japanese participants would account for fully one-half of the field. Three years after that, in 1991, the Japanese component hit a high of 70 percent. Between 2004 and 2014, 58 percent of all runners who started the marathon came from Japan. It was therefore largely thanks to Japanese participation that the Honolulu Marathon kept pace with the New York, Boston, Chicago, London, and Berlin marathons during the early to mid-1990s, when the rise of the so-called marathon middle class—recreational runners inspired by Oprah Winfrey and Al Gore, for whom simply finishing 26.2 miles was sufficient accomplishment—swelled top fields into the tens of thousands.

Though Japanese participation in the Honolulu Marathon exploded in the 1990s, the result of increased interest in long-distance running in Japan and the independent marketing efforts by race sponsor Japan Airlines and its subsidiary tour agency JALPAK, the relationship between the marathon and the Japanese advertising firm that represents JAL dates back to a 1979 meeting between then HMA president Jack Scaff and Jiro Kitamura of Asatsu (now ADK). Scaff was interested in creating a sister race in Japan. Kitamura had worked with the Ohme-Hochi 30K on behalf of another client, Mitsubishi Fuso, a truck and tractor company that wanted to encourage physical exercise for its drivers. The two men worked to identify a suitable location. As Kitamura recalled:

Since Hawaii is an island and people are used to being close to the ocean, they were looking for a site close to the ocean—and not too far from Tokyo—and that's why they chose Miura City in Kanagawa. They were happy about the idea because in the summertime they have many visitors but their visitor industry suffers in the winter. [. . .] Of course they want to have a little fun after they finish and accomplish finishing the full marathon, just like you guys having a little party afterward at Kapi'olani Park. So we planned finishing the event with a congratulatory event for the finishers on the beach in Miura. The concept was not to just run and compete and finish and go home but to have fun with everybody—not only the runners and organizers but also the people in the community.[1]

The first Miura International Citizens Marathon was held in February of 1981. (The race is actually a half-marathon; in Japan, the term "marathon" has been used to refer to any long-distance race.) As with other Japanese races, only elite-level competitors participated. Each year, a lottery is held in which three finishers are invited to participate in the Honolulu Marathon. In one of the earliest Honolulu Marathon promotions in Japan, the host of the annual Miura Marathon broadcast on the Tokyo Broadcast System invited runners to join him in running the race. Coupled with another promotion headed by former Olympian and longtime Honolulu Marathon supporter Frank Shorter and his Japanese sponsors that brought 150 Japanese runners to the race, the number of Japanese runners in the 1982 Honolulu Marathon jumped from 977 the previous year to 1,500.

Not long after he resigned as president of the HMA, Scaff had a visit from Jim Barahal and Jon Cross. Barahal had invoked Scaff's name in his takedown of the HMA executive board, accusing the leaders of turning their backs on those who had established the race—a highly ironic charge, given that under Barahal the HMA would eventually disassociate itself entirely from the race's founder. In a rare meeting between the marathon's past and imminent future, Barahal and Cross sought Scaff's advice about starting up a Christmas fun run. The informal sit-down took place at Scaff's Round Top Drive residence, the site of his popular pre-marathon carbo-load party for Honolulu Marathon Clinic participants and old friends like Shorter, Kenny Moore, and others. The conversation drifted to the challenges Barahal

faced as leader of the HMA. Scaff's advice, recalled frequently o\
years, was simple and direct: "Whatever you do, don't lose the Chun\

Scaff was acknowledging Jeanette and Ron's indispensability in the administrative and operational areas, but also perhaps their less visible roles as key intermediaries with Asatsu. As a naval engineer, Ronald Chun made regular visits to Japan, and Jeanette frequently tagged along. Early on, Scaff asked Jeanette to meet with Asatsu executives to discuss race management. Over a series of meetings in Japan and Hawai'i, the Chuns built close relationships with Kitamura and Asatsu CEO Masao Inagaki, their Hawai'i-Asian sense of decorum proving a comfortable match with the two Japanese gentlemen. Once, when Asatsu executives were visiting Honolulu, Jeanette noticed Inagaki looking worn and hungry. She made a quick trip to a Japanese eatery to buy him a bento (box) lunch. The small gesture left a deep impression. The next time they met, Inagaki presented her with a neatly wrapped box containing a necklace. "Here is your bento,"[3] he said. Over the years, the Chuns and Asatsu/ADK and JAL executives exchanged countless visits, sewing friendship and business together in ways that are increasingly rare. For some new ADK employees, visiting the Chun's Mō'ili'ili home is making a pilgrimage to a historic site.

Asatsu had long wanted to broker a title sponsorship agreement between JAL and the marathon, but had been stalled by an HMA board not prepared to cede the marketing and promotional control required for significant financial support. And yet, HMA leaders continued to accept all-expenses-paid trips to Japan to meet with Asatsu and JAL, irking the Chuns with their seeming willful disregard of cultural protocols and general lack of courtesy and cultural sensitivity. Ron Chun said that HMA visitors repeatedly promised to move forward with sponsorship agreements while in Japan, only to have the executive board vote the proposals down back in Hawaii. "I felt bad," Chun said: "Everybody—(John) Kelleher, John Maughan, Gary (Murfin)—everybody went to Japan and just strung them along. They'd tell them, "Yeah, we're going to do it." Then (they) come back to Hawai'i (and) the boss says 'no.' And I'd say, 'Why are you taking it back?' So it would never get done."[4] Kitamura was more forgiving:

> Rather than opposition, there was maybe confusion among the board members for understanding the concept of having a sponsor pay for the event. The organization is a (non-profit organization) and members of

the board are doing it on a volunteer basis. But if we want a public corporation to be a sponsor of the event, we need to pay something in return like, for example, something we promised them we were going to do, like putting a logo in the printing as an advertisement. This kind of thing wasn't understood clearly by some of the board members. In Hawai'i, people have friends everywhere. Some people had friends in a beverage company and they donated some beverages to the event so they said, we can put your logo in the printing, whereas, actually, that was the space for the official sponsors and not everybody who helped out on the way. That was the kind of confusion we met with in the beginning.[5]

The impasse dissolved as Barahal assumed control of marathon sponsorship and he and Cross, in the wake of the Benson faction's walkout, carried through with a gradual culling of the HMA board. In 1986, just prior to Barahal becoming HMA president, Asatsu delivered a proposal for JAL to become the Honolulu Marathon title sponsor to Jeanette Chun, who then took the offer to Barahal. Kitamura had assured Barahal that the Japanese market was primed for a mass embrace of the Honolulu Marathon, a race the unique characteristics of which—no qualification, no field cap, no time limit—made it an ideal match for Japanese recreational runners shut out of the major competitions in their home country. By that point, however, the response was hardly in doubt. "Jim wasn't dumb," said Ron Chun. "He wasn't a bigot."[6]

A Perfect Tsunami

Barahal needed only to scan the lobbies of the hotels where his clinics operated to see that Hawai'i's fortunes were becoming increasingly bound to the Japanese. The political and economic movements that set the stage for massive Japanese investment in Hawai'i overlapped with Hawai'i's own transition from an agriculture and military-based economy to one strongly dependent on tourism. Following the 1964 Olympic Games in Tokyo, Japan eased international travel restrictions, allowing its citizens to visit other countries for pleasure as well as business. In an effort to limit the amount of money leaving the country—money necessary for importing modern machinery to spur post-war economic recovery[7]—the government limited the amount of money Japanese could exchange for overseas vacations. These restrictions remained in place until 1976, when Japanese economic prosperity, high-volume jet travel, and affordable group tour packages all contributed to a foreign travel boom. The 1985 Plaza Accord elevated Japanese tourism and investment in Hawai'i to unprecedented levels. Spurred by a 50 percent appreciation of the U.S. dollar against top world currencies, and a resulting threat of reactive international trade restrictions, the United States, Japan, West Germany, France, and the United Kingdom agreed to a devaluation of the dollar against the Japanese yen and the German mark. According to the University of Hawai'i Economic Research Organization, Japanese businesses seeking to take advantage of the suddenly powerful yen invested some $12 billion in Hawai'i between 1985 and 1995. (In the preceding ten years, the total had been $850 million.) Japanese tourism followed suit. Drawing upon overseas departure statistics from the Japan Ministry of Transport, UH economics professor James Mak evaluated this rapid growth.

Due to its relative proximity, year-round temperate weather, relative safety, and large local Japanese population, Hawai'i was ideally suited to become the No. 1 destination for Japanese tourists. According to Mak, Japanese accounted for one-fourth of all visitor arrivals, and even more significantly, more than one-third of visitor spending in 1992. In their 2005 study "Japanese Runners in the Honolulu Marathon and Their Economic Benefits to Hawaii," Jerome Agrusa, John Tanner, and Dan Lema also noted that Japanese tourists are group travelers whose sense of safety and comfort is shaped by the concept of *amae,* roughly translated as a presumption of and dependence upon the benevolence of others. Assumed within Japanese society, *amae* often extends to foreign locations. And as Agrusa et al. observe, "Hawaii, a core American culture with Japanese cultural influence, is a reflexive antithesis of Japan, a core Japanese culture with American cultural influence. And so, Hawaii and Japan symbolize a diacritical synthesis of psychological *amae* affinity."[8]

For Japanese recreational runners, Hawai'i offered the rare opportunity to compete in a real marathon in a place perceived to be safe, accommodating, and sufficiently compatible culturally. Although often overlooked

Table 2 Japanese International Departures, 1964–1989

Year	Departures
1964	127,749
1974	2.3 million
1984	4.7 million
1989	9.7 million

or underappreciated, Japan's contributions to the marathon as a sport have been longstanding and highly significant. Sponsored by the Mainichi newspaper chain, the first Japanese marathon was staged on March 21, 1909 along a course stretching from Kobe to Osaka. Later dubbed the Lake Biwa Mainichi Marathon, the race was revived in 1946 to inspire the Japanese to rebuild their war-torn nation, and has been staged every year since, often headlined by such international stars as Abebe Bikila, Frank Shorter, and Karel Lismont. The Asahi Marathon debuted in 1947, operating for the first seven years as a Japanese-only competition. Renamed the Fukuoka International Marathon Championships in 1966, the race has since served as a de facto world championship, with winners of each year's top international marathons competing under sanction of the International Association of Athletics Federations.

Individually, Japanese runners ranked among the world's best from the 1950s through the rise of the big-city marathons in the 1970s and '80s, this despite a strange and inauspicious debut on the world stage at the 1912 Olympic Games in Stockholm. Marathoner Shizo Kanakuri and middle-distance runner Yahiko Mishima were the first Japanese athletes to compete in the Games. Reportedly fatigued from his journey from Japan and unaccustomed to the local fare, Kanakuri, running in traditional wooden tabi, collapsed on an unsupervised stretch of the course and was taken in by a local family. Returning to Japan without checking in with race officials, he was listed as "missing" for fifty years, even though he competed in subsequent Olympics.[9] Japan's supposed breakthrough in international competition came at the 1936 Games in Berlin when Kitei Son (né Sohn Kee-Chung) and Nan Shoryu (Nam Sung-Yong) took the gold and bronze medals, respectively, in the marathon. However, this milestone was darkened by the reality that the both Sohn and Nam were Korean athletes compelled to compete as representatives of Japan, which had annexed Korea in 1910.[10] An iconic photograph from the awards ceremony showed Sohn and Nam bowing their heads in what they later described as "silent shame and outrage."[11]

For its role in World War II, Japan was shut out of international athletic competition—including the 1948 Olympics in London—until 1951, when Shigeki Tanaka, Shunji Koyunagi, Yoshitaka Uchikawa, and Hiromi Taigo were invited to participate in the Boston Marathon. Tanaka, a witness to the 1945 bombing of Hiroshima, won the race in 2:27:45, wearing split-toe running shoes in the style of Japanese tabi. This victory ushered in a golden age of Japanese marathon running. From 1951 to 1981, Japan tied

Finland for the second most Boston Marathon victories (seven), behind only the United States (eight). In 1968, Kenji Kimihara placed second to Mamo Wolde in Mexico City, still the best finish by a Japanese national in the Olympic marathon. At that point, Japan boasted arguably the world's deepest reserve of elite marathon runners. In 1964 alone, Japanese athletes had run forty sub-2:20 marathons. United States marathoners that year ran exactly one. Runners such as Tanaka, Kimihara, and 1981 Boston Marathon champion Toshihiko Seko were revered in their homeland, sparking a national fascination with long-distance running.

By the 1970s, major Japanese road races were broadcast via television and radio to rapt audiences. The marathon was a major spectator sport, if not yet a participatory one. Analyses of Japan's running traditions almost invariably note that the marathon's grueling test of character resonates within a society that considers tenacity and perseverance—*konjou*—as matters of national pride. And yet, for the first century of marathon running in Japan, for pragmatic and traditional reasons, races were largely inaccessible to all but the best distance runners. Despite great popular interest, the strict time limits and tight caps on entry, deemed necessary to avoid disrupting traffic and community life in the high-density cities, prevented a mass-participation running boom like the one the United States experienced in the 1970s.

Asatsu's Inagaki and Kitamura clearly recognized the desires of Japan's recreational runners, and when the HMA accepted a JAL title sponsorship, the floodgates suddenly opened. Tour companies immediately began developing packages focused on the race, complementing promotions by a prominent Japanese radio station, and by the Japanese publication *Runner's Magazine* in cooperation with the JTB, Japan's largest tour agency. Honolulu Marathon tour packages soon became so numerous and varied that Asatsu/ADK began offering annual seminars to apprise travel agencies of the latest Honolulu marathon developments, and to share video clips and other promotional materials. Asatsu was also behind an hour-long Honolulu Marathon highlight special that debuted on the Tokyo Broadcast System (TBS) in 1989. In a country where live broadcasts of collegiate and professional *ekiden* races are watched with the same rapt attention Americans pay to the NCAA Men's Basketball Final Four or the National Football League playoffs, the highlight program is a reliable staple of TBS winter programming, attracting upwards of 2.5 million viewers each year, and planting a dream of participating in the minds of countless Japanese recreational runners. Even in the earliest days of the JAL title sponsorship, with

Table 3   Japanese Entrants in the Honolulu Marathon, 1986–1995

Year	Total Entrants	Japanese Entrants	% of Field
1986*	10,354	3,553	34.3
1987	10,413	4,551	43.7
1988	10,205	5,094	49.9
1989	10,813	6,004	55.5
1990	13,268	8,674	65.4
1991	14,605	10,236	70.1
1992	30,905	18,286	59.2
1993	29,514	19,001	64.4
1994	32,771	21,291	65.0
1995	34,434	21,717	63.1

(Honolulu Marathon Association, "Entrants from Japan 1973–2007")
*First year of JAL title sponsorship.

the Japanese running boom still a decade away, Asatsu's marketing and promotion led to a transformative influx of Japanese participants into the Honolulu Marathon.

JAL's heightened profile was immediately apparent in the mid- to late 1980s. HMA's most symbolic concession was allowing JAL's name to be featured on the runners' race bibs. For road-racing purists, the race bib is a sacred space, akin to a professional football, baseball, or basketball uniform. Granting any portion to advertising, in the manner of NASCAR vehicles or European football jerseys, signified a loss of institutional integrity, a fatal compromising of a race's duty to its runners and host community. Although this may now seem quaint, this was some runners' response when the bright red "JAL" appeared on the otherwise black-and-white Honolulu Marathon bib. The logo and other notices of Japanese sponsorship and patronage spread out along the course, from JAL-emblazoned tents, scaffolding, and other infrastructure, to Japanese-language signage at the start and finish. JAL asked for and received space for its logo atop each mile marker. In deference to the Japanese competitors, the race also introduced kilometer markers in Japanese. Ron Chun usually was the one who figured out how to accommodate JAL's requests without breaking the budget. When the sponsor wanted a leader board with its logo on top, Chun built one himself. When the board fell into disrepair after several years, Chun and his sons created another one out of aluminum piping. When it was time to update the old mile markers, Chun designed new eleven-foot models, topped with framing for the JAL logo and a large digital clock. To test its sturdiness, Chun left the proto-

The Honolulu Marathon has relied on Japanese participation to maintain its position as one of the world's largest marathons. Photo by Bruce Asato. Courtesy of the *Honolulu Star-Advertiser.*

type, fortified by sandbags, in his front yard during Hurricane Iwa. His justifiably anxious neighbors were very happy that the massive marker didn't budge. He also created space for some twenty large tents near the finish area for JAL officials, tour agencies, and the large contingent of Japanese media on hand to cover Japanese celebrities in the race.

Increased Japanese presence not only transformed the appearance, but to some degree the personality of the race as well. The crowd behind the starting line became wider and deeper, swollen by battalions of runners in matching tops milling beneath the colorful banners of one of a dozen or more tour companies. Japanese entrants also ran in elaborate costumes—Playboy bunnies, robots, American superheroes, emaciated sumotori in cheek-chafing *mawashi*—invoking both traditional European festival pageantry and modern Japanese *kawaii* culture. Nor did the runners come alone. Family members, friends, local Japanese organizations, and junior employees from Japanese sponsors and tour agencies lined the course, beating clappers and drums and shouting Japanese words of encouragement. The rise in Japanese participation coincided with an overall slowing of the field, a fact some have attributed to the high number of Japanese participants who arrive at the race having done little or no training. Foolhardy on its face, such impetuousness has links to Japanese festival traditions like *mikoshi* or *danjiri,* in which participants work together to transport massive floats at frightening speeds through their village, or to endurance rituals like *kanchu-misogi,* in which participants immerse themselves in freezing water or hug giant blocks of ice—or both. Such traditions are expressive of the Japanese virtue of *gamanzuyoi,* the ability to "endure the unendurable," or to exhibit stoic forbearance in the face of difficulty. Thus, it's not uncommon to see suffering back-of-the pack joggers link arms in solidarity as they trudge to the finish line.

For the most part, the local running community embraced the visiting runners, but pockets of discontent appeared as Japanese influence in Hawai'i increased generally in the early 1990s. For some residents, the spectacle of thousands of Japanese runners disrupting local traffic on East Honolulu roads, now lined with Japanese language signage, became distressingly emblematic of how conspicuous Japanese spending—$5 billion in 1989 alone— had led to in the proliferation of exclusive golf courses, separate standards of customer service for local consumers and the more coveted Japanese clientele, and, along the Kāhala and Diamond Head stretch of marathon course itself, the long swath of empty beachside homes held as investment properties by absentee Japanese owners. Such changes account for the results of a study conducted by Market Trends Pacific and John M. Knox Associates for the Hawaii Tourism Authority. Between 1998 and 2006, the number of Hawai'i residents who agreed that their island "is being run for tourists at the expense of the local people" rose from 43 to 62 percent.

Barahal and other MHA officials found that they had to fight off similar accusations about their road race, repeatedly insisting that local runners were important to its present and future, while at the same time promoting it as "the world's biggest destination marathon." In deference to Asatsu and JAL, the marathon in fact came to work almost exclusively with Japanese sponsors, abandoning all but token efforts at U.S. and non-Japanese international marketing. Since then, the marathon has enjoyed a largely uninterrupted level of Japanese patronage that assures its ongoing success—just as Kitamura had promised.

CHAPTER 9

The Living Legacy of Bikila and Wolde

Ibrahim Hussein's record-setting performances in the 1985 and 1986 Honolulu Marathon vindicated Jon Cross's belief that modern African runners could be the standard bearers for the Honolulu Marathon, and paved the way for Jim Barahal gaining control of the HMA. But these records only hinted at what the graceful and articulate young man from Kapsabet, Kenya, would come to represent for the future of his sport, his tribe, and his country. With Barahal and Cross serving as his de facto coaches, Hussein returned to the New York Marathon in 1987 intent on improving on his fourth-place finish from the year before. Following a race plan plotted by Barahal, Hussein easily outpaced the competition, finishing in 2:11:01. (Gianni DeMadonna of Italy was second, in 2:11:53, followed by Pete Pfitzinger in 2:11:54.) "I needed something like this, a big win, to happen for me," Hussein said after the race: "There are so many great runners from Kenya. I am one of many."[1]

Hussein is Nandi, one of several tribes comprising the Kalenjin people of the Great Rift Valley. A member of the Kalenjin's tiny Muslim minority, Hussein had a relatively comfortable upbringing, thanks to the family general store and farm. He attended the prestigious St. Patrick's Secondary School in the town of Iten, where he distinguished himself as a top middle-distance runner. Like many Kenyans of his generation, he grew up idolizing fellow tribesman Kipchoge "Kip" Keino. In the 1968 Mexico City Olympics, Keino took gold in the 1,500 meters and silver in the 5,000. Four years later in Munich, when Frank Shorter's marathon win sparked the American running revolution, Keino won the 3,000-meter steeplechase and took second in the 1,500 meters. As he ran the three-mile stretch to and from his school each day, Hussein would daydream that he was Keino. Hussein's accomplishments on the track earned him a scholarship to the University of New Mexico. In Albuquerque, Hussein dazzled as a 400-meter runner while earning a degree in economics.

Just a month after his New York victory, Hussein ran the 1987 Honolulu Marathon. Battling wind, rain, and his own tired legs, he extended his winning streak to three consecutive years, despite finishing in 2:18:26, well off his record pace. The following year, with Barahal and Cross again serving as his handlers, Hussein went to Boston, one of three dozen African runners ready to vie for the top prize of $45,000 and a Mercedes Benz. Like any other Olympic year, the top American runners stayed away, wanting to stay fresh for the Olympic trials. Their absence was more than offset by a strong field of international runners whose countries used the Boston Marathon as an Olympic qualifier. The field that day included defending champion Steve Jones of England, 1987 Beijing Marathon champion Juma Ikangaa of Ethiopia, two-time New York Marathon winner Orlando Pizzolato of Italy, and 1984 Olympic silver medalist John Treacy of Ireland. Two of Cross's original Honolulu Marathon recruits, Zach Barie and Gabriel Kamau, were also running. The frontrunners stayed in two large packs through the first ten miles, with the lead group reaching the halfway mark at 1:03:12, ahead of world-record pace. After twenty miles, this furious pace had dropped all but three serious contenders: Hussein, Ikangaa, and Treacy. Ikangaa surged, attempting to break the other two men. Hussein betrayed no distress in responding to each challenge, but Treacy, a late entry, fell behind. Down the stretch, it was Hussein's superior kick—a powerful weapon honed during his collegiate days as a 400-meter runner—that made the difference. He broke the tape in 2:08:43, followed by Ikangaa just a second later. Treacy finished third in 2:09:15. With this win, Hussein became the first black man to win the Boston Marathon. Ethiopian Belayneh Densamo had won the Rotterdam Marathon two years in a row, setting a world record the day before Hussein's Boston victory. But the Rotterdam race, started in 1981, had not yet risen to the ranks of the top marathons. It was therefore Hussein's triumph in the world's most storied race that truly announced the ascendancy of African runners in the modern marathon.

His breakthrough also created a well-defined niche for the Honolulu Marathon. While it ranked among the top races internationally in terms of participation, it could not compete financially with Boston, New York, and other major marathons in securing established top-tier talent. Hussein's victory, and strong showings by Barie and Kamau, confirmed that Barahal and Cross had turned the Honolulu Marathon into a proving ground for the elite runners of the future. Hussein followed his 1988 Boston victory with disappointing showings in the 1988 Olympic Games in Seoul and the 1990 Commonwealth Games in Auckland, New Zealand. But in 1991 and 1992, he recovered with back-to-back victories in Boston, thereby cementing his legacy. Hussein would attempt only one more title defense in Honolulu, understandably saving himself for more lucrative races. The road he had helped to pave there for other rising African runners, however, would only broaden over the years. Starting with Hussein's three consecutive victories, African competitors would win twenty-eight of the thirty Honolulu Marathons between 1985 and 2014—and if not for some truly bizarre circumstances, the figure might stand at twenty-nine.

Who Is Brant Nava?

A week before the 1988 Honolulu Marathon, Cross got a call from agent Larry Heidebrecht, asking if he could bring over a young prospect from Paraguay. Cross was wary of Heidebrecht, whose most famous client, Canadian sprinter Ben Johnson, had been stripped of his Olympic gold medal earlier that year, having tested positive for steroids. After consulting with Barahal, though, Cross told Heidebrecht that the runner and his coach could come at their own expense. If the runner finished in the top five, the race would reimburse his travel costs. It seemed like a safe bet for a race committed to identifying and nurturing young talent.

"Brant Nava" arrived in Honolulu at 5 p.m. on December 11, exactly twelve hours before the race, accompanied by his coach, identified at the time as Paul Stefanos from Greece. Showing no signs of jetlag, Nava headed out with the lead pack the next day, and gradually built a significant lead. But he seemed to falter down the stretch, and did not respond to a late surge by Italian runner Gianni Poli, who won in 2:12:47. Poli, who was celebrating his honeymoon in Honolulu, was the sort of charming and telegenic personality that marathon organizers and race media love. His victory however was overshadowed by curiosity about the mysterious Paraguayan, who but for a reported case of stomach cramps seemed to be the superior runner. The next day, the *Honolulu Star-Bulletin* ran an above-the-fold article by Pat Bigold titled "Marathon's Mystery Man Almost Won It." It led with the question on everyone's mind: "Who is that guy?"

The question wasn't just prompted by a runner appearing out of nowhere to almost win one of the world's largest marathons, but by Bigold's intuition that something was fishy. Bigold was well versed in marathon chicanery. In 1980, while working for the *Lawrence Eagle Tribune,* he had watched as a similarly unknown runner named Rosie Ruiz crossed the finish line at the Prudential Center to win the Boston Marathon's women's division in a course record of 2:31:56. Bigold had a rooting interest in Boston native Patti Catalano, a four-time winner of the Honolulu Marathon, who finished third behind Ruiz and Jacqueline Gareau. Catalano was a fiery competitor but never a sore loser, so Bigold was surprised when he caught up with her and found her apoplectic at Ruiz receiving the ceremonial laurel wreath.

> (Catalano) and I both watched her come up on the stage. I remember Patti saying, "She's fat! She's fat!" She was mad. She was yelling. She was just livid. I said, "Where did you finish?" She said, "Third. That girl over there beat me" and she looked over at (Gareau). "The fat girl didn't win."[2]

Catalano wasn't the only one outraged and suspicious. New York City Marathon founder and race director Fred LeBow was there, and when he saw Ruiz being celebrated as the winner, he approached Boston Athletic Association officials and told them that he believed Ruiz had cheated to an 11th place finish in his race the previous year. Bigold quickly latched on to the story, even recruiting a French-Canadian security guard from his newspaper to help him interview the Quebecois Gareau. In the following days, spotters at various checkpoints reported that they had not seen Ruiz pass. Then witnesses came forward to testify that during the New York City Marathon, they had seen Ruiz on the subway. Eventually, LeBow disqualified Ruiz, retroactively making her ineligible to run in Boston. The BAA then stripped Ruiz of her title,[3] and declared Gareau the rightful winner. It remains one of the most notorious moments in Boston Marathon history.

Although he didn't have much to go on, Bigold felt certain that Brant Nava was not who he was claiming to be. This put him at odds with Barahal and Cross, with whom he had always enjoyed a cordial relationship:

> I remember being there, pursuing this thing, continuing to ask questions about this guy whereas Barahal and Cross wanted me to focus on

the winner and the fact that this guy (Nava) had come out of nowhere to challenge him. [. . .] I tried to follow (Nava) and find where he was going. I got a tremendous amount of opposition from the Honolulu Marathon guys, both Jon and Jim. More so from Jon. Jon was adamant that I was not going to ruin this guy's day.[4]

As Cross recalled the situation, Bigold insisted on interviewing Nava, and Cross said he would arrange an exclusive interview later in the day if Bigold would leave him alone in the interim. A disagreement ensued. Depending on who is telling the story, it ended either with Cross shoving Bigold into a wall, or Cross politely asking Bigold to wait for his interview. But even without Bigold's prodding, the sense that something was amiss only intensified. A post-race interview with Nava's coach, "Stefanos," on KHON-2's highlight special captured him hurriedly answering questions in an accent that did not seem Greek, while a visibly nervous Nava turned away from the camera. In longer interviews with print and broadcast media, Stefanos's claim that he had discovered Nava through another unnamed Paraguayan client, and had taken him to England just a year earlier to train, seemed at best a stretch. After the race, New York Marathon winner turned broadcaster Alberto Salazar, who was born in Cuba, attempted to speak to Nava in Spanish, only to be met with a confused stare.

Cross and Barahal arranged to take Stefanos and Nava to the airport the following evening for their flight back to California. But when Cross arrived at the hotel lobby, they weren't there. Minutes passed, and he asked the hotel manager to check on their room. It was empty; the two men were gone. As Cross recalled:

> That's when it started to hit me. I went to Jim and said, "Here's the phone bill." I could see the phone records for this room and it was Paraguay, Paraguay, Johannesburg, Johannesburg, Johannesburg, Paraguay, Paraguay—because they were, like, freaked out. And so then I realized that we had been duped.[5]

The calls to Johannesburg seemed to confirm Cross's worst fear. The mystery man from Paraguay was probably from South Africa, whose system of apartheid, or racial segregation, had prompted the Athletics Congress to ban its athletes—white and black—from international competition. Cross knew

South African runner David Tsebe competed in the 1988 Honolulu Marathon as "Brant Nava" of Paraguay. Photo by Dennis Oda. Courtesy of the *Honolulu Star-Advertiser.*

that the presence of a South African athlete in the Honolulu Marathon field could therefore potentially cost the race its TAC sanction, guaranteeing that no elite athlete would ever return.

While Cross and Barahal prepared to report the incident to the Athletics Congress, Bigold was working international phone lines, following whatever lead he could to find out who Nava and Stefano really were. Eventually, Bigold made contact with Illinois sports agent Glenn Lattimer, who told him that Nava was actually a black South African runner named David Tsebe, and that Stefano was South African Paul Coetser (misidentified in the subsequent story as Paul Coetze), a partner in a sports management company specializing in helping South African athletes circumvent the international ban. As the story unfolded, Barahal speculated that the runner posing as Nava had been exploited, possibly under the threat of imprisonment. In a Bigold article six days after the race, Barahal claimed that he and Cross "believed they could learn more about the frightened runner's background by quietly and sensitively winning his confidence," and that the reason they did not immediately contact the TAC was because Barahal "believed he had found a 'great runner' and did not want to scare him away by jumping to conclusions."[6]

The TAC dispatched special assistant Alvin Chriss, the man who had designed the trust system that allowed athletes to receive appearance fees and prize money without losing their amateur status, to Honolulu to investigate the case. He was particularly interested in Heidebrecht's involvement, since he had previously been accused of commercially representing student athletes in violation of NCAA rules. During the investigation, Coetser called Chriss, confessed to the scam, and confirmed that Nava was in fact Tsebe. Coetser also admitted that he had "invested" $400,000 in buying fraudulent passports for three other South African athletes. Chriss called the operation "a major conspiracy." He also interviewed Heidebrecht, who claimed he was merely doing a favor for Coetser, whom he knew as Paul Stevens. Ultimately, Chriss absolved the Honolulu Marathon Association of any wrongdoing: "The association has a history of favoring its athletes and not getting involved in the bureaucracy of the sport. They offered the benefit of the doubt and were taken in by (Coetser)."[7]

In a 1990 *Los Angeles Times* series of articles about South African athletes, Coetser described his operation. Through bribery and deception, for example, he had obtained a Lesotho birth certificate for South African marathoner Annette Falkson, which he then used to get her a passport that would circumvent the ban by presenting her as a citizen of Lesotho—an independent country located within South Africa. But the ruse failed. When she attempted to run the 1988 Los Angeles Marathon, she was identified by U.S. track officials. In the article, Coetser bragged about his groundwork for establishing false identities for his clients:

> I can't tell you the number of big races we have run in the U.S. and everywhere else. We have people registered with TAC, we are members of the New York Road Racing Club. I try to run as many races under as many names as I can, to get a name established (and pass on to other South Africans). So when race directors ask where my athletes have run, we can show results. I have run many times under women's names.[8]

For Tsebe, a promising young South African runner, Coetser took advantage of a Paraguayan government initiative that made farms in the northern part of the country available to foreign investors. As part of a deal, Coetser obtained four passports, which he then used to register his athletes with the Paraguayan track and field federation. "There is corruption like you cannot believe," he was quoted as saying. "Anything is possible with money."

The incident troubled Barahal and Cross—and not just because they had been duped. They sympathized with Tsebe, a black South African clearly capable of competing with the best in the world, but caught in a political struggle in which he had no agency. Just twenty-one when he competed as Brant Nava, Tsebe was an accomplished high school runner who received support from a platinum mine (in the form of a "welfare officer" position) that allowed him to train and compete as one of the country's top marathoners. Before arriving in Honolulu, Tsebe had won the Sun City Marathon and come second in the South African championships in Cape Town. The international ban cost him some of his prime running years. But once apartheid was overturned, and the ban on South African athletes lifted just prior to the 1992 Olympics in Barcelona, he wasted no time in making his mark. David Tsebe won the 1992 Berlin Marathon in 2:08:07, the fastest time in the world that year. Then that December, at the invitation of the Barahal and Cross, Tsebe returned to Honolulu to compete under his own name. He finished third, behind Benson Masya and first-time marathoner Cosmas Ndeti. In addition to his third-place earnings, Barahal arranged for Tsebe to receive an extra $5,000—the amount he surrendered when he was disqualified in 1988.

Success and Its Burdens

Disruptive as it may have been, the Tsebe incident only underscored the vast potential of African marathon runners. In the pre-Internet age of recruiting, true obsessives like Barahal and Cross had an advantage over race directors who only paid attention to major marathon results. During his travels with Hussein, for instance, Cross caught notice of an unorthodox Tanzanian runner named Simon Robert Naali:

> He was just totally erratic. I mean, he would take off and get a big lead and then he would look around and he would back off. They would catch up and he would take off again and he was just crazy. But he didn't die. He still ran like fifth or something like that even though he was doing this herky-jerky pace. I thought, "That guy's got potential."

Cross turned to his old contact Filbert Bayi to secure Naali for the 1989 race, setting up an intriguing battle of contrasting styles between Naali and defending champion Hussein. But the race itself proved anticlimactic. The twenty-three-year-old Naali broke away from the pack just before the half-mile mark, and contrary to Cross's scouting, he never looked back. His 2:11:47 finish was just four seconds off of Hussein's course record. Hussein himself finished second, followed closely by Gidamis Shahanga of Tanzania. Two other Tanzanian runners, Suleiman Nyambui and Agapius Masong, finished fourth and fifth—an all-African sweep. The following year Naali faced a stiffer challenge from his own younger brother, Thomas Robert Naali. Battling strong headwinds, the brothers broke from the pack early and stayed within a few seconds of each other until the final 500 yards, when Simon Robert Naali pulled away in a dead sprint. He finished in 2:17:29; his brother thirty-four seconds later. Masaki Oya of Japan finished in 2:20:22 for third place, the highest-ever Honolulu finish for a Japanese male runner.

By the early 1990s, African runners were the dominant force in international marathon racing, and with this came more a more organized training and management infrastructure. Cross and Barahal had recruited African runners through an informal network of coaches, teammates, and in Hussein's case, shoe company representatives like Ernie Severn. But the turn of the decade saw more athletes from Kenya, Tanzania, and Ethiopia represented by professional agents. Nevertheless, Barahal and Cross's ahead-of-the-curve investments secured the long-term prospects of the marathon's elite athlete division. Zane Branson was one of the first agents for African runners to work with the Honolulu Marathon Association, and his ability to deliver top up-and-coming runners made him one of the small handful of agents whom Barahal and Cross trusted implicitly. A standout runner at Staunton River High School in Virginia, and one of the top members of East Tennessee State's impressive cross country teams of the late 1970s, Branson moved to England for graduate school, promoting concerts to cover his tuition. He eventually expanded to sports management through associate Gerry Helme, who represented Douglas Wakiihuri, a Kenyan runner who trained in Japan as part of the S&B Foods running team. Wakiihuri placed first in the 1987 World Championships in Rome and second in the 1988 Olympics in Seoul. It was Helme who brought Wakiihuri to the 1989 London Marathon and the 1990 New York City Marathon. He won both. Branson's first Kenyan client was Benson Masya, a former boxer with tantalizing running ability and unshakable self-confidence, but also frailties that would prove tragic.

Masya, a member of the Kamba tribe, came to Honolulu in 1991 having never run a full marathon. Under less than ideal conditions, and in one

Agent Zane Branson was responsible for bringing top Kenyan runners to the Honolulu Marathon. Photo courtesy of Brittny Ing-Lee.

of the most competitive races to that point, his raw talent prevailed as he outkicked defending champion Naali and former world record holder Steve Jones of Wales to win in a time of 2:18:24. Masya defended his title the following year, beating close friend and countryman Cosmas Ndeti and the recently liberated David Tsebe with a 2:14:19 victory. Ndeti would rebound the following year with the first of three consecutive victories in the Boston Marathon, further establishing the Honolulu Marathon as a proving ground for runners on the cusp of the big time.

Coming off an injury, Masya lost the following year to Bong-ju Lee,[9] the only non-African male runner besides Poli to win the Honolulu Marathon after Hussein's breakthrough in 1985. Masya returned the following year, and won his third title with a stirring come-from-behind victory over Thabisco Moghali of South Africa and Andy Green of England. Although he never enjoyed the success and fame of his friend Ndeti—outside of Honolulu, his only major win was the 1997 Stockholm Marathon—Masya was widely considered one of the top runners of his generation. As Barahal remarked years later, "Benson was a huge talent and the No. 1 road racer in the world at one time when he ran here. It was a big thing for us that he would run here. It showed the world we could attract a top runner again (after Ibrahim Hussein)."[10]

But Benson was as well known for his hard living as he was for his running. He trained with Ndeti and other Kenyan runners in Albuquerque, New Mexico. Unlike the deeply religious Ndeti, however, Masya enjoyed spending his free time drinking and carrying on with his college-aged cohorts. "At the time, in the late '80s and early '90s, it was quite common for distance runners from Kenya to go for training then go to the pub," said Branson, who from his base in Liverpool, England, found it difficult to keep tabs on Masya: "It was more of a rowdy crew than it is now and it was just the way running was. It was still very much college based. It wasn't funny but it didn't seem like that big of a deal—until I found out the real extent of what was going on." By 1996, two years after his last win in Honolulu, it was clear to Branson that Masya's lifestyle and drinking were putting his career, and even his life, in jeopardy. After a strong showing in a 10-mile race in Southampton in October 1996, Masya turned his attention to the New York City Marathon. Earlier that year, Branson had arranged for Masya's wife Joan and their son Willis to come to the United States. They were a stabilizing force. According to Branson, Masya stopped drinking for the six months they were there. A few weeks before the race, however, Joan was stricken with what doctors feared might be cerebral meningitis, and hospitalized for two weeks. She recovered, but it was decided that she and Willis would return to Kenya while her condition was still stable. Masya would follow them a week later, after the race. Branson volunteered to take Joan and Willis to the airport; when he returned ninety minutes later, Masya was gone, lost to the city for what would be a two-day bender. He reappeared in time for the race, but was in no condition to give it his best effort, struggling to a disappointing twentieth place finish. Instead of then returning to Kenya and his family, Masya told Branson that he wanted to try again in Honolulu. Reluctantly, Branson brokered the deal with Barahal and Cross, who were in New York to observe the race.

A month later in Honolulu, Masya struggled again, finishing sixth in a race he had once dominated. Branson pleaded with him to return to Kenya to regroup and prepare for Boston the following year. But Masya was adamant that he wanted to return to Albuquerque. As Branson recalled:

> I knew that if he went back to Albuquerque that he would be finished.
> I was worried about his own life, not necessarily the running. I wrote

him a letter. He was in my house and I sat up one night and wrote him a letter on yellow memo pad and I explained to him my reasoning and I said, "If you want to go back to Albuquerque, I don't want to feel responsible. I can't tell you not to go. You're a grown man . . . but I know it's not the right thing to do for you." But he wanted to go, and he went. And then I stopped managing him.[11]

Branson kept in sporadic contact with Masya in the years that followed, using his connections to help him with visa issues when, for reasons Branson was never told, Masya was deported from the UK and Sweden in the late 1990s. After one extended silence, he contacted Branson from Germany, where he had hoped to restart his career. But he was wasting away from an unidentified disease, and clearly could no longer compete. "He was very ill and basically . . . the only nutrition he had was milk," Branson said: "He couldn't have anything else. (Fellow Kenyan runners) Tegla Laroupe and Pamela Chepchumba were taking care of him in Germany and they got him back to Kenya." Masya died shortly thereafter of what Branson later acknowledged were likely complications of AIDS. In one of their last conversations, Maysa said he had found Christianity and reformed his bad habits. "It was a blessing knowing that he was at peace with himself and he wasn't off the rails like he had been before," Branson said. "I think he was remorseful."[12]

In fact, the triumphs of African marathon runners on the world stage in the late 1980s and 1990s distracted attention away from the difficulties many of them faced due to their success. Sports writers who booked flights to Kenya, Tanzania, and Ethiopia to explore the origins of these seemingly superhuman athletes often returned with novelistic narratives about barefoot boys and girls running for miles each day in high-altitude villages, or about shocking coming-of-age rituals,[13] or about military-style training camps and shady agents and talent brokers lurking around every corner. There were few stories about how overnight wealth and celebrity made young African runners targets in their home countries. In many cases, returning runners were expected to support not only their family and friends, but their neighbors and communities as well. Their relative wealth amidst the surrounding poverty made them vulnerable. Josiah Thugwane, the gifted South African runner who followed up his 1995 Honolulu Marathon victory with a gold medal in the 1996 Atlanta Olympic Games, was attacked by robbers wanting to steal the car he had bought for himself with his earnings from

Honolulu. He escaped, but only after a bullet had grazed his chin. Ondoro Osoro, winner of the 1998 Chicago Marathon, had to withdraw from the 2000 Olympic Games in Sydney after being shot in the neck during a car jacking in Kenya. While he was recovering, his oldest son was kidnapped in an apparent ransom plot, but managed to escape. Osoro rebounded from a nerve injury suffered in the shooting to take third in the 2002 Honolulu Marathon and win the 2003 Rock 'n' Roll San Diego Marathon.

Nor have wealth and adoration insulated African athletes from political and social strife in their countries. In late 2007, violence broke out in Kenya when Kalenjin-backed presidential candidate Raila Odinga lost to incumbent Mwai Kibaki, a member of the politically dominant Kikuyu tribe, in what Odinga supporters claimed was a rigged election. An estimated 1,200 people were killed and approximately 300,000 displaced in four months of fighting. Among the casualties were Olympic relay runner Lucas Sang, hacked to death while walking home in Eldoret, and Wesley Ngetich, killed by an arrow. Luke Kibet, who placed first in the marathon world championships in 2007, had his Olympic training upended due to a concussion from being hit with a stone during a political disturbance. At another time, he had to pull out a gun to fend off a mob attack. Many other Kenyan runners couldn't train due to roadblocks, civic disruptions, or threats of violence. In one case, Kalenjin runners scheduled to compete in the United States and elsewhere had to cancel when opposition forces surrounded their training camp, making it impossible for them to leave the country. Kalenjin runners were particularly vulnerable, due to accusations that the prize winnings they had given to their communities had been used to purchase weapons wielded in the struggle. In an interview with *Salon,* Colm O'Connell, an Irish coach based in Kenya, addressed the issue: "Of course they use their money to help their communities. They practically have a moral obligation to do so. And in the end, who knows whether the money is really used to buy a sack or corn or a bow?"[14]

A Defining Rivalry

The most storied rivalry in Honolulu Marathon history played out over eight years in the late 1990s and early 2000s between two Kenyan runners with long and strong ties to the race. Mbarak Hussein first came to Honolulu in 1986 to watch his older brother Ibrahim defend his championship. Nineteen at the time, and with no running experience beyond what he needed to get around in his home village, the younger Hussein decided to give the race a try. He finished in under three hours. At Ibrahim's urging, Mbarak moved to the United States for school, first at South Plains Junior College in Texas, where he starred in the 800- and 1,500-meters, and then at Lubbock Christian University. After Ibrahim's breakthrough victories in Boston, many young African runners decided that moving from middle distances to the marathon was the wisest and most lucrative post-collegiate path. His younger brother was no different, and in 1993, Mbarak Hussein returned to Honolulu, hoping to retrace his brother's journey to international stardom. He finished fourth, behind Bong-ju Lee and brothers Cosmas and Josphat Ndeti.

Jimmy Muindi, the 1992 world junior steeplechase champion, was also at the 1993 race. Brought in by Branson as a pacer for Masya, Muindi dropped out at the 30K mark as planned, but not before getting a feel for the course and what it would take to win in Honolulu. He returned the next year, finishing fourth behind Masya, Thabiso Moqhali, and Green. He was third in 1995 and second in both 1996 and 1997. By that point, a Muindi victory seemed inevitable and overdue. Muindi seemed poised to claim his first marathon win the following year when he, Hussein, and two-time defending champion Erick Kimaiyo descended Diamond Head Road together for the final one-mile push. But, just like the previous year, Muindi was overcome with stomach problems. Weakened by vomiting, Muindi's body seized just as the trio passed Poni Moi Drive, the final intersection before Kapi'olani Park. Kimaiyo led Hussein with 50 yards to go but it was Hussein's superior kick and a bit of inspiration from Ibrahim Hussein that proved decisive. Calling upon the explosive sprinting ability that made him a junior college champion, Hussein surged forward, beating Kimaiyo to the finish in less time that the race clocks were equipped to measure. "The last few miles, the last 100 meters, I was thinking that my brother would say I can't lose the race," Mbarak Hussein later revealed. As for Muindi, he was crushed by the defeat. "It was my victory," Muindi told *Race Results Weekly,* "I was so disappointed."[15]

This initial encounter became a rivalry the following year, when Hussein, Muindi, and Kimaiyo once again found themselves shoulder to shoulder heading down Diamond Head Road. This time, however, Muindi didn't falter, outsprinting Kimaiyo and Hussein in the last twenty yards to capture his first Honolulu win in six attempts. He defended his title the following year, but then Hussein took the next two in 2001 and in 2002—the latter in spite of a bit of trickery by Muindi:

Kenyan runners Erick Kimaiyo, Mbarak Hussein, and Jimmy Muindi combined for 11 Honolulu Marathon victories. Photo by Dennis Oda. Courtesy of the *Honolulu Star-Advertiser.*

That year, I remember making a big break, but I had stomach problems and had to slow down. (Hussein) thought I was finished, so he made a break, going very, very fast. When he passed, I told him, "Just go.'" But he didn't know I had a lot left and I tried to make a kick to the finish before him. After he won (by 4 seconds), he said, "I thought you were done! Oh man, you are killing me."[16]

While neither one enjoyed losing to the other, Hussein and Muindi were good friends and frequent training partners. They were both proud of together dominating the race for nearly a decade. "When we're in competition, we assist each other very much," Muindi once said. "He'll make a move and take over the pace. Then, I'll make a move and take over the pace. At the end, sometimes he beats me and sometimes I beat him. It's part of the game."[17] Hussein was thirty-seven when he won the 2002 race—elderly by marathon standards, but still a more-than-able competitor. Muindi, however, was just hitting the peak of his powers. He beat Hussein by more than two minutes in 2003, drawing them even at three wins apiece. He then won three of the next four, becoming the first six-time male champion in the race's history. Both men found their greatest success in Honolulu, but they performed well in other high-profile races. Muindi won the Rotterdam Marathon in 2005, and placed in the top five at the Chicago Marathon three times. Hussein won the Twin Cities Marathon in 2005 and 2006, and placed fourth in the 2002 Boston Marathon.

Branson, Muindi's manager, said both men were top-flight marathoners who achieved great success at least partly because of the Honolulu Marathon's nurturing environment:

> It was Jon and Jim inviting Jimmy back here. Jimmy was always in the top three. The money they were paying him and his earnings from here kept him moving for a few years until he got to really crush it. Without Honolulu, Jimmy would not have ever really made it as a marathoner. Without Honolulu, I'm sure Cosmas (Ndeti) would not have made it as a marathoner because (he) wouldn't have got the chance in Boston, and Boston is the only place he ran well. Cosmas with three victories in Boston—it would have never have happened if he hadn't run here. You can make that connection with a lot of racers. [. . .] I really have a personal admiration and respect for Jon and Jim because they weren't making financial choices a lot of times when they brought somebody in. They gave guys chances and they wanted to see guys develop. These opportunities don't exist in a lot of places.[18]

There is no question that Barahal and Cross have been highly supportive of the African runners and coaches who have come through Honolulu. They brought back Tsebe when the international ban lifted, and paid him an additional $5,000, to make up for the money he lost when disqualified in 1988. In 1989, they decided that if Naali had not stopped to tie a shoelace, he likely would have set the course record instead of falling four seconds short. So Barahal signed off on giving him the $10,000 bonus he would have earned for breaking the record. And when Filbert Bayi, the renowned Tanzanian runner and coach who helped bring Naali, James Munyala, and others to Honolulu could not afford a knee operation, Barahal enlisted orthopedic surgeon and former HMA race director Kent Davenport to perform the surgery. Three-time Honolulu Marathon champion Duncan Macdonald was the anesthesiologist, and Barahal himself handled the blood work. All gratis.[19]

For Cross and Barahal, it only made sense to build and maintain such goodwill with agents and athletes who might later steer young up-and-comers to Honolulu. In 2010, Branson was looking to prepare a prized client for an ambitious project. Patrick Makau had made his debut at the 2009 Rotterdam Marathon, finishing fourth in 2:06:14. A year later, he won it in 2:04:48—the fourth-fastest marathon ever recorded. Branson knew that Makau had the potential to set a new world record, but he also knew that he needed the right place to broach the subject. He called Barahal and Cross to ask if they would be willing to fly Makau and his family to Honolulu in exchange for Makau running the first 15 kilometers of the race as a pacesetter. "I wanted him to come because I knew this environment was an inspiring and relaxing place and this is where it was discussed that he would try to break the world record," Branson said. The agreement worked for both sides. Branson got the setting he wanted to prepare Makau for the attempt. The Honolulu Marathon got to boast of having arguably the world's fastest marathon runner in its field.

Ten months later, Makau set a new world record of 2:03:38 at the 2011 Berlin Marathon. "Honolulu was what set that up," Branson said.[20]

CHAPTER 10

Challenges of the Big Time

It is a common misperception that Japanese participation generated by JAL sponsorship and marketing efforts in the mid-1980s lifted the Honolulu Marathon to the ranks of the largest marathons in the world. In fact, Honolulu consistently ranked just ahead of Boston and not far behind the New York City Marathon in the number of finishers in the mid- to late 1970s. In 1982, the London Marathon ranked No. 1 with 15,116; New York City (13,599) and Honolulu (10,023) were the only other races with more than 10,000. What the Japan connection did do, however, was keep Honolulu near the top during the 1990s and early 2000s, when both the number of races and number of runners worldwide markedly increased. In 1980, after the first American running boom had dissipated, some 143,000 people in the United States finished a marathon. In 1990, that figure was 224,000, and in 2000 it reached 353,000.[1] These numbers were consistent with the overall increase in road-race participation. In 1980, the 100 biggest American races of any distance accounted for some 350,000 participants. By the mid-1990s, the total was more than a million."[2]

While this period of growth received neither the attention nor the analysis that the 1970s running boom did, it changed things more dramatically by redefining what a marathon is, and who it is for. The first running revolution was sparked by American runners like Frank Shorter and Bill Rodgers, who fueled the American public's desire to emulate their competitive excellence. By the late 1980s, American distance running had fallen into mediocrity, run off the road by a rush of gifted African runners whom casual American sports fans had no interest in following, or even telling apart. But the sport itself flourished as a recreational pursuit, a marker of personal achievement for the fitness-minded upper and middle classes. In an age of high-participation fun runs, the belief that the marathon should be the exclusive province of the most fit runners, dedicated to excellence at the limits of human exertion, gave way once and for all to the idea that simply completing 26.2 miles was a success, and that performance need only be measured against personal standards.

Out of this new ethos emerged some unlikely heroes, from then-Vice President Al Gore, who ran a 4:54:25 at the 1997 Marine Corps Marathon at the age of forty-nine, to John Bingham, the outspoken champion of back-of-the-pack runners, whose "Penguin Chronicles" ran in *Runner's World* from 1996 to 2014. No figure was more influential than talk-show host Oprah Winfrey, who took up running during one of her well-chronicled weight-loss campaigns. Shedding some seventy-two pounds with the help of a professional trainer, Winfrey completed the Marine Corps Marathon in 1994. Her time of 4:29:20 gave rise to the term "the Oprah Line," a standard of respectable marathon performance for recreational athletes of merely average ability. Winfrey's achievement, and the noticeable effect training had on her physical appearance, inspired many who probably never would have considered themselves marathoner material. As author and runner Edward McClelland observed, "This was not a spindly 24-year-old Yalie gliding through Old World Munich. This was a middle-aged woman hauling her flab around the District of Columbia. If Oprah could run a marathon, shame on anyone who couldn't." As the emphasis on competition declined, the marathon became primarily a personal venture, a way to give your aspirations, beliefs, or convictions physical expression. For some, completing one was the climax for journeys of achievement, recovery, or re-creation. For others, it became a public expression of support, friendship, sympathy, political beliefs, and even protest.

In 1984, the London Marathon set aside entries for the Sports Aid Foundation, initiating a powerful driver of marathon participation for the next three decades: charity running. In 1988, for instance, Bruce Cleland, a forty-year-old non-runner whose two-year-old daughter was diagnosed with leukemia, recruited thirty-seven volunteers to join him in running the New York City Marathon as a way to raise funds for the Leukemia and Lymphoma Society. With the help of friend and former New York City Marathon champion Rod Dixon, Cleland got thirty-eight entries. Each team member had to raise a minimum of $5,000 to claim a spot. He also got corporate sponsors to contribute for a place on the team's official training jersey. In all, the very first Team in Training raised $320,000 for its charity.[3] Soon, other Team in Training programs were established in cities across the United States, and scores of other charitable organizations have created similar initiatives. The practice has had its controversies. Because the New York City Marathon has a cap on participation, and awards entries on a lottery basis, guaranteed spots for charity runners lowered the available entries by 11 percent.[4] Even in Honolulu, where the marathon does not cap participation, individual runners have complained that large contingents of charity runners representing different organizations have created a sense of cliquishness out on the course and among the spectators. Nevertheless, charity running has proved to be a potent fundraising vehicle for charities, and a boon to individual marathons.

Fast Company

With the battle over professionalizing the elite ranks largely over, and the waves of first-time recreational runners driving participation ever upward, the major marathons had to find their own places in the new order of road racing. David Monti, editor and publisher of *Race Results Weekly,* and professional athlete consultant for the New York City Marathon, explained:

> Then each race started to decide what their identity was vis-à-vis the professional sport. The Portland Marathon in Oregon decided, along with the Marine Corp Marathon in Washington, that they would not be a factor in the professional sport at all. They don't spend any money on it at all. They have no top athletes. They are somehow a people's race. They've both been very successful with that market position. So, ordinary athletes go there and enjoy the race like that. Another group of marathons decided that they were going to remain in the "pro only" avenue, like Fukuoka, where they were only going to be for top athletes. They didn't care about these other developments. So Fukuoka gets 90 percent of its funding from the TV broadcaster that puts it on. All they care about is what you can see on the screen. Then, the rest of us, New York, Boston, and London saw this huge opportunity to marry all of that under one tent and add to it this very critical charity component that didn't exist at all previously. [. . .] They all have a huge charity component. They are large and inviting to runners of all abilities. New York has runners of all abilities, so does Los Angeles and Berlin and London.

David Monti, founder of *Race Results Weekly* and the professional athletes consultant for the New York Road Runners, has become a key consultant for the Honolulu Marathon Association. Photo courtesy of Brittny Ing-Lee.

At the front end, a very, very good elite field where athletes are paid, either through prize money or appearance fees or bonuses or some combination of all three. Depending on the kind of sponsor you have and the amount of money they have for you, you can tailor that front end of the race to meet your budget.[5]

The Honolulu Marathon Association clearly wanted to be part of the third group of be-all marathons, as president Jim Barahal and race director Jon Cross took their cues from New York and Boston in creating the overall race experience they sought to provide. As Cross explained:

At some point, I don't know when, we just decided that we wanted to be an international race. We wanted to be newsworthy, but we wanted to make sure that the average runner or the regular athletes had a great experience. We need it to have enough invited runners to make it newsworthy, but not spend so much money that we can't have good entertainment on the course and malasadas at the finish line.[6]

Of course, the Honolulu Marathon would always be very different from its would-be peers. While all the major marathons had large numbers of out-of-area participants, the local/non-local distinction in Hawai'i was much more pronounced, with roughly half of outside participants coming from a single country (Japan) and with little attention paid to attracting runners from anywhere else. The Honolulu Marathon also received far less direct financial support from its sponsors. The estimated $2 million from JAL and other Japan-based sponsors hardly resembled the other big marathons' title sponsorships from financial institutions like John Hancock (Boston), Manufacturers Hanover (New York), and LaSalle Bank (Chicago). Unlike the New York Road Runners or the Boston Athletic Association, with their broad organizational infrastructures and deep personnel resources, the HMA, as part of a Barahal plan endorsed by Asatsu, had reduced its executive board from more than thirty members to an effective core of Barahal, Cross, Ron and Jeanette Chun, Tommy Kono, and legal counsel Richard Sutton, and relied heavily on a mix of volunteers and paid contractors to carry out its work. The Honolulu Marathon therefore rivaled other major marathons in terms of participation, but had the organizational structure of much smaller races. In a sense, then, the race mirrored its host city, a place rapidly transformed into a major metropolitan area, but continuing to hold on to many small-town habits. Such distinctions however did not shield the HMA from all of the headaches involved in staging one of the biggest marathons in the world.

Side Ventures

In the late 1990s and early 2000s, with Japanese participation at its peak, the most obvious signs of Barahal's leadership were the HMA's attempts to expand its capabilities and offerings. In addition to leading HMA and working as a physician, Barahal had tried his hand at stand-up comedy, hosted a sports radio show (as "Doctor Sports," his tag line was "Maybe I'm wrong, but I don't think so"), and even wrote a screenplay about a baseball player frozen during the sinking of the Titanic who is unthawed decades later to lead a team to a championship.[7] At Barahal's impetus, HMA explored taking over the Great Aloha Run, its only real rival among local road races. The packet pick-up was relocated to the Hawai'i Convention Center, resulting in a major expansion of the expo. He flew in Shorter, Rodgers, and other running luminaries each year for public appearances. And he staged ancillary events like the popular but short-lived Waikīkī Mile.

Some ventures at this time were indulgences of Barahal and Cross's Baby Boomer tastes. In 2001, Barahal invited infamous gonzo journalist Hunter S. Thompson to report on the Honolulu Marathon for a new ESPN online column. He had covered the race in 1980 for *Running* magazine. Later excerpted in *Playboy,* that piece became the basis for Thompson's book *The Curse of Lono.* HMA flew in Thompson and his friend and actor Sean Penn, who owned the movie rights to *The Curse of Lono.* The resulting column read like a pastiche of Thompson's classic works: a predictably paranoid take on the race that showed little evidence of his having actually witnessed it. But he enjoyed the hospitality, and with the help of friend John Wilbur, a former NFL lineman and University of Hawai'i assistant football coach, he talked Barahal into paying for him to return for the next two years. The arrangement foundered, however, when the famously temperamental Thompson broke his leg two days before the 2003 race. Rejecting his first-class seat on a commercial airline, he spent much of the following week threatening lawsuits and badgering famous friends to "rescue" him from his ninth-floor room in the luxury Kahala Mandarin Oriental Hotel. Eventually, Penn chartered an air ambulance to fly Thompson, his wife, a personal assistant, and a nurse to Colorado.

Thompson's visits overlapped the introduction of headline-worthy live music acts to the marathon's annual carbo-loading party, now held at the Waikīkī Shell. The offerings started modestly with the Beatles tribute band GetBack! in 2001. The following year, the association brought in Beach Boys founder Brian Wilson to perform. Wilson, slowly emerging after decades of voracious drug use and subsequent psychological debilitation, was warmly received before rain, audio issues, and Wilson's own stupefied performance resulted in a slow but steady exodus to the gates. But hopes were high in 2003, when the HMA announced a special concert by Van Morrison. Zane Branson, agent for many of the top Kenyan runners, had referred race officials to New York-based promoter Kenneth Vangel. Starting in October 2002, HMA sent Vangel a series of four checks totaling $47,500 to pay Morrison to perform at its December 12 pre-race luau. But in May 2003, Morrison's booking agency contacted HMA, telling them that the singer knew nothing about the concert, and would not be performing. After an FBI investigation, a federal grand jury indicted Vangel of four counts of mail fraud. The following year, the HMA tempered its ambitions by booking Riders on the Storm, a band made up of original Doors members Ray Manzarek and Robbie Krieger and former Cult singer Ian Astbury performing

Doors music. In 2006, the HMA tried to appeal to a younger crowd by booking Gavin DeGraw, but were dismayed when many Japanese attendees left after seeing opening act Jake Shimabukuro, the Hawai'i-born ukulele whiz who was popular in Japan. Subsequent concerts have featured local entertainers (often Shimabukuro), with the occasional Japanese pop star.

In 2003, Barahal also teamed with HMA contractors Mitch Kahle and Holly Huber to start Sports Media Productions LLC, which would produce MyMarathonDVD custom race videos. A technological update of similar customized VHS products available for the New York City Marathon and other races, the DVD spliced together footage of the customer running the course and highlights from the race. Though technically independent of the association, the company had full course access and was actively promoted by the HMA and its recently hired media consultant, former *Honolulu Star-Bulletin* reporter Pat Bigold. The service was later adopted by the Los Angeles Marathon, the Boston Marathon, and the Kona Ironman Championships. But conflicts soon arose when the Delaware-based YourDay Video Technologies Inc. sent letters to the HMA, Sports Media Productions, and MyMarathonDVD customers alleging a "striking similarity" between MyMarathonDVD's video capture system and one that YourDay had patented six years earlier. In a pre-emptive strike, Barahal and Sports Media Productions filed suit against YourDay Video, charging that its letters to MyMarathonDVD customers was an unfair and deceptive trade practice that sought to affect adversely its ability to do business with its two existing clients—the HMA and the World Triathlon Corp.[8] No record of further legal action between the two companies exists, indicating that Barahal and his partners successfully warded off a potential lawsuit. MyMarathonDVD enjoyed relatively modest success, with its greatest value realized only in the wake of the Honolulu Marathon's biggest operational mishap.

Timing Disaster

The 2007 Honolulu Marathon will be remembered as one of the most costly and trying events the HMA ever staged. The problems started the evening before the race when heavy rains soaked east Honolulu, saturating the grounds of Kapi'olani Park and short-circuiting four of eight large generators powering the race's newly adopted timing system. The rains persisted through the start of the race and continued intermittently throughout the day, slowing the overall progress of the race and rendering the once grassy finisher's area a nearly impassable expanse of thick, shoe-sucking mud. All along Kalaniana'ole Highway were left narrow paper tags loosened by rain and torn away from flapping laces by the slightest frictions—unnoticed indicators of a day that was about to get much more complicated for race organizers.

The Honolulu Marathon was one of the first major marathons to use microchip timing. The Burns Computer Services' ChampionChip system, acquired in 2000, involved radio frequency identification transponders housed in a plastic disc attached to a runner's shoes, and timing mats placed at the start, the finish, and select points in between to record the chips as the runners passed over the mats. While many smaller races collect the timing chips at the finish line for later reuse, Honolulu Marathon officials found it more practical to issue single-use chips. Accurate and reliable, the system was also expensive, costing about $250,000 a race. Over the years, Barahal developed a strong relationship with timing expert David Simms, who had been advising the Honolulu Marathon for twenty-one years, and who had partnered with Mike Burns to develop and market the Champion-Chip. Simms had recently started his own company, SAI Timing and Tracking, to market a new system he had developed that used laminated paper tags rather than solid plastic discs to house the transponder, and replaced bulky timing mats with more portable computer stations. Most attractive to the HMA, though, was that this system promised to save them $300,000 over five years. Barahal trusted Simms, and accepted his claim that that the new system had been beta tested at forty road races, and successfully implemented at the Philadelphia and Las Vegas Marathons. Had anyone at the HMA checked the Las Vegas Marathon website, however, they would have learned about missing split times for hundreds of runners, and found lengthy discussion threads dedicated to complaints about timing issues at the Las Vegas and the Philadelphia marathons.

Reporters from the *Honolulu Advertiser* at the finish line knew something might be amiss nearly four hours into the race, when confusion arose about the winner of the local finishers division. Former Hawaii Pacific University cross country runner Esben Dalgaard crossed the finish line at 2:36:40, but his name did not appear in the list of division leaders. Throughout the day, reporters at both daily papers received calls from runners complaining that their split and finish times were either incorrect or missing from the Honolulu Marathon website. When the release of the complete race results to the media was delayed by several hours, the scale of the problem became clear. The following morning, reporters were summoned to Kapiʻolani Park, where Barahal gave the HMA's first official response. "We screwed up," he said, assuming responsibility for a situation no one yet fully understood. Marathon officials believed that the split and finishing times of hundreds, and perhaps thousands, of runners had been incorrectly recorded, with as many as 3,500 not recorded at all. According to Simms, the short-circuiting of the four generators prior to the race had shut down and reset incorrectly the remote electronic readers that tracked the runners' progress. The heavy rains also led to many chip tags detaching from runners' shoes. Simms guessed that the finishers' data was still "98 percent correct" with individual split times probably 95 percent accurate. "Five percent is a lot of people," he said at the time: "We're pretty good from a statistics standpoint, but from a marathon standpoint, we suck."[9]

He had no idea. To correct as many times as possible, and to determine how many runners had not been recorded, the HMA enlisted marathon officials and specially trained contractors for the mammoth task of reviewing seven hours of finish-line video captured by Sports Media Productions. Over the course of two months, 1,200 to 1,500 man hours were expended— as many as four hours were required to scan each minute of video—at a cost of about $50,000. Because of the density of runners at the start, the reviewers could not determine how many people actually began the race. By subtracting the number of unclaimed race bibs from the total number of verified entrants, however, the association determined that the maximum number of starters was 24,769. SAI's original readings had only 20,582 begin the race, even though it claimed to have recorded 20,865 finishers. The review came up with 22,839 finishers. Ultimately, only 1,798 finish times reported by SAI proved to be accurate. The HMA later sued SAI to recoup damages.[10]

Problems with the 2007 race were not confined to the timing issues. City officials and the public were furious about of the damage inflicted on Kapiʻolani Park's rain-soaked grounds by runners, tents, and delivery trucks on marathon day. Soccer teams and other park users were displaced, and acres of grassy picnic area were soaked and rutted for weeks after. As always, the HMA turned to vice president Ron Chun to fix the mess. Drawing on his extensive connections and his personal corps of volunteers, Chun removed 70 cubic yards of mulch, replacing it with 170 cubic yards of top soil. His crew then laid tropic turf sod over the damaged areas. The repairs cost an estimated $70,000. But even after the grounds were restored, and the timing fiasco was put to rest, HMA officials had to deal with one last headache.

Drug Controversies

In 2006, thirty-five-year-old Lyubov Denisova, an elite Russian runner who paid her own way to Honolulu, left a stacked women's field behind en route to a new women's course record of 2:27:19. A two-time Los Angeles Marathon winner (2002 and 2005) with nine sub-2:30 marathons under her elastic band, her dominant performance in Honolulu was still something of a surprise, since her competition included defending champion Olesya Nurgalieva, former winner Eri Hayakawa, and dark horse favorite Alevtina Biktimirova. What with the prize money and incentives, Denisova left Honolulu with $67,000, the most for a female competitor in the race's history. Race officials were so taken with the shy but personable Denisova that two months later they brought her back for a series of public appearances. But shortly afterward, representatives from the World Anti-Doping Agency visited her home in Gainesville, Florida, and administered a random "out-of-competition" blood test. The results showed elevated levels of testosterone, an indicator of performance-enhancing drug use. Denisova's agent, Andrey Baranov, said she had taken a supplement purchased over the Internet, unaware that it contained the anabolic steroid prostanozol. The International Association of Athletic Federations (IAAF) banned Denisova from international competition for two years, effectively ending her career, and voided her finishes in three races she ran between her drug test in March and the announcement of the findings in May. Because the test was administered after she had competed in Honolulu, her Honolulu Marathon championship and prizes were hers to keep—much to Barahal's chagrin. "We can't go back in time and take back the money and the title, but it's a reasonable conclusion that that if she was cheating in February and March, it's likely that she was under the influence in December."[11] Denisova's failed test led Barahal to institute mandatory drug tests for the top three finishers in the men's and women's elite divisions, and random tests for ten finishers in both categories—all at HMA expense. (Periodic drug testing had previously been conducted at the Honolulu Marathon, but at the discretion and expense of USA Track & Field.)

Denisova's male counterpart in the 2006 marathon was Ambesse Tolossa of Ethiopia, who defeated five-time winner Jimmy Muindi in a hard-fought race that ended with Muindi accusing Tolossa of deliberately bumping him, clipping his heels and spitting on his shoes. In the wake of the Denisova scandal, the HMA was hoping for a spirited rematch in 2007 that would return the focus to racing. It almost happened. Toiling through the same rainy conditions that were about to wreak havoc on the new timing system and turn Kapi'olani Park into a marsh, Tolossa and Muindi spent most of the race less than an arm's length apart. Finally, on the long, gradual climb up Diamond Head Road heading toward Triangle Park, Muindi fell victim to an upset stomach, vomiting several times while struggling not to break stride. Realizing that Muindi could not respond to a challenge, Tolossa broke away with a controlled sprint to win in 2:17:26. Afterward, Barahal praised Tolossa's tactics, and said he hoped that Tolossa would become the race's next dominant champion. "I'd love to see him win six or seven times," Barahal said.[12]

In keeping with the drug-testing policy implemented after Denisova's suspension earlier that year, Tolossa took a blood test immediately after the race. Following standard protocol, the blood was divided into "A" and "B" samples for independent testing by the U.S. Anti-Doping Agency. Results from Tolossa's "A" sample indicated the presence of opiates. Subsequent testing of the "B" sample confirmed the finding, resulting in a two-year IAAF suspension for the Ethiopian runner. Honolulu Marathon officials learned about the findings when they saw Tolossa's name on the IAAF's periodic list of banned athletes. The case was puzzling. As Barahal explained, although included on the list of banned substances, opiates are not considered performance enhancing for runners. The HMA, which had withheld the prize money pending the results of the tests, quickly voided Tolossa's victory, giving Muindi his sixth Honolulu Marathon championship. Though disappointing, the result vindicated Barahal's decision to implement mandatory testing at the marathon's expense. "You don't do this sort of thing if you aren't ready to deal with the results," he told the *Honolulu Advertiser.* "If you test, you will get positives and you have to be willing to face that. I'm glad we did it. The system was successful and it's what it's here for."[13] In fact, Barahal's proactive approach to matters of race safety and integrity may be his best quality as HMA president, a conclusion borne out by an impressive history of life-saving actions on the course.

Matters of Life and Death

When tens of thousands of people, some well trained and others less so, challenge their personal thresholds of exertion and endurance under unpredictable conditions, it is a virtual certainty that over the course of decades there will be some tragedies. The Honolulu Marathon has certainly been no exception. In 1982, sixty-two-year-old Bob Johnson of Waikīkī collapsed shortly after completing the race. Resuscitated and taken to the hospital, he died soon after, becoming the Honolulu Marathon's first official casualty. Two years later, Anthony Lewis, a forty-nine-year-old British engineer living in Hong Kong, suffered a heart attack near the nine-mile marker and died. In 1994, a fifty-two-year-old electrician from Japan named Kunihiko Kono collapsed near Mile 17 about four hours into the race. Spectators performed CPR, but Kono died at the hospital. Then in 2002, thirty-three-year-old Grant Hirohata-Goto, running the race with his seasoned marathoner father Norman, and his young first-timer brother Gregg, collapsed at the finish line and died of apparent heart failure.

Given the scale of the race, such events are as inevitable as they are unpredictable. Nevertheless, every race official is acutely aware of how quickly situations can turn dire, and every HMA president from Scaff to Barahal can rightly claim to have gone to great lengths to control the factors they can, and to anticipate the greatest threats to the safety of the field. In 1995, for instance, marathon officials spent a week worrying about a heat wave that had settled over the islands. More importantly, they took steps to prevent related emergencies on race day. Since the water for aid stations was drawn from fire hydrants, access to fluids was not a concern. But anticipating greater demand, the organizers increased the order for cups. They also chartered tour buses in case large numbers of runners had to be removed from the course. These preparations proved necessary. High temperatures and humidity during the first three to four hours of the race led hundreds of runners to seek medical attention for dehydration and heat exhaustion. Race volunteers commandeered water hoses from private residences along Kāhala Avenue to spray runners as they passed, and race officials patrolled the course, encouraging people to drop out if they felt unwell. According to Barahal, medical personnel used more than 170 intravenous lines, and many runners were transported swiftly to the hospital. As the morning wore on, Barahal, Cross, and other race officials discussed calling off the race if conditions worsened. Barahal took the danger very seriously:

> We . . . had to weigh the moral and ethical question of how much re-
> sponsibility do we assume and to what degree were runners responsible
> for making their own decisions about whether to continue. It went di-
> rectly to how we view society. Is someone else responsible for you at all
> times, or do you take responsibility for your own safety? That's what
> running is all about. It's about training and preparation and ultimately
> personal achievement.[14]

Thankfully, the number of runners dangerously affected by the heat decreased as the race wore on, suggesting that those in the middle and back
were less prone to overexertion, and were more likely to be hydrating at regular intervals.

These efforts in 1995 showed the HMA's ability to identify and prepare
for potentially hazardous situations. But its most remarkable success in pro-
tecting the lives of its runners resulted from Barahal using his intuition as a
medical professional. Following the heart-related death of a runner in the
Marine Corps Marathon, Barahal stationed eight portable external defibrillators at different points along the course. They arrived just two weeks
before the 2006 Honolulu Marathon. Running that year was a thirty-nine-
year-old pharmacist from Tokyo named Koji Takano, who had successfully
completed fourteen marathons. Takano enjoyed a strong race up until the
30-kilometer mark, when he began feeling unusually fatigued. He carried
on all the way to Kapiʻolani Park. Just thirty yards from the finish line,
however, Takano, feeling increasingly ill, started walking. With the encouragement of the crowd, Takano rallied to run the final yards to the finish line
but then suddenly collapsed—just as race doctor Lawrence Rotkin was
rushing over to check on him. Takano had no pulse and no respiration. The
medical staff immediately brought over one of the portable defibrillators,
and administered two powerful shocks to Takano's chest. The second one
restarted his heart. In the ambulance en route to the hospital, a confused
Takano begged his caretakers to take him back to the course so he could
finish the race.[15] At a special presentation the following day at Kapiʻolani
Park, Barahal told Takano that he was "the most amazing finisher in this
year's race . . . maybe ever."[16]

PART III

HONOLULU MARATHON INC.

CHAPTER 11

An Economic Engine

It has been a matter of both consternation and insulating pride for Honolulu Marathon Association leadership that ever since the city and county of Honolulu withdrew in-kind support in the early 1980s, the race has operated without government support—no subsidies, no preference or standing consideration for its permit applications. Each year, Tommy Kono or some other representative must submit the paperwork to obtain the necessary permits. Each year, Jeanette Chun cuts checks in excess of $150,000 for Honolulu Police Department personnel, whose work on marathon day is considered "special duty." The lack of funding is not really an impediment. Through sponsorships, entry fees, and merchandising, the race has more than covered its expenses. The HMA consternation, however, comes from knowing that the Honolulu Marathon's positive impact on the local economy—in excess of $100 million each year, according to HMA-funded studies—equals, or often exceeds, the total impact of all the so-called sporting "signature events" that the Hawaii Tourism Authority underwrites each year. For years, HMA leadership tried to convince the state that the race deserved support based on the value it returned. But as long as the marathon continued to thrive on its own, there was no incentive for the state to make even a goodwill gesture. As HMA president Jim Barahal remarked after the NFL decided to move the Pro Bowl from Honolulu to Florida for 2009:

> There was a time when we were jealous or resentful of the incredible amount of money given to the Pro Bowl, as well as to a large number of smaller events, some athletic and some not. But the NFL always had a

lot of leverage because they could always take their ball and go, which is what they've done. We might have some leverage if we said that we were going to move the race to Orlando, but that's absurd and it will never happen. We finally understood that we were never going to get (funding) so we just got on with our lives, and over time it's become clear that it's better to stand on our own two feet.[1]

Recognizing the superior resources that rival tourist destinations like Florida and Nevada were devoting to advertising, in 2005, the Hawaii Tourism Authority adopted a ten-year strategic plan explicitly designed to "narrowly target marketing efforts with a focus on Hawaii's best prospects to counter competitors' larger marketing budgets." One announced goal was "developing and supporting sports events that can establish Hawai'i as a world-class venue and generate media exposure for the destination, and those that may not have media but can assist in leveling out shoulder periods."[2] Out of the HTA's annual budget of about $71 million, $8 million is earmarked for its sports marketing program, intended to generate visitor spending and positive media coverage, and also to enhance the quality of life for residents. Historically, the Pro Bowl and the PGA Tour events have received the most substantial state sports funding.

The Pro Bowl was held annually in Hawai'i from 1980 until 2009, and then again from 2011 to 2013. The NFL recognized early on that Honolulu was well suited to host this all-star event. For the players, selection meant a free vacation to a warm and exotic destination that they could enjoy with their families. That alone stems the tide of all-Pro selections fearful of injury who might otherwise decide to begin their offseason early. As for the NFL, its incentive was more pragmatic: a state subsidy of between $4 million and $5 million each time the game is played in Hawai'i. For the HTA, this investment paid off not just in an estimated $26 million in direct visitor spending each year, but also in the more difficult-to-measure marketing value of displaying Hawai'i's sunny skies, white sand beaches, and lush mountains in January to twelve million winter-weary TV viewers. The game returned to Honolulu in 2016 but the NFL has since indicated that it is exploring the possibility of staging future games in Brazil, Germany, and other international locations.

The PGA Tour's relationship with the state dates back to 1965, with the debut of the Hawaiian Open at the Wai'alae Country Club. The HTA started officially sponsoring Tour events in 2001, as a way to publicize the state's golf courses and support Hawai'i's $1 billion golf industry. Under the terms of a four-year deal with the Tour signed in 2015, the HTA will contribute approximately $1.9 million to sponsor the Hyundai Tournament of Champions at Kapalua (Maui), the Sony Open in Hawai'i (O'ahu), and the Mitsubishi Electric Championship at Hualalai (Hawai'i Island). The HTA claims that these events generate approximately $65 million in direct tourist spending.

The HTA has also financially supported the Vans Triple Crown of Surfing, a prime example of "intrinsic" events that showcase the unique qualities of Hawai'i's environments and lifestyles.[3] An economic impact study conducted by Brigham Young University-Hawaii's Alliance of Marketing Professionals and Students found that the 2010 Triple Crown generated $20.9 million in spending from surf enthusiasts who flock to O'ahu's North Shore for the event. In 2014, the other sporting events receiving HTA subsidies were the Diamond Head Classic (college basketball), the Hilton Honors Beach Volleyball Challenge, the Ironman World Championship, the LPGA Lotte Championship, the Pacific Links Hawai'i Championship, the Hawai'i Bowl (college football), the Xterra World Championship (off-road triathlon), the Xterra Trail Run World Championship, the EA Sports Maui Invitational (college basketball), the Kaua'i Marathon, the Queen Lili'uokalani Canoe Race, and the 'Ohana Cup (rugby).

Although the marathon generates significant visitor spending during a tourism shoulder period (the span between high and low seasons), attracts regular international coverage (including an annual highlight special on Japanese TV), and draws not just huge numbers of out-of-town runners but thousands of local participants—thereby producing the HTA's three desired outcomes for a subsidized signature event—nevertheless, the Honolulu Marathon does not figure into the Tourism Authority's stated plans for future sports marketing. At the same time, however, the marathon's independence and oft-invoked economic impact have pre-empted criticism of the race's annual takeover of East Honolulu roads and allowed the HMA to operate largely unencumbered by state bureaucracy and politics.

The Worth of a Marathon

While the marathon has not figured into the state's long-term sports marketing plans, it has nonetheless been in the interest of marathon officials and the state tourism officials to understand just how much the event impacts tourism and visitor spending. In 1982, when Japanese entries jumped from

977 to 1,500, HMA research director Gary Murfin worked with the Hawaiʻi Visitors Bureau to produce the first Honolulu Marathon economic impact study. From a survey of participants, the study concluded that roughly 4,000 out-of-state runners accompanied by 4,500 friends and relatives put $8 million into the local economy. A more sophisticated survey two years later estimated that more than 10,000 out-of-state runners and companions contributed $12.3 million. In 1995, the Honolulu Marathon surpassed the New York City Marathon as the largest marathon in the world, with 34,434 entries and 27,022 finishers. According to Hawaiʻi's Department of Business, Economic Development and Tourism (DBEDT), an estimated 24,000 out-of-town runners and 11,000 visiting spectators generated $140 million, allowing Barahal to boast: "We think we have the biggest (marathon) by any measure, whether the criterion is the number of starters or finishers or the economic impact."[4] In 2002, following four years of declining participation bottoming out at 23,513 runners, as Japanese entries fell from 14,282 to 9,159 following 9/11, DBEDT estimated the race's economic impact at only $61 million.

But that figure was far below the $92.4 million that a newly hired Hawaiʻi Pacific University professor named Jerome Agrusa arrived at through an independent study. Born and raised in New York, Agrusa had been a stockbroker, entertainment director, sales representative, and restaurant manager before turning to education. As a child, he'd watched "these weird guys" huffing and puffing up and over the Verazzano Narrows Bridge at the start of the New York City Marathon. Years later, as a visiting student at Northeastern, he had also watched runners pass the Prudential Building near the finish line of the Boston Marathon. Agrusa first came to Hawaiʻi in 1989, just as he was finishing a master's degree in hospitality management at the University of Houston. He taught summer school at what was then Hawaiʻi Pacific College, and he returned several times until Chuck Gee, dean of the University of Hawaiʻi at Mānoa's School of Travel Industry Management, convinced him to pursue a PhD. Completing the degree at Texas A&M University, Agrusa spent several years teaching at the University of Southern Mississippi and the University of Louisiana at Lafayette. It was in Louisiana that he started attempting to gauge the economic impact of high-profile events likely to draw visitors. As Agrusa recalled:

> What happened is I used to ask the local government of Louisiana how they determined the economic impact and in the city of New Orleans,

they stated they weigh the garbage. They have this much garbage this week, and then during the Mardi Gras it's this much more garbage, so they figured out how much more money was spent. I came up with this brilliant idea of asking the tourists how much money they spent. Let's ask them. I did that for a number of years. Once I did it for the Mardi Gras, I did it for the Festivals Acadiens, and the Festival International.[5]

When Agrusa joined the HPU faculty in 2002, the Honolulu Marathon and the number of Japanese visitors it attracted immediately caught his attention. He created a survey like those he had used in Louisiana, then had it translated into Japanese by HPU student Atsuko Hirobe. "We went to Costco and bought Tootsie Pops and little candy canes," he recalled: "We went to the finish line at Kapiʻolani Park while people were hanging out after the race and just started surveying people with clipboards."[6] Three-hundred runners completed the survey. Though too small a sample size to produce data reliable enough for publication, the survey caught the attention of local news media and of HMA media liaison Pat Bigold. The following year, the HMA gave Agrusa $5,000 to conduct a formal economic impact survey. Agrusa and his students set up shop at the Outrigger Reef, the official marathon hotel and site of packet pick-up, and surveyed about 1,000 visiting marathon participants. From that sample, he estimated that the race contributed $86.8 million to the state economy—a significant infusion, since tourism arrivals had declined due to the SARS epidemic and the war in Iraq. This survey also yielded useful data about the respondents themselves: 91 percent stayed in a hotel; 40 percent of English-speaking runners and 31 percent of Japanese runners said they were visiting Hawaiʻi for the first time; and perhaps most importantly, 93 percent of first-time visitors from English-speaking countries and 87 percent of first-timers from Japan said they would return for a vacation.

For the next decade, Barahal green-lighted funds for Agrusa to continue his work. These yearly analyses extended positive news coverage into the new year, and gave the HTA quantified data to demonstrate the marathon's value to lawmakers and the community at large. With Bigold actively promoting the story, and Agrusa delivering reliably good quotes with an Emeril Lagasse flair, the Honolulu Marathon economic impact story became standard February fare on the business pages of the daily newspapers, with the data usually repeated ten months later in the stories leading up to the next race. What Agrusa and his students collected annually also tells a story

Table 4 Honolulu Marathon Economic Impact, 2003–2013

Year	Total Entries	Japanese Entries	Estimated Economic Impact (in millions)
2003	25,283	15,149	$86.8
2004	25,671	15,723	$90.7
2005	28,048	17,345	$100.1
2006	28,637	17,905	$101.6
2007	27,829	17,507	$108.9
2008	23,230	14,396	$100.7
2009	23,469	14,402	$100.1
2010	22,806	13,492	$106.5
2011	22,615	12,359	$107.7
2012	31,083	16,283	$132.9
2013	30,568	13,585	$101.4

In 2003, JAL flights reduced due to SARS and Iraq war (Sokei, "Run Brought $86.8M"). In 2006, hotel room availability was reduced by Waikīkī Beach Walk renovations (Nichols, "Room Shortage"). The year 2008 marked the start of the Japanese recession. In 2010, the yen hit an all-time high. In 2011, the Japanese earthquake and tsunami negatively impacted Japanese tourism to Hawai'i. In 2012, there was increased marketing by JAL and Adidas for fortieth anniversary race; encouragement from the Japanese government that citizens resume international travel to re-establish normalcy following the disasters of the previous year; and an increase in airline seat capacity.

about a period when Japanese participation especially reflected how outside influences like the SARS and H1N1 epidemics, the wars in Iraq and Afghanistan, and the Japanese recession affected the marathon, and how JTB Global Travel Service and JAL tried to overcome these challenges.

Quantifying Impact

Between 2002 and 2012, Agrusa refined his HMA-funded surveys not just to determine the economic impact of the marathon and its affiliated Race Day Walk more accurately, but also to identify and understand the factors driving the results. His 2012 report is only eleven pages long, including several large photographs, but it provides a compelling insight into why Hawai'i tourism officials so highly value Japanese tourists. Of the 31,083 people who entered the 2012 race, 16,283 were from Japan, 12,124 from Hawai'i, 1,883 from the U.S. Mainland, and 793 from other foreign countries. The Race Day Walk attracted an additional 3,248 participants, 2,625 from Japan. The 2,152 surveys—1,569 in Japanese and 583 in English— that Agrusa collected showed that Japanese runners, each accompanied by 0.98 friends or family members who did not compete, stayed for an average of 5.78 days, spending approximately $351.22 per day. U.S. runners accompanied by 0.97 non-participating companions stayed longer (8.79 days) but spent much less per day ($158.20). Runners from countries other than Japan brought more non-participants with them (1.34), stayed the longest (9.1 days), and spent $211.25 per day. Using DBEDT's economic impact formulae, Agrusa calculated that out-of-state runners generated $132,852,000 in total sales. Of that, $62.43 million was the total direct, indirect, and induced income; of special interest to the government, $6,181,562 was total direct, indirect, and induced tax revenue. A 2013 report, which indicated a dramatic decrease in overall economic impact (to $101,447,710) and direct, and induced tax revenue (to $4,720,360) was not released and the HMA has continued to cite the previous year's $132.8 million figure as the event's economic value to the state.

Agrusa attributes the high level of Japanese spending to the strength of the yen relative to the U.S. dollar,[7] and to the Japanese customs of *omiyage* (buying small gifts for family and friends) and *kinen* (buying souvenirs to "legitimize and commemorate" their visit to a noted place). Such spending is especially marked in first-time visitors, who account for 52 percent of all runners from Japan. He also concludes that recently the Honolulu Marathon has benefited from a huge increase in first-time female Japanese runners:

> They didn't just decide (to run a marathon) today. They decided that a year ago or maybe longer. They actually train for a whole year. Four days a week, they're getting up before work to do this run. When it comes to doing the race, they say to themselves, "Hey, I trained for a year or two years and I'm not just coming for a few days. I'm coming for a few days before to make sure I'm acclimated and I'm ready . . . then I'm going to stay a few days later to reward myself." And if they have family members, they bring them with them. They make it a vacation.[8]

The studies also found high levels of satisfaction with the marathon—98 percent of the respondents had a positive experience—and with Hawai'i as a tourist destination. Roughly half of the Japanese respondents intended to run the Honolulu Marathon again within the next two years, and more than 98 percent said they would visit Hawai'i again without running the marathon. Finally, the survey indicated that marathon tourism not only benefited O'ahu, but the neighbor islands as well, where hotel occupancy typically drops 10 to 20 percent during the December shoulder period. Thirty-five percent of English-speaking respondents and 22 percent of Japanese respondents said they would be visiting another island during their stay.

Problems of Comparison

Soonhwan Lee, an associate professor of kinesiology at Indiana University-Purdue University Indianapolis, has identified four reasons for communities and event sponsors to invest in economic impact research:

> First, because many sport events in our communities were financed by public tax support, economic impact studies continue to be an important public relations tool for city government. Secondly, there is doubt that sporting events may actually help develop a community relative to its economy. Therefore, accurate estimates should be proposed and the results should be reported to community members. Thirdly, as sport is not just an entertainment but an industry, the results of economic impact may be a cornerstone to develop many related businesses in communities. Finally, positive or negative economic results of spot events may be an important method to determine communities' draft budget for the coming year.[9]

Because many such reports are funded by the events themselves, the results are often skeptically received. The HMA-funded studies by Agrusa employed relatively conservative multipliers and relied on the same calculation formulae as government agencies. But the data can still be difficult to evaluate, due to huge disparities between the report results for similar events. In a 2007 review of economic impact studies and press releases, Steven Cobb and Douglas Olberding of Xavier University noted that per-runner impact estimates range from less than $1,000 in Washington, DC, to as high as $4,200 in Boston. Why?

> A closer examination of the methods used to construct these estimates reveals evidence that race analysts used a wide range of both assumptions and methodologies to estimate marathon economic impact. For example, estimates of the economic impact of the Napa Valley Marathon were constructed using only direct spending data and therefore failed to include any secondary (or multiplier) effects. Another study, an

analysis of the Florida Gulf Coast Marathon, relied on proxy data (e.g., "typical" visitor spending data from their local Chamber of Commerce) as the basis for their direct spending estimates. Even more significantly, many of the small city studies reviewed completely ignore any potential contribution from local race participants.

Although Agrusa's studies do not factor in local contributions, it is reasonable to assume that given the Honolulu Marathon's large field and high percentage of out-of-town participants, and most notably of high-spending Japanese entrants and their companions, the race will rank among the top marathons in terms of economic impact. Agrusa claims that geographic isolation is a key factor:

> Here . . . the spending is just so much higher because there is no (other) way to get here (than by airplane). Nobody can drive here. If you're flying, the longer you fly, the longer you stay. That's just statistically accurate. People who fly ten hours stay longer than a person who flies five hours. A person that takes twenty-four hours to come, they don't turn around and fly back.

In terms of financial contribution to the community, however, Honolulu trails the Chicago Marathon, with its much larger field but fewer international participants. In 2013 Chicago reached its cap of 45,000 runners. Twenty-three percent (10,264) were from outside the United States. Mexico accounted for the largest contingent, with 2,375. An economic impact study conducted by the University of Illinois at Urbana-Champaign's Regional Economics Applications Laboratory concluded that the marathon contributed $253.5 million to the city, prompting Don Welsch, president and CEO of Choose Chicago, to dub the race "a demand generator."[10] Using the Chicago Region Econometric Input-Output Model, the study identified $101.8 million going directly to main sectors of the tourism industry, with another $151.7 million in indirect activity. This estimated impact was a significant increase over 2008, when a field of 33,033 runners had an estimated $143 million in economic impact.

But again, differences in specific conditions and in methods for collecting and analyzing data make comparisons impractical. For instance, the 2013 Marine Corps Marathon's 23,380 finishers generated $88 million for the Washington, DC, area, according to Towson University's Regional

Economic Studies Institute. This is about $54 million less than the 2012 Honolulu Marathon—but the Washington race produced an estimated $9.1 million in state and local tax revenue[11]—roughly 33 percent more than in Honolulu. The 2014 Boston Marathon attracted 35,660 runners, with only 5,330 from outside the United States, and generated an estimated $175.8 million for its city, according to the Greater Boston Convention and Visitors Bureau.[12] In stark contrast, the 2014 Rock 'n' Roll Marathon in Raleigh, North Carolina, with a field of 10,918 entrants, supposedly attracted 18,074 out-of-state runners and their non-participating friends and family. Here the economic impact report commissioned by the Competitor Group, Inc., the owner of the Rock 'n' Roll Marathon series, and conducted by San Diego State University researcher Scott Minto, determined that the race generated $8.1 million for Raleigh. Again, the variance in methodologies and subsequent results makes comparison between analyses subject to so many qualifiers as to make the exercise hardly worth the effort. To begin to understand the potential worth of an event like the Honolulu Marathon, it is necessary to first identify what its chosen mode of economic analysis can and cannot measure.

Caveats and Limitations

In the wake of Hurricane Sandy, the New York Road Runners famously cancelled the 2012 New York City Marathon. While considered an appropriate response, given the large-scale regional suffering, many were alarmed at the supposed loss of the $340 million anticipated to be injected into the five boroughs. In response, Patrick Rishe, CEO of Sportsimpacts, a market research and planning company, challenged what he called a "grossly inflated" estimate of economic impact. According to Rishe, the way to measure actual revenues is to "capture 1) the amount of visitor spending which flows into the defined impact region that 2) is retained locally as new income after the money has initially been spent." A credible study would therefore focus on non-local participants (roughly 80 percent of the field of 40,000) and their travel partners, non-local spectators who came specifically to watch the race, and non-local media, contractors, security, and other ancillary personnel. By these criteria, Rishe estimated direct spending at $75 million to $85 million, with a maximum impact of $144 million—"a far cry from $340 million."

When examining the New York City Marathon's calculations, Rishe took into account the most common blind areas in economic impact research: substitution, crowding out, and leakages. In their study "Bowling in Hawaii: Examining the Effectiveness of Sports-Based Tourism Strategies," Robert Baumann, Victor Matheson, and Chihiro Muroi discuss how considering these blind spots affected their study of the Hawaii Tourism Authority's sports marketing activities. In the case of substitution, consumers spend money at an event that would have entered the local economy anyway. So, for example, the money local consumers put into the Pro Bowl or the Honolulu Marathon represents a "reshuffling of local spending," not new economic activity. Neither HTA nor Agrusa take this into account in their economic impact analyses. Substitution may also occur when "casual visitors," who would have been in Honolulu anyway, attend or participate in an event. Again, such spending presumably would have occurred elsewhere in the local economy. "Time switching" can also lead to miscalculations. In this case, visitors who would have come to Hawaiʻi anyway schedule their stay to coincide with the event.

"Crowding out" occurs when visitors participating in or attending an event displace visitors who would have come during the same time period. As the authors note, "While a city's hotels may be full of fans during the Pro Bowl, if the city's hotels are generally full of vacationers or conventioneers anyway, the Pro Bowl simply displaces other economic activity that would have occurred. In other words, even if the gross economic impact of a mega-event is large, the net impact could be small." The Honolulu Marathon, for example, occurs during a shoulder period, when arrivals are lower and more hotel rooms are therefore available. Nevertheless, Baumann, Matheson, and Muroi conclude there is ample evidence of crowding out. Although the marathon brings in about 15,000 Japanese runners, the net gain for arrivals is estimated at only 6,519. Or to take an even more extreme example, in 2006, ongoing construction of the Waikīkī Beach Walk significantly reduced room availability at a time of extremely high demand, thanks to the marathon, the sixty-fifth anniversary of the attack on Pearl Harbor, and a U2 concert at Aloha Stadium, all taking place on the same weekend. Crowding out was inevitable.

Agrusa himself notes that leakage is the most difficult factor to take into account. This occurs when the money spent during an event-specific stay does not remain in the local economy. For instance, what a Honolulu Marathon runner spends at hotels, restaurants, and stores owned by non-local companies is unlikely to remain in Hawaiʻi. And while wages paid to local workers will stay, as Baumann, Matheson, and Muroi note, it is more than likely that these workers will be asked to do more for the same pay, increasing return to capital at the expense of labor. Economic multipliers based on input-output models that take into account inter-industry relationships in a given region and an area's normal economic patterns are typically applied in *ex ante* (before the event) analyses like Agrusa's for the Honolulu Marathon. According to Baumann, Matheson, and Muroi, such multipliers tend to be overstated in analyses of mega-events, although Agrusa said he errs on the side of caution to account for leakage:

> There's a difference between economic impact and economic spending. Economic spending is one number and then we have a multiplier. Our multiplier is very conservative and we do that because we use DBEDT's model. I do my own input-output model and then we look at DBEDT and align them. Anybody with a multiplier more than 1 isn't telling the truth because here we have to import so much product. That's why our multiplier is lower. If you grew the food here, when there's spending going on the multiplier could be higher because the money is spent first: The tourist spends it and he spends it here. So (leakage) is actually in the formula, but it's not a separate line.

Ultimately, though, Barahal and the HMA have never spent much time explaining the nuances of economic impact research. What is trumpeted in press releases and interviews is the "total sales generated" figure—like the $132,852,000 estimated in 2012—and not the less impressive but more telling tax revenue that indisputably remains in Hawai'i ($6,181,562 in 2012). The big number stands as evidence that as a significant economic engine, the marathon is the most valuable sporting event in Hawai'i. But in itself, this total has still not been enough to cause the state to consider the marathon as a candidate for future support under a new sports development initiative. Headed by Lt. Gov. Shan Tsutsui, it is intended to make Hawai'i a "premier sports destination for professional, amateur and youth athletics."[13] Even so, the constantly advertised number reminds state officials that what is good for the Honolulu Marathon is good for Hawai'i.

CHAPTER 12

Behind the Scenes

The Honolulu Marathon Association office sits in the middle of what is known, sometimes ironically, as the Kaimukī Business District in East Oʻahu. In the late 1800s, part of the area served as an ostrich farm for Hawaiʻi's last king, David Kalākaua. Later, farmers grew carnations there for funerals. In the early twentieth century, the neighborhood attracted businesses displaced by the Chinatown fire of 1900 and benefited from the extension of a streetcar line from Kapahulu to the top of Koko Head Avenue. The main road, Waiʻalae Avenue, was first paved in 1925 and served as the central conduit for traffic between Downtown Honolulu and East Honolulu during Kaimukī's commercial heyday.[1] But construction of the H-1 Freeway in the 1960s let motorists bypass the district, effectively ending new commercial investment, and leaving the area to molder as a badly aging collection of restaurants, bars, and mom-and-pop stores.

In the late 1990s and early 2000s, cafes, crafts shops, and a hipper brand of eatery took advantage of Kaimukī's affordable rental spaces and retro-cool vibe, ushering a period of gentrification that transformed the upper slopes of Waiʻalae Avenue. Located above what used to be Magoo's pizzeria, and is now Town, a trendy New American restaurant favored by young professionals and the local arts crowd, the HMA office sits on the dividing line between the gentrified upper Waiʻalae area and the lower slope, where pawn shops, liquor stores, and fast food restaurants still operate. The space itself—a small office crowded with files and memorabilia and an adjoining conference room—remains largely unchanged after more than three decades of steady, volunteer-led operation. Once the domain of legendary volunteer managers Sylvia "Sam" Martz and Edith Leiby, the office is now the preserve of Valerie Lawson, who, despite her intentionally low profile, is viewed internally as every bit as indispensable as Ronald and Jeanette Chun because of her handling of registration operations. Smart, discreet, and usually clad in one of her innumerable road-race finisher shirts, Lawson is representative of the HMA's evergreen volunteers. Over some twenty years, she has met her responsibilities largely without relying on input from above—an important quality, given president Jim Barahal's tendency not to micromanage, and the HMA's own culture of operational areas staying in their own lanes. "My job is within these walls and I am just waiting for the next new thing that the (HMA executive) board brings me," Lawson says.

A former aerobics instructor, Lawson ran her first marathon in the early 1980s. Like countless other first-timers, what she really wanted was a finisher's shirt. She participated each year, later joining friends to help clean up the finish area at Kapiʻolani Park. This brought her into contact with the Chuns. Lawson had been recently laid off from her job at a computer company and Jeanette Chun took advantage of the opportunity to recruit Lawson to help out at the marathon office. The volunteer job was the sort of low-pressure situation that Lawson found appealing at the time: "After coming from a full-time work environment with a lot of responsibility, to come and just be told what to do—and as a volunteer you could do no wrong (and) no one would ever scold you even if you made a mistake—it was great."[2] Lawson found an early mentor in Leiby, who taught her the ins and outs of the association's painstaking manual registration system. Lawson recalled volunteers working late into the night, some at makeshift workstations lining the hallway, stuffing packets or manually inputting tens of thousands of names, addresses, ages, birth dates, and T-shirt sizes. She eventually took over as office manager, learning from Chun how to serve as the go-between for the various operational areas. In 2003, after Leiby's retirement, Lawson took over registration duties, though flatly refusing to take the title of registrar. "Oh no," she said. "That's Edie." The registration process has been updated several times, with computers lessening the need for intensive labor. Lawson credits her volunteers for the office's quiet efficiency:

> They've been here so long, they know a lot. They know what needs to be done. [There is] really very little management. With the volunteers that I have, they each have their own duties and they know what to do and they do it well. [. . .] They just come to volunteer. I think it's the camaraderie, the old friendships.[3]

As race day approaches, the number of volunteers swells to upwards of 150, including two groups of University of Hawai'i students and about twenty JAL junior employees.

The week of the race, Ronald Chun's crew transfers five truckloads of equipment and supplies from the office to the Hawai'i Convention Center, where Lawson and her volunteers will set up late registration and packet pick-up command centers. Volunteer training is on Monday and Tuesday; pick-up opens on Wednesday. "It's generally chaos," Lawson said. "It's a matter of coordinating all the deliveries of the T-shirts that have to come in, and the packets."[4] From Wednesday to Saturday, Lawson will work from 7 a.m. to 10 p.m., then return home, and send a message to the HMA executive board about the day's packet pick-up and expo numbers. Lawson's volunteers take race day off, or are assigned elsewhere, returning Monday to assist in distributing finisher certificates. Tommy Kono, the last active link to the founding days, always knew best the value of Lawson's contributions.

> She is really something special because I know that she gets a lot of squawk from everybody, the runners and all that, but she is so cool. [. . .] It's amazing how she can handle everything without blowing her stack. She is something special. You couldn't find a better person working. [. . .] I would say those three persons—Jeanette, Ronald, and her—are the key persons. Everybody else can be replaced but not those three.[5]

Like many of the managers outside of the executive committee, Lawson focuses on her own responsibilities, to the exclusion of most other concerns:

> My thinking is just very restricted [to] my area. Whenever something new comes up, my response to Jim or Jeanette or whoever it is that brings it to me is, "Bring it on. We will handle it." In other words, it's your job to go out there and advance our cause and it's my job to handle whatever it is you bring us. I can't think beyond what my job is.[6]

She therefore avoids the personality conflicts that occasionally flare up and does not second-guess board decisions. And her volunteers are so reliable that when she was treated for cancer a few years ago, "because of my staff, I don't think anyone in the organization realized I was ill."[7]

Year-Round Preparations

Like those serving under him, Jim Barahal's responsibilities are clearly defined. He explores avenues for growth and expansion, consults with Jon Cross about the elite-runners field, and perhaps most importantly, works closely with Jeanette Chun and the advertising company ADK (formerly Asatsu) to maintain relationships with the Japanese sponsors. Barahal and the Chuns travel to Japan each January to review the race with ADK and to meet personally with funders. As president of the HMA, Barahal's presence is important, but JAL officials and Asatsu representatives work most directly with Jeanette Chun. As Barahal told the *Honolulu Advertiser* in 2002, "We speak to our sponsors in one voice, and that's Jeanette's voice. She's the conduit that maintains the flow of information and keeps up the critical relationships."[8] Jiro Kitamura, the HMA's primary contact at ADK, agrees: "Jeanette has been working as a window between HMA and our side and she's a very competent lady. [. . .] If there is a printing request, it has to first go through her, then she shows it to us and we discuss it. Everything has to go through her."[9] Barahal has a hands-off policy on ADK's marketing and promotions in Japan, where the race is promoted as the "JAL Honolulu Marathon." The two sides communicate frequently, but mostly to keep each other aware of what is happening, not to consult or to ask permission.

The Chuns' own home marks out duties and territory. The main house is Jeanette's work area, which by default makes it the hub of the Honolulu Marathon's administrative activities. Dozens of file cabinets and plastic storage boxes filled with contracts, receipts, maps, tax materials, and other records are stacked in nearly every available space. The largest open area, the kitchen, has two industrial-sized refrigerators and cupboards well stocked with anything the Chuns' many, many visitors might conceivably want to eat—and nobody may leave without taking something to snack on later. Barahal stops by regularly on his way to work, often just to spend time and have a cup of coffee. According to the Chuns, if there's something new he wants them to do, and especially if it might be an unwelcome surprise, he'll blurt it out as he's walking to his car to leave.

The outside four-car garage is Ron Chun's domain, the sort of work area one might imagine a career Navy engineer would create for himself if tasked with rigging and constructing just about everything a growing marathon needs. Ron assembled and maintains the marathon's massive storage facility at Honolulu Harbor. In the early days, the barricades, signage, mile markers, and other supplies were kept in a shipping container at the Kapiʻolani Park Bandstand. When the city and county evicted them, Chun got a second container and set up at Pier 40 of Honolulu Harbor. Four more containers and two further moves down the pier later,[10] Chun now oversees a miniature city connected by covered alleyways. For lighting, he rigged up disposed-of streetlights to gas generators. Discarded racks have been re-covered to create the walls of a storage space that houses literally tons of pipe, wiring, lumber, and other materials that Chun acquired for free or at minimal cost, then refashioned into signage, boards, and other infrastructure.

While Jeanette's duties keep her on the phone or the computer for hours every day, most of Ron's work comes in the weeks before and after the race, when he and his longtime volunteers transform one corner of Kapiʻolani Park into the massive finishing area. Chun's trusted core includes George "Bubba" Jones; Kenneth "Smiley" Lawson (Val Lawson's husband); and several of Chun's son's old friends from Maryknoll School. "They've been with me thirty-five years," Chun says: "They're all retired but they all come back. Skinny little kids to 500-pound men. They're willing to work. I tell them, 'If you're going to help, help with your heart. I'm going to ask for blood.' "[11] While those closest to him know that he barks far more than he bites, Chun is an unapologetic taskmaster. During the park set up in 2013, he arrived one morning wearing a lobster hat, complete with dangling red claws, which he purchased during a trip to Maine. Jones and the others spent the morning calling him "Crabby," to which Chun, trying not to break a smile, replied: "It's not a [expletive] crab, it's a [expletive] lobster!" This crew has worked together for so many years that Chun really has little direction to offer. It takes 1,200 volunteers and contractors roughly ten days to set up the tents, the announcement tower, the photographer's bridge, and other structures. After the race, it takes roughly four hours to strike it down. "On Monday, you see nothing," Chun says: "It's like it never happened."[12]

Building the Field

Jon Cross's efforts to build world-class men's and women's fields are never ending. He studies race results year-round, stays in close contact with the clutch of agents he trusts most, and builds and maintains relationships with every elite athlete he comes across. Always receptive to a tip, a referral, or an opportunity for mutual benefit, he is the primary contact for agents, leaving the financial negotiations to Barahal. Over the years, Cross has become a master at the art of assembling a competitive field. Citing a frequent re-mark by race commentator Toni Reavis, he says the race is best when a well-balanced group of runners can regulate and push each other. Depending on who is in the field, Cross may recruit a talented middle-distance runner as the designated "rabbit" or pacer. He carefully selects runners who are com-petitive by nature, so as to avoid having the top runners collude to stay to-gether, and therefore not push themselves in the early stages of the race.

While he himself does not negotiate appearance fees, Cross keeps in mind that inviting a top-level elite runner could break the budget for the rest of the field. But as agent Zane Branson noted, the sheer number of tal-ented African marathoners coming out of training centers, often established by retired runners, has tipped the scales in favor of the races: "Economic conditions for a marathoner have actually decreased considerably, well over fifty percent if not more, and that's because of the saturation with so many Kenyans."[13] David Monti, the elite athlete coordinator for the New York City Marathon, agrees that the number of worthy runners and the num-ber of available elite spots have flipped since Africans became the dominant force: "Now, there's an athlete surplus by far. [. . .] There's way more guys in Kenya and Ethiopia than the big marathons can accept. Like in my job for New York, we have to turn away eighty to ninety percent of people that ask us. I'm talking about people that are qualified."[14] Top runners today also tend to avoid short- and middle-distance races that do not pay nearly as much as the major marathons. According to Branson, then, top runners make less today than they did twenty years ago. All this benefits race direc-tors like Cross, who work within restrictive elite athlete budgets. But his vigi-lance and his connections to influential agents allow him to take advantage of the occasional fluke availability. When for instance Hurricane Sandy forced the cancellation of the 2012 New York City Marathon, Cross leveraged the Honolulu Marathon's position as the last major marathon of the year to get Olympic bronze medalist and future world record holder Wilson Kip-sang at what has been described as a "deep discount." The next year, Cross lured Martin Lel, three-time winner of the London Marathon and two-time winner of the New York City Marathon, at a similarly discounted rate when Lel was forced to drop out of the New York City race.

Partly because he noticed early the rise of Russian women marathon-ers, Cross has been successful in assembling compelling women's fields in recent years. Working closely with agents like Konstantin Selinevich and Andrey Baranov, he improved overall quality and depth by acquiring such gifted female runners as Boston and Chicago Marathon winner Svetlana Zakharova; Irina Bogacheva, who won fifteen international marathons over a nineteen-year career; and Alevtina Biktimirova, who holds marathon titles in Frankfurt and Tokyo as well as Honolulu. Top female African runners, including Ehitu Kiros of Ethiopia and Joyce Chepkirui of Kenya, have appeared in Honolulu as well.

Next to Jeanette Chun, Cross has been the HMA official most prone to overwork. In addition to his invited runner duties and responsibilities as race director, Cross is also part of the hospitality committee with Farley Simon and Dennis Kurtis. "Jim is not always the friendliest guy," Cross explains: "He can be and he can not be. I'm almost always that way. I'm the outgoing one."[15] But as the race has gotten bigger, Cross has had to learn to pace himself. In 1992, an utterly exhausted Cross was bedridden for weeks after the race. "He was in very bad condition," Branson recalled: "He was ill for about a month after that. He couldn't even sit up."[16] It was Ron Chun who taught Cross the art of starting people on a job, checking in to make sure it's being done correctly, then making sure it's completed. "I finally figured out that a race director should direct," says Cross.[17] When he presides over meetings now, he is less frazzled, and more secure.

> We have three meetings. Three. That's it. [. . .] Jeanette gives me a list and I'll say, "Start line," and then Rick goes—it's almost a joke, as if people are trying to see how few words they can say—"all's good." Meetings can last less than an hour because it's the same people that are doing the same things and you have confidence and faith in them that they are going to do the job.[18]

The Longest Day

The joke (not his own) is that Rick Taniguchi is the most untouchable man in Honolulu because he secures sweet-paying special-duty assignments for 425 police department officers each December. If he's ever actually received a nod of appreciation from Honolulu's finest, he certainly wouldn't say so, but his duties as deputy race director certainly have waves of impact in the community. His responsibilities, and his overall status, increased as others left or became less active in the HMA. When longtime race codirector Ken McDowell left amid ongoing conflicts with Cross, Taniguchi, and other race officials, Taniguchi took over representing the marathon in government-related matters. As Tommy Kono scaled back his activities, Taniguchi became involved in obtaining permits, and meeting with representatives from the Department of Transportation Services and the state Department of Transportation. These tasks are tedious, but essential. As Kono explained, most applications need to be submitted a year in advance to ensure that another event seeking road usage that December weekend does not displace the marathon, despite its five decades of history. The HMA even reserves the Waikīkī Shell concert venue, simply so it can secure parking next to the finish area. Taniguchi's work pace picks up in October, when he begins meeting with the Honolulu Police Department to arrange for special-duty officers. He also meets with neighborhood boards and businesses along the route to discuss ways of minimizing negative impacts. His style can be brusque, but media consultant Pat Bigold insists that Taniguchi is effective—very effective:

> With Rick, there's no chatter. There's no talking out of school. There's no, "Hey Pat, this is what I heard" or "Did you hear that?" You don't get that out of Rick. Rick is down to business. "I've got this problem, Rick, where do I park this media truck?" "O.K., give me five minutes." Five minutes later I'll get a call. He's got a solution. He's really good at that. Not a great personality. This was the difference (between) him and Ken (McDowell). You're not getting any stories. He cuts to the quick.[19]

The day before the race, Taniguchi and his volunteers head to the starting line early in the morning to post race banners, assemble equipment, and check thoroughly the communication system. He returns later that night to patrol the four-mile area and to coordinate with police the removal of illegally parked cars. As midnight approaches, he goes to the control area to oversee the setting up of the barriers that will keep runners and spectators away from the neighboring high-rise properties. The first shuttle buses start to arrive around 2 a.m., and even as he prepares for the start, Taniguchi greets dignitaries and sponsors. Once the last runner is underway, Taniguchi leads his crew of some 120 volunteers in cleaning up the area—an enormous task completed within two to three hours. He will then typically work through the afternoon to pack, inventory, and return rental equipment. "At about 4:30 to 5 p.m., I'm pretty much out of it," he says. "Doing management takes upwards of twenty, twenty-one hours. That's pretty much the maximum anyone can do."[20]

Taniguchi's counterpart in course operations, and probably his main rival for becoming race director if Cross ever steps down, is J. J. Johnson. A former elite miler and old running friend of Cross and Barahal, Johnson has a fitness consulting business in Japan, and serves as race director for the Honolulu Triathlon, the Ko Olina Triathlon, and the HMA's Hapalua Half-Marathon. With a background in logistics from his time in the military, Johnson oversees the sixteen aid and medical stations along the course. Former high school track coach and longtime marathon volunteer Happy Chapman, who has worked under Johnson for the several years following the departure of McDowell, said "J. J. is not the easiest guy to work with, let me tell you that, but he's very organized. He's very good at doing a lot of things."[21]

Each aid station requires as many as 150 people, but as the race has grown, finding and keeping pure volunteers has become more and more difficult. In the early days, the Outrigger Canoe Club, Compadres Bar and Grill, and other organizations would take responsibility for finding volunteers as a community service and to promote their cause or business. But the work is demanding, the race day long, and with the proliferation of races, plenty of organizers are looking for volunteers. For some time now, therefore, the marathon has paid honoraria to sports teams and other groups looking for a reasonably lucrative one-day fundraising opportunity. As Taniguchi explains:

> We're out there to help the community. By doing this event, we have seventeen[22] aid stations and many of them are volunteer groups that are out there wanting to get $750 to $1,000 for their efforts. I mean, it's not easy money. You've got to work your butts off. [. . .] Hey, everybody has costs up there, you know? All your Gatorade and all your water and all your stuff. If you want nice uniforms and they cost fifty bucks, hundred bucks, maybe you do this event. Maybe you get $20 off or something for each team member.[23]

Chapman also notes that the military is a reliable source of volunteer labor, often working the difficult two-way aid stations along Kalaniana'ole Highway.

Following the example of Japanese race directors, some time ago Cross put together the first comprehensive manual for course operations, complete with hand-drawn illustrations of every intersection to aid with police placement. Updated many times as the race has evolved, the manual continues to guide procedures. As part of the race day protocols, several sweeps of the course take place before the runners hit the road. Chapman says occasional problems arise—stations are improperly set up or manned, signs are facing the wrong way—and are addressed immediately. The preparation that goes into the course operations is essential to a smooth race.

> It's tremendous work because you've got to get up early. You've got to get there. The preparation alone is a lot of work. Then the runners start coming in. Then eventually it gets to a point where it's non-stop. They'd be there and there are not that many runners because you only have the elite people coming by. Eventually, the problem is there's going to be a three- or four-hour period where you can't even see a separation. It's just incredible.[24]

The great, often exasperating unknown each year is when the last finisher will cross the line. To return roads to full public service as soon as possible, race infrastructure is pulled from the course throughout the day. The goal is to open up Kalaniana'ole Highway by 2 p.m.—nine hours after the start. In years past, walkers have taken twelve or more hours to finish. Some are merely untrained; others have significant disabilities. If participants at the back are injured, fatigued, or likely to jeopardize their health by continuing, officials will encourage them to stop, and in extreme cases, pull them from the course. But in keeping with the marathon's commitment to letting physically able participants set their own pace, organizers will not close the finish area until the last participant arrives. This policy has been a key selling point, and particularly for Japanese recreational runners. To avoid possibly shaming themselves, Japanese runners often will not attempt a race if they are not reasonably sure they can finish it. But the 2013 race sparked a debate about whether it was time to institute a time limit. According to Taniguchi, a group of local participants left the course at different points during the day to eat lunch, to rest, and to have dinner, leaving frustrated race officials and volunteers waiting at Kapi'olani Park until the group finally crossed the line at 1 a.m.—twenty hours after starting.

Selling the Story

From 2001 until the abrupt termination of his contract in 2014, nearly every story read or watched about the Honolulu Marathon was researched, pitched, facilitated, vetted, or managed by Pat Bigold, the former *Honolulu Star-Bulletin* reporter turned media consultant. The HMA was the first to hire him after a mass layoff at the *Bulletin* set him adrift. Race officials have called the hire a lifeline thrown to an old media ally; Bigold considers it an example of the HMA's predilection for bargain shopping. In any case, he quickly showed that he was as dogged a PR man as he was a reporter, ferreting out story angles from previously overlooked corners, studying the tendencies of different assignment editors and reporters, sowing goodwill through targeted exclusives, and ensuring that the marathon was covered not only as a serious sporting event, but as a subject for features, business stories, and editorials. Though at times exasperating to pitch-weary editors, Bigold used his understanding of daily journalism to become a reliable and accommodating resource to reporters. He gathered contact information, arranged interviews, compiled useful statistics, and identified secondary sources—all without overtly attempting to shape coverage. He had a particular talent for identifying human interest stories that could provide depth and breadth to marathon coverage. Through his efforts, for instance, Gladys "The Gladyator" Burrill became a local celebrity during her bid to break the world record for fastest marathon by a woman in her nineties. It was Bigold who made elite runners more accessible to the local community by arranging for top competitors like Mbarak Hussein to visit schools and run with cross country teams. When negative news broke, Bigold was an important go-between for scoop-hungry reporters and Barahal, whose composed demeanor in front of the camera often contrasted with his impulsive and temperamental reactions behind closed doors. "I can't count the number of times he's fired me," Bigold said of Barahal before his most recent and apparently final termination in 2014.[25]

In recent years, Bigold's own work with traditional media was complemented by an expanded social media initiative headed by Barahal's brother-in-law Fredrik Bjurenvall. Based in London, Bjurenvall spends race week helping to manage HMA's media center. According to Bigold, Bjurenvall's marketing savvy, facility with Facebook and Twitter, and mild temperament made him a welcome and effective ally in promoting the race and navigating personalities within the organization.

> He's working at the [social media] stuff at all hours, posting stuff. I don't particularly care for the grammar sometimes. Sometimes with his choices, what he thinks is newsworthy. [But] he keeps a constant flow

of information coming. Plus he's answering questions from readers who ask them. He actually has drawn in a lot more people to the race internationally because of this social media interaction. [. . .] Also, I'm not the nicest guy. I'm a little clumsy. I may say the wrong thing. Fredrik is very, very polished. It was good to have him there. He has become much more influential in the organization.[26]

In retaining Bjurenvall, Barahal and the HMA seem to be anticipating the eventual retirement of those executive board members with the strongest local ties, moving toward more power concentrated within the presidency, and more operational responsibilities outsourced to contractors outside of Hawai'i. It's a transition plan that makes sound business sense, even as the organization moves further away from its origins.

CHAPTER 13

The Road Ahead

The lead pack in the 2013 Honolulu Marathon reached the one-mile mark in five minutes and thirty-two seconds—the slowest start in course history. The only person who seemed to be running with a purpose was a lone Japanese runner about twenty seconds ahead of the pack. No one in the lead truck—not HMA president Jim Barahal, or veteran race commentator Toni Reavis, or any of the print media reporters—recognized him. He looked fast, and didn't show any signs of tiring, but his high number (24193) indicated he was not a serious contender. All agreed he was probably one of those goofballs who wanted to get on Japanese TV and brag to his friends that he once ran ahead of the world's best African runners. But the goofball didn't let up or falter, and when he hit Mile 4 in 21:03, stretching his lead to a minute and a half over the trailing pack, it was clear that he had some ability. Still, through much of the first half of the race, Barahal and Reavis bemoaned the apparent agreement among the African runners to hang back, take it easy, until the late stages. They noted the absence of six-time champion Jimmy Muindi, agreeing that he would never have allowed this to happen. "Jimmy kept people honest," Reavis said. There would be no new record set that day.

As race officials settled in, they learned that the mysterious leader was Saeki Makino, who had run a 2:21:42 marathon in Dusseldorf, Germany, a year earlier. More significantly, Makino was a training partner of Yuki Kawauchi, who had gained international celebrity by competing as a "citizen runner" operating outside of Japan's restrictive corporate running system. Top Japanese runners are essentially salaried employees of their sponsor: their training, nutrition, coaching, and sometimes housing are all provided.

A full-time government worker, Kawauchi trained independently, and unlike his corporate peers, who are obligated to appear in a limited schedule of mostly Japanese races in the professional *ekiden* system, he competed almost monthly, and in races outside Japan. And he was very good. In 2013, Kawauchi ran eleven marathons, all faster than any completed by an American runner that year, and four of his finishes were under 2:10. It is no secret that Honolulu Marathon officials would love to see a Japanese overall champion. The impact such a breakthrough would have on audiences for the highlight show on Japanese TV would be huge, and it would give an immense bump to marketing efforts there. But the marathon takes place during the professional ekiden[1] season, when corporate-sponsor athletes must compete. As Cross explains, "The ekiden corporate system thing, the Japanese federation, is like the AAU was. It's very controlling. They rule the athletes there. The athletes don't have a lot of power. They don't have unions yet."[2]

While no male Japanese runner has ever won his Honolulu Marathon division, there have been two women's division champions: Japanese college student Eri Hayakawa in 2003, and Kyoko Shimahara in 2008, when another Japanese runner, Kaori Yoshida, came in second. Hayakawa was affiliated with a training center founded by Susumu Nakajima and the revered marathoner and TV host Mari Tanigawa that operated outside the professional ekiden system. Hayakawa's win in Honolulu was hailed as a positive omen for Hawai'i tourism, following a drop in Japanese participation due to 9/11 and the SARS scare. As Kristen Scharnberg of the *Chicago Tribune* wrote, Hayakawa "is the prototype of the visitor with whom Hawaii has been looking to reconnect: She is young, upwardly mobile and—perhaps most of all—Japanese." Hayakawa played a major role in promotions for the 2004 race. Her image was everywhere at the Honolulu Marathon Expo and in Waikīkī during race week. Years after her victory, Japanese tourists were still snapping photos of the shoes she wore in 2003, on display at the Niketown on Kūhiō Avenue. Shimahara and Yoshida also attracted tremendous attention in Japan and Hawai'i following their 2008 performances. Both were members of Second Wind, a team sponsored by makeup giant Shiseido, which had broken away from the Japanese federation.

While no one in the pace truck thought Makino could win—not with the sun just peeking out over Diamond Head, and more than half the race ahead—his two-minute lead over the pack at the 10K mark could not be ignored. While the pace truck was twenty yards ahead of Makino, the vehicles carrying the photographers and TV camera men were back with the

African runners, unaware that Makino had not dropped out yet, or certain that he wasn't worth tracking. Only when Barahal sent a motorcycle escort back to talk to the camera crews—"Get them up here! They're missing the story!"—were the first close-up images of Makino captured. As Makino lengthened his lead heading into Hawai'i Kai and back down Kalaniana'ole Highway, Barahal, Reavis, and Barahal's son Sebastian, a high school runner, watched Makino's form for signs of degradation. The first hints came shortly after the 17-mile mark, when Makino's elbows began to drift outward, and his head started to loll ever so slightly. A half a mile back, the pack of seven shifted gears, and began to reel in the faltering leader. The issue now was mathematics. What pace could Makino maintain down the stretch? Could the pack, now dashing through sub-5-minute miles, make up the distance in time?

By the time Makino rounded the corner off Kalaniana'ole Highway and onto Keala'olu Avenue, just past the 22-mile mark, the dream was over. As Makino grimaced in agony, a group led by Gilbert Chepkwony and two-time champion Nicholas Chelimo glided by, their strides effortless, faces impassive. The real race was beginning. Chepkwony made a winning gambit heading up Kāhala Avenue, shedding Chelimo and the others as he blitzed through Mile 23 in just 4:36. Victory in hand, he slowed to 4:56 in Mile 24 and 5:11 in Mile 25, finishing in 2:18:47, the slowest winning time in six years. Chelimo was second at 2:19:22, followed by Solomon Bushendich at 2:19:38. Makino eventually limped over the finish line in twelfth place, at 2:37:12.

The scene at the park was unusually chaotic. As the first pace truck pulled to the side, the large digital clock mounted on its roof hit a crossbar holding a banner and landed on volunteer Dennis Swart's head. Across the way, Bigold was leading the winners to a press tent to rest before their interviews, but Barahal decided that those should happen immediately in an open space closer to the finish line. As Bigold headed to the tent, Barahal, adrenaline still pumping, barked, "Pat, get over here!" Bigold glared. It was going to be one of those days. Bigold had already sparred with ADK account executive Ayako Ito over Japanese media members who were leaking into restricted areas. Ito's dismissive reply left him fuming. In fact, Bigold was already disturbed by ADK's decision to use JAL funds to bring in the Super Girls, a 12-girl pop act, to appear at the marathon. Still irritated a year later, Bigold questioned HMA's relationship with its ad agency: "[ADK is] getting $1.5 million a year so why does it seem like they're running us rather than employed by us? Why is Jim so careful? Why doesn't he ever admonish Ayako? What's the deal? The tail's wagging the dog."[3] As it turned out, it would not be Bigold's problem for much longer.

A plastic chair appeared, and Chepkwony sat nervously as a half-dozen reporters leaned in.

> "Congratulations," one said.
> "Yes."
> "How do you feel?"
> "Yes."
> "How does it feel to have won the race?"
> "It is very special."

After a minute or two of quizzical looks and clipped answers from the exhausted winner, the reporters turned to Chelimo for more of the same. Afterward, they compared notes, stitching together what they agreed to report as direct quotes. The "interview" played worse on TV than in the newspapers.

Many top Kenyan and Ethiopian runners have real difficulties in conducting such interviews, limiting their ability to connect with English-speaking audiences. Agent Zane Branson, who died in Kenya in 2015, identified this as a significant problem for a sport relying heavily on sponsorships:

> There's a push for managers to try to connect the elite runners with the back of the group, and doing question/answer stuff, and using social media more, trying to build personalities more. The approach before was to do media training but the way that media training (works) for pretty much any athlete is through their experience and their confidence. You can do some kind of set up of how interviews are conducted and how to do this and get them used to the cameras but they're speaking their third language, not even their second language. Their tribal tongue is their first language and then they learn Swahili and then they learn English. Nobody has ever taken time and a lot of managers don't care. All they care is about if they race well, then that's where they make their money. They don't make money by taking time to media train, but they're going to have to. This is essential.[4]

The elite athletes were back in their hotel rooms well before the bulk of what would eventually be 22,096 finishers had reached the turnaround in Hawai'i

Kai. The overall field was consistent with recent years: 30,568 entries, including 13,585 from Japan and 13,918 from Hawai'i. It was the first time since 2001 that local entries outnumbered Japanese ones but following recent trends, only 7,251 local runners actually finished. Even if all 435 runners who started but did not finish came from Hawai'i, it would still mean that about 45 percent of local registered entrants did not actually run. (In 2012, only 7,011 of 12,124 local entrants finished, with only 303 overall starters who did not). Officially, in 2013, the Honolulu Marathon ranked as the fourth largest marathon in the United States, and the ninth in the world. But that spot rightly belonged to the Boston Marathon, where notoriously more than 5,000 starters were pulled from the course after two bombs exploded at the finish area. The previous year, Honolulu had been the second-largest American marathon, and seventh internationally. But again, its ranking was misleading, because the New York City Marathon, with an expected field of about 47,000, was cancelled due to Hurricane Sandy.

Overall, 2013 continued what Running USA has called the second great American Running Boom. Since 1990, overall road-race participation has increased every year with the exception of 2003, and Running USA's 2014 State of the Sport report indicated that more than nineteen million people had participated in some event the previous year—an annual increase of 22 percent. 5K races were most popular, accounting for 44 percent of all runners, but adventure runs and other untimed, non-traditional races saw dramatic increases, with some four million athletes competing. Female participation drives this overall growth. Women made up 25 percent of racing fields in 1990; by 2013, it was 57 percent. While the kinds of races have multiplied greatly over the last twenty-five years, the marathon has enjoyed steady growth. In 2013, approximately 541,000 people completed a U.S. marathon—an annual increase of 11 percent. A record 1,100 events took place, and ninety-two boasted fields of more than 1,000. The typical second running boom participant is older and considerably slower than those competing at the tail end of the first boom. In 1980, the average age of marathon participants was thirty-four for men and thirty-one for women. In 2013, the men were forty, and the women thirty-five. In 1980 the average male finisher clocked in at 3:32:17, with the women at 4:03:39. In 2013, it was 4:16:24 for men and 4:41:38 for women.

The Honolulu Marathon is in the vanguard of these trends. In 2013, it not only had the highest number of finishers over sixty, but also claimed the title of the slowest U.S. marathon-distance running event, with an average finish time of 6:07:32. (New Mexico's Bataan Memorial Death March had a median time of 8:13:54, but it is promoted as a march, not a run.) Honolulu's lack of a time limit therefore continues to ensure its viability. If the race had a six-hour time limit, as in Denver, Houston, San Francisco, or even the Island of Hawai'i, half the field would have been disqualified. Particularly in the last decade, the second running boom has greatly benefited the top big city marathons. In 2005, 32,995 runners finished the New York City Marathon; in 2014, it was 50,433. Over the same time span, Chicago grew from 32,995 to 40,801, and Boston from 17,549 to 31,805. Honolulu's numbers have actually decreased slightly—from 24,291 in 2005 to 21,824 in 2014, with a dip to 19,078 in 2011.

At least one commentator suggested that HMA's virtually exclusive focus on the Japanese market for its out-of-state participants has cost it opportunities for growth. David Monti of *Race Results Weekly* and the New York City Marathon acknowledged that the Honolulu Marathon has carved out a remarkably successful niche for itself, but noted that more could be done:

> Can we just assume that there's always going to be more customers? I don't know. If I were organizing the race, I wouldn't change the basic components of the formula: December date, open finish line, aloha spirit, Japanese emphasis. I don't think I would change any of those things. I think changing any of those things would be suicide. What I would do more of is try to get more people to come here from the mainland. There's a perception of the mainland that Hawai'i is too far away and too expensive. Neither of those things is true. [. . .] It's amazing how few people I meet here that are from the mainland. I think a similar number came from Europe, which doesn't make any sense.[5]

Perhaps the greatest danger to the Honolulu Marathon, however, is the fast-developing reality that it is no longer the last and best option for Japanese recreational runners who will never qualify for one of the exclusive corporate marathons. In 2007, the Japan Track and Field Federation and the city of Tokyo created the Tokyo Marathon, Japan's first "citizens road race." Open to amateur and professional runners, and offering a generous seven-hour time limit, the race took deliberate aim at joining New York, London, and Berlin as a premier open-field marathon. This race sparked a running craze. Training centers and running programs proliferated, and by 2011, more than

Title sponsor JAL's influence is visible throughout the race course. Photo by Jamm Aquino. Courtesy of the *Honolulu Star-Advertiser.*

300,000 people were submitting lottery applications for one of the race's 32,000 spots.[6]

Jiro Kitamura, chairman of the ADK-operated Honolulu Marathon office in Japan, credited Honolulu for some of the Tokyo race's success:

> Because the Tokyo Marathon was new, there were many issues and problems but the good thing was that many of the participants had run the Honolulu Marathon before so they had the experience. [. . .] The organizers didn't have the experience, but the runners did, so they knew the rules about how you don't rush at the start line because it will cause confusion. In that way, even though it was the first time, it turned out pretty good and the Honolulu Marathon contributed to that.[7]

The Tokyo innovation led to a host of new open races, including marathons in Osaka, Kyoto, Saga, Kita-Kyushu, and Okayama. Formerly for elite athletes only, the Nagoya International Women's Marathon went public in 2011, and even the field for the Naha Marathon in Okinawa, a public jogging event started in 1985 to celebrate the twenty-fifth anniversary of a sister-city agreement with Honolulu, has increased significantly in the last few years. By 2013, of the fifteen largest marathons in the world, four were Japanese: Tokyo (fifth, with 34,832 finishers), Osaka (seventh, with 26,937), Naha (twelfth with 19,118), and Kobe (thirteenth, with 17,816). Even so, Kitamura feels that Honolulu will survive the competition, thanks to its positive reputation among Japanese runners, and the overall quality of the race:

> The number of bigger marathon events in Japan is expanding. We now have Osaka, Nagoya, Kobe, Kyushu and all of these have 20,000 to 30,000 runners. Unfortunately, because the concept is still new in Japan, when you look at the quality of the organization or the environment for the runners, it's far from ideal yet. The Tokyo Marathon is a good one, but if you want to run in it [. . .] the race has places for about 35,000 but 400,000 apply to run. So, if you want to run in a good quality event, you have to be lucky. In Honolulu, you don't have to worry about that. As long as you have a will to run and have saved some money to come over here, once you are here the quality of the event is such that everybody is satisfied afterward.[8]

Whither the Aloha Spirit?

When David Monti lists the factors that make the Honolulu Marathon a success, along with the December race date and lack of a time limit, he points to the aloha spirit. And when Jim Barahal and other HMA officials not originally from Hawai'i speak of Jeanette and Ron Chun, or Val Lawson or Tommy Kono (even though he is originally from California) they point to the aloha spirit of these people as a commodity—a valuable asset to be leveraged for the benefit of the race. Barahal's and Cross's affection and admiration for the organizational stalwarts are undeniably genuine, but as is the case for all of Hawai'i tourism, aloha has long been tied to practical considerations. For the nearly thirty years now that Barahal has led the HMA, relying on the Chuns' broad local connections and their talent for working with the Japanese advertising partner has made solid business sense. Having Rick Taniguchi or Tommy Kono represent the marathon at neighborhood board meetings has also made things easier. But as in all matters of business, calculations are continually made, costs and benefits are weighed, and opportunities are considered.

Months after the 2013 Honolulu Marathon, Ron Chun was still turning over in his mind how the digital clock on the pace truck could have struck that banner and fallen on Swart. Everyone else had laughed it off—a minor incident, and Swart wasn't hurt. But Chun needed an answer. Was the new truck higher than the old one? Was the banner too low? Was the timing mat so thick that it had raised the truck just enough for the clock to strike the banner? Lurking behind these questions was a concern that this accident could be held against him, to be used later as evidence that he was slipping. A year or so before, Jeanette Chun had made a relatively minor error in the HMA's tax filing. She corrected it, and it ultimately had no impact. But there were murmurs that perhaps she was getting too old to be handling the accounting duties, and that an outside CPA should be retained. As for Ron's oversight of the finishing area, although the free labor his personal corps of volunteers provides would seem to assure his security in the HMA, the Chuns and other old timers have been noticing for several years how once-internal matters—registration, aid station management, even gift bags—are being parceled out to paid contractors.

A decade ago, Barahal told the *Honolulu Advertiser* that when the Chuns retire, "I'll be right behind them to turn out the lights."[9] This probably will not be the case. Barahal is in his early sixties, and as David Monti has noted, race presidents tend to stick around well beyond retirement age. But the Chuns are now both in their late seventies. Prior to his death in April 2016, board member Tommy Kono was unequivocal about what would happen when the Chuns left the HMA:

> I work closely with them so I know most of what they do, whereas the others have no inkling what they do. The Chuns' friends are supporting them, not the marathon. They support them. So if [the Chuns] quit, everybody else in their group would quit. There's no way the marathon could survive.[10]

The Chuns' importance to the HMA as an organization may be just as significant. As Val Lawson remarks: "The difference between Jeanette and Ron and Val as opposed to Jim and Jon and Rick would be family thinking versus business thinking. There is part of us that realizes that there is a human, personal-contact aspect versus the other side that needs to keep the business in business and think financially."[11] According to Kono, "The only reason Jeanette stays is because she feels obligated to the Japanese groups. She doesn't want to drop the ball and leave the Japanese groups stranded."[12] Kono, who was 85 when he died, had been looking forward to winding down his marathon duties. In 2013, he told Jeanette that he wanted to retire. She urged him to stay because she said she needed him on the board. With his passing, the board was reduced to just five members: Barahal, Cross, the Chuns, and legal counsel Richard Sutton.

While Barahal claims not to be thinking about the future of the board, for Cross, the path forward is clear enough:

> I don't see that [Jeanette] is irreplaceable even with the Japanese. Ron is the one I worry about the most. What will we do when he can't do it anymore? [. . .] Basically you would have to hire contractors. You'd have to hire contractors and stuff to do it. But you know, it's not that far in the future that we're going to have to deal with it probably. Does he really want to do this when he's in his eighties? I don't know. So the clock is ticking on some of these people.[13]

The Transition Begins

Barahal and some other board members periodically claim that they are not compensated for their work—an odd and easily-disproved fiction, since by law a non-profit organization's tax filings are publicly available. What each HMA officer receives is well within major marathon standards, considering the concentration of responsibility within a very small executive board, the scale of the event, and the net profits it generates. Tax documents from 2002 to 2014 show that executive compensation takes up about 10 percent of the marathon's gross earnings. Barahal's annual compensation has fluctuated broadly, from $31,875 in 2002 to $257,000 in 2012. Only one board member, Jeanette Chun, recorded a year with no financial compensation. In December 2013, in a well-researched and straightforward report of the HMA's business dealings, the online news site *Civil Beat* listed the officers' 2012 compensation. Nick Grube, the writer of the article, noted that Barahal's compensation was comparable to what other presidents of major marathons receive, and quoted Barahal as saying, "I think I'm grossly underpaid, but we think it's a number that reasonable people would not find objectionable. We worked for many, many, many years where we were not being paid."[14] According to marathon staffers, Barahal was furious about the article, calling it a "hit piece" and vowing never to speak with "print" media again. His ire may actually have had less to do with the disclosure of his compensation to the general public than with the possible response of volunteer staffers, contractors, and especially fellow HMA board members unaware of what others were being paid. Some months later, when Adidas withdrew as a sponsor, Barahal announced an across-the-board 25 percent pay cut for all executive staff and employees. In a rare display of opposition to a Barahal edict, board members and staffers revolted, forcing him to rescind the order within hours.

Barahal had declared numerous media boycotts in the past, but they typically lasted a few days, or even hours. His anger about the *Civil Beat* piece, however, lingered for months, and became a frequent reference point when the HMA received routine media requests for comment about stories he deemed negative. When KITV-4 reporter Brianne Randle requested a response to a resident's complaint, received via the ABC affiliate's "Action Line" consumer advocacy service, about litter left over from the marathon, an angry Barahal directed Bigold to tell the station's assignment editor Sheryl Turbeville that he would no longer talk to KITV-4 reporters and that the marathon was going to withdraw its advertising from the station. Shortly after, he cancelled a longstanding subscription to Dateline Media, which tracks media "hits" to measure an organization's overall public presence. And finally, he replaced Bigold's monthly retainer with an as-needed services agreement. For Barahal—who had used local media to stage his takeover of the HMA, readily participated in positive profiles and marathon retrospectives that celebrated his leadership, and regularly deployed Bigold to champion the newsworthiness of Dutch princes, Irish nuns, and octogenarian record chasers running the marathon to local newspapers and TV stations— traditional media had outlived its usefulness. Barahal told Bigold that henceforth, the HMA would only communicate with the public via social media; that is, through Barahal's brother-in-law Fredrik Bjurenvall in London. This shift to out-of-town media contractors continued later that year, when Barahal fired Bigold outright and hired the New York-based Monti as a media and race consultant.

Kono, the Chuns, and the others who Barahal inherited when he took over as president are nearing the end of their runs with HMA. He can now choose whom he wants to work with, and groom them for the future. Having benefited for many years from the work of the organizational stalwarts identified with the aloha spirit that makes the Honolulu Marathon a unique experience, Barahal is turning increasingly to family—insiders note that his wife Helena's presence is growing—and to friends like J. J. Johnson, whose ambitions to become race director, and perhaps more, are widely assumed. Such movement threatens the delicate if volatile balance of personalities and abilities that has helped the marathon achieve its greatest successes. As the HMA's ambassadors of goodwill begin to leave, they will take with them profound institutional knowledge and a vast networks of local businesses, contractors, and volunteers whose loyalty is not to the race, and certainly not to its leadership, but to the people whose word and handshake are the foundation for decades-long friendships. By necessity, then, and by choice, the HMA is turning to paid contractors, many from Barahal and Cross's home state of Michigan, to ensure a smooth transition of operations, if not relationships. For a race that has always catered to outside expectations of local Hawaiian culture versus the genuine article, all that is left are awkward pantomimes of connection with the host culture—an opening chant in Hawaiian, shell lei imported from Taiwan for the finishers, malasadas at the finish line. In 2014, the race revived its old motto: "In the footsteps of the kings' runners," a supposed nod to ancient kūkini despite the fact that the race course was never modeled after ancient running routes. The motto is prominent in web advertisements for the race, always next to or below a photo of a beaming young female Japanese runner.

The marathon's present state is a familiar one on the Hawai'i business landscape: a race, operated by transplanted businessmen whose social and professional networks share space but not connection with the local culture, staged on state and city and county roads for a largely foreign clientele, everything justified by vague and disputable claims of positive economic impact. It is how business is done these days.

A Final Visit

It is mid-afternoon, a respectable time of day for Jack Scaff to fill a glass from his home tap and contemplate the issue of legacy. But as always, he needs to let the shaggy dog out for a bit of a run first. He's in good spirits these days. A bout of cancer two years ago led to widespread rumors of his imminent demise, fanned at times by his chilly acquaintances in the HMA. But he's in full remission now, and looking as healthy as he has for years. He moves gingerly due to spinal stenosis but once he finds a comfortable seat and sets his drink down, the old mile-a-minute brain begins to crank. He starts and abandons a couple of promising threads, one about his annual trip to Brazil for Carnival, and another about some ideas for marketing the Honolulu Marathon in Australia and New Zealand, before he settles in on an anecdote about the night he was named a Living Treasure of Hawai'i by the Honpa Hongwanji.

They told me, "Dr. Scaff, we believe in reincarnation. If you could come back as anybody but yourself, who would you come back as?' " I said, "Well, if she'd let me, I'd like to come back as Mrs. Scaff's next husband." I'd never thought about it, but it's probably the best thing I've ever said.[15]

It was at another recent reception, this one for visiting Chinese runners, that Scaff and Barahal renewed acquaintances after many years. Barahal had walked past Scaff's table without a word but responded brightly when Scaff's wife Donna called out to him. ("I'm a troublemaker," she joked.) The two exchanged pleasantries and posed for a photo together. Afterward, Barahal mentioned the possibility of the HMA "helping" Scaff's new health venture. It was an amiable if not totally comfortable encounter between two men who have not always been on such friendly terms.

For many years, the two were consistent in their public stance regarding each other: They had no relationship, good or bad. Scaff had already left the Honolulu Marathon Association by the time Barahal arrived in Hawai'i. For a time they shared a common enemy in the HMA executive board faction that effectively forced out Scaff and attempted to do the same with Barahal. But over the last twenty years, the marathon's two most recognizable leaders have seemingly been unable to resist antagonizing each other from a distance. When approached by the media, Scaff has never shied away from sharing his honest assessment of the marathon's shortcomings in marketing, administration, and service to the community. And while Barahal has generally avoided overtly negative comments about Scaff's various projects, including the Great Aloha Run and the Great Trans-Koolau Trek, his actions sent clear signals that he did not welcome any association with his predecessor. For Scaff, the turning point came in the early 1990s when the HMA went after Scaff's Honolulu Marathon Clinic. While the clinic has no official affiliation with the Honolulu Marathon, it has nonetheless served as an important bridge between the race and local participants. It's Scaff's proudest accomplishment, the grassroots program he considers his most significant legacy. Thus, when the HMA, represented by intellectual property attorney Martin Hsia, attempted to keep Scaff from using "Honolulu Marathon" in the name of the clinic, essentially setting the race that Scaff helped to found in conflict with the program he had created to perpetuate it, the famously loquacious doctor was left incredulous. Hsia's threatened legal action never materialized, however, thanks to an attorney who had been running with Scaff's clinic. With the help of another intellectual property expert, the attorney determined that since Scaff had been using the Honolulu Marathon Clinic name some nineteen years before the Honolulu Marathon Association officially registered it, the clinic had legal standing to retain the name. "Who owns the name? It belongs to me," Scaff says. "I just haven't asked for it back."[16]

To Scaff, the push to have former Honolulu Mayor Frank Fasi recognized as the "true" father of the Honolulu Marathon was an even more obvious attempt at a personal slight. Scaff was part of the inaugural class inducted into the Honolulu Marathon Hall of Fame in 1995 and he still has the plaque recognizing him as the "father of the Honolulu Marathon." Yet, shortly after Fasi died, Barahal claimed to have discovered a letter written by Fasi encouraging Col. C. H. Greenley of the Mid-Pacific Road Runners Club to establish a Honolulu Marathon that could serve as the "Boston of the Pacific." The letter was actually the mayor's reply to the MPRRC's request to use city roads for the marathon it was already planning as a result of Scaff's initiative. Nonetheless, Barahal offered the letter as proof that Fasi was "the true father" of the Honolulu Marathon. When Fasi was himself inducted into the Hall of Fame in December 2010, Barahal presented his family with a plaque praising the former mayor for having "conceived of the idea of a marathon in his beloved Honolulu and organized the efforts to make it happen," a claim that ignored more than a century of marathon running in the city. The challenge to Scaff's standing may have been a counterpunch. Coincidentally or not, the week before Barahal announced his discovery of the letter, Scaff had angered marathon officials by tipping off the *Honolulu Advertiser* to the impending bankruptcy filing of Honolulu Marathon title sponsor JAL, leading to an article in which an irritated Barahal was called on to affirm the sponsor's ongoing commitment to the race.

In isolation, the periodic enmity that has flared between Scaff and Barahal seems nothing more significant than the friction of egos, an unsurprising ruffling of feathers between two proud men of polar dispositions and motivations. Scaff co-founded the first Honolulu Marathon but served as president of the Honolulu Marathon Association for just three years. Yet he remains the figure most broadly associated with the race, in part because of the widespread attention he attracted in the event's audacious infancy and in part because of the legion of loyal acolytes he has amassed through his running clinic. Barahal has served as president of the association for nearly 30 years, far longer than all the other HMA presidents combined. On his watch, the race has become the largest destination marathon in the world, a launching point for some of the most successful athletes in the sport, and a positive economic contributor to the state. The legacies of both men are assured, yet a sense of competition exists. In the broader context of the race's history, the tension between the two men is emblematic of both the conflicting forces that have shaped the identity of the race over more than four decades and resonates in the uneasy but effective balance of disparate personalities atop and within the Honolulu Marathon Association itself.

Scaff claims not to think about the Honolulu Marathon much, but there's very little going on with the HMA that he doesn't know about. If he feels any disappointment about what became of his most famous project after he left it, he is still very proud of what the race has meant to the thousands of Hawai'i residents who have crossed its finish line. That's why he still spends every Sunday at Kapi'olani Park, instructing new generations of novice runners on the finer points of long slow distance, proper hydration, and talk tests. And while he remains wary of Barahal, he's willing to entertain notions of détente. "I'm getting older," he says. "Maybe it's time to bury the hatchet."[17] Indeed, there are other things to think about. Lately, Scaff's been devoting a fair amount of time to an ambitious new project that will use organized sports as a means of preventing diabetes. It could work. Nearly a half-century ago, he and a friend chased a similarly wild idea.

Notes

Chapter 1: A Good Day for a Marathon

1. Tymn, "Sore-Legged."
2. Tymn, "Sore-Legged."
3. Tymn, "Marathon Has Record Field."
4. Bigold, "Race Too Japanese?"

Chapter 2: Birth of the Honolulu Marathon

1. Jacob.
2. Louie.
3. Jacob.
4. Laskow.
5. Gallagher.
6. Gallagher.
7. Goldstein.
8. Scaff, Interview.
9. Scaff, Interview.
10. Scaff, Interview.
11. Scaff, "A True."
12. Scaff, "A True."
13. Cisco, 227.
14. Ferris.
15. Scaff, Interview.
16. Fasi.
17. Fasi served three consecutive terms from 1968 to 1980. Following his defeat by fellow Democrat Eileen Anderson, he won his last three elections as a Republican. He resigned mid-term in 1994 to make yet another unsuccessful bid for Hawai'i governorship, this time as part of his own newly created "Best Party."
18. Mak, 15–17.
19. Tsai, "Tourism Leads Economy."
20. U.S. Census.
21. Hooper.
22. Martin, "Frank F. Fasi."
23. Hooper.

24. Altonn, "Runners Gird."

25. Hogan.

26. Scaff, Interview.

27. Osmun, *Marathon,* 60–61.

28. Hunter, "They'll Put Their Hearts."

29. Hunter, "They'll Put Their Hearts."

30. Avrasin.

31. Kalb, "Honolulu Marathon: 151 of 167."

32. Kato.

33. Kato.

34. "Tommy Kono."

35. "Tommy Kono."

36. Bass.

37. Kono.

38. Scaff, Interview.

39. Wood.

40. Scaff, Interview.

41. Osmun, "Foster."

Chapter 3: Rapid Growth Years

1. Kono.

2. Avrasin.

3. Scaff, Interview.

4. Osmun, *The Honolulu Marathon.*

5. Chun, Jeanette.

6. Chun, Jeanette.

7. Chun, Jeanette.

8. Chun, Jeanette.

9. Chun, Jeanette.

10. Chun, Ronald.

11. Chun, Ronald.

12. Chun, Ronald.

13. Kreifels.

14. Taniguchi.

15. Moore, "The Rules."

16. Osmun, *The Honolulu Marathon.*

17. Scaff, Interview.

18. The growth phase of the so-called first American Running Revolution was in fact already beginning to taper. The Honolulu Marathon's first decline in participation occurred in 1980, with a negligible net loss of eighty-one

runners from 1979. But the following year, the field narrowed to 7,270 (Honolulu Marathon, Statistics 1973–2009).

19. Scaff, Interview.

Chapter 4: Transitional Times

1. Osmun, *The Honolulu Marathon.*
2. Luis.
3. An HMA board member and sales executive for the local ABC affiliate KITV-4, Kelleher would later serve as Honolulu Marathon race director.
4. Murfin.
5. Luis.
6. Roberta "Bobbi" Gibb completed the Boston Marathon as an unofficial participant in 1966, 1967, and 1968. At the time, AAU rules barred women from competing in races longer than 1.5 miles, based on the belief that women were physiologically incapable of running long distances. Emboldened by Gibb's example, Switzer entered the 1967 Boston Marathon as "K.V. Switzer." A famous series of photographs captured the moment when race official Jock Semple, realizing that Switzer was a woman, tried to forcibly remove her from the course, and was knocked aside by Switzer's boyfriend and race escort Tom Miller. In 1972, the first year that women could officially enter the Boston Marathon, Semple was on hand to personally welcome Switzer to the event.
7. Tymn, "Boss."
8. Tymn, "Boss."
9. In 1975, Hall, a Massachusetts native who survived polio as a child, secured a promise from Boston Marathon race director Will Cloney that he would be given a finisher's certificate if he completed the race in under three hours. He finished in 2:58. He was not, however, the first wheelchair athlete to complete the race. In 1970, Eugene Roberts, who lost both legs to a landmine while serving in Vietnam, had competed in the race without official sanction, finishing in just over six hours (Derderian, 610).
10. Peace.
11. Tymn, "Boss."
12. Leavy.
13. Leavy.
14. Now known as USA Track and Field.
15. Meyer, "1981."
16. Stewart.
17. "Mini-Rebellion."
18. Meyer, "1981."

19. Roe, who won both the Boston Marathon and New York City Marathon that year, subsequently returned the prize money and was reinstated.
20. Reavis, "The Road to Go Pro."
21. Kurtis, "Crim."
22. Meyer, "The TAC."
23. "What a Difference a Year Can Make."
24. Williamson deferred the issue of instituting a cap on entries, but said that such a move would only be made to ensure the safety and overall quality of the race experience.
25. Miller, "Won't Sell Out."
26. Miller, "Won't Sell Out."
27. Murfin.
28. Murfin.
29. Tymn, "Marathon Faces."

Chapter 5: The Marathon from Myth to Modernity

1. Clark.
2. Clark.
3. Plutarch, 158.
4. Browning, 34.
5. Watson.
6. "Marathon History."
7. Rader, 69.
8. Martin and Gynn, 67.
9. Martin and Gynn, 73.
10. Martin and Gynn, 75.
11. Doyle.
12. Burnton.
13. Cisco, 225.
14. "Australian Wins."
15. Cisco, 225.
16. "Race over Real Marathon."
17. "Australian Wins"
18. "League Defers," 3.
19. Rader, 69.
20. Beckwith, 337.
21. Beckwith, 337.
22. Malo, 219.
23. Malo, 219–220.
24. Malo, 219.
25. "Kaoo Running."

26. "King Cops."
27. Osmun, *Marathon,* 112.
28. Osmun, *Marathon,* 116.
29. Carroll.
30. Hamilton, "MPRRC," 3.
31. The race was renamed the Maui Marathon in 1974, and continues today under the auspices of the Valley Isle Road Runners.
32. Chapman.
33. Tymn, "The Marathon Has Come a Long Way."
34. Tymn, "The Marathon Has Come a Long Way."

Chapter 6: The Michigan Guys

1. Cross.
2. Cross.
3. Cross.
4. Cross.
5. Cross.
6. Judah.
7. Martin and Gynn, 235.
8. Moore, "Tears."
9. Cross.
10. Cross.
11. Tymn, "Can't Take Money."
12. Wyatt, "Fast Men's Field."
13. Wyatt, "Numbers Down for Marathon."
14. Bigold, "Honolulu Paid Price."
15. Luis.
16. Bigold, "Honolulu Paid Price."

Chapter 7: The Coup

1. Bigold, "Honolulu Paid Price."
2. Christensen.
3. Neff.
4. Cross.
5. Bigold, Interview.
6. Bigold, Interview.
7. Bigold, Interview.
8. Bigold, "Marathon Threatened."
9. Millar, Interview.
10. Tymn, "Expectations."
11. Tymn, "Barahal, Cross Team."

12. Tymn, "Déjà Vu."
13. Millar, Letter.
14. Bronstein, 128.
15. Straub later purchased Doctors on Call from Barahal.
16. "Wheelchair Race."
17. Lawhead.
18. Bigold, "Problem for Every Mile."

Chapter 8: A Japanese Marriage

1. Kitamura.
2. Cross.
3. Chun, Jeanette.
4. Chun, Ronald.
5. Kitamura.
6. Chun, Ronald.
7. Mak, 21.
8. Agrusa, Tanner, and Lema, 264.
9. In 1967, as part of a publicity stunt by Swedish media, Kanakuri returned to Stockholm and "finished" the race, recording an unofficial time of 54 years, 8 months, 6 days, 5 hours, 32 minutes and 20.3 seconds (Corkill).
10. In 1950, two years after Korea was liberated from Japan, Sohn coached a contingent of South Korean runners—Ham Kee-Yong, Song Gil-Yun, and Choe Yun-Chil—that swept the top three spots in the Boston Marathon. Sohn had previously coached Suh Yun-Bok in the 1947 Boston Marathon. Suh became the first Asian athlete to win the race, finishing in a world record time of 2:25:39.
11. Bull.

Chapter 9: The Living Legacy of Bikila and Wolde

1. Robb.
2. Bigold, Interview.
3. Ruiz continues to maintain that her victory in Boston was legitimate. In 1982, she was arrested on suspicion of embezzling $60,000 from a realty firm. The following year, she was arrested for attempting to sell two kilograms of cocaine to an undercover police officer.
4. Bigold, Interview.
5. Cross.
6. Bigold, "Mystery Man."
7. Bigold, "TAC Official."
8. Cart.

9. Though unexpected, Lee's victory was no fluke. Arguably the most accomplished Asian male runner of the modern era, Lee used Honolulu as a springboard for international success, earning a silver medal in the 1996 Olympic Games in Atlanta and placing first in the Fukuoka Marathon in 1998. In 2001, Lee won the Boston Marathon, the first non-African runner to do so since 1990.

10. Reardon.

11. Branson.

12. Branson.

13. The most oft-repeated of these is a Kalenjin initiation ceremony in which boys are made to endure circumcision without anesthesia. The boys' faces are covered with a thin layer of mud. If the boy reacts to the pain by wincing or cringing, and a crack appears in the mud, he is labeled a coward unworthy of the respect of his village. Most western accounts link the ceremony and the value the Kalenjin place on enduring pain stoically with the seemingly placid demeanor Kenyan runners display during races.

14. Thielke.

15. Monti, "Inseparable."

16. Abramo.

17. Abramo.

18. Branson.

19. Bigold, "Doctors Operate."

20. Branson.

Chapter 10: Challenges of the Big Time

1. Running USA, *2014 Annual Report*.

2. Longman, "New Running Boom."

3. Banowetz.

4. Robbins.

5. Monti, Interview.

6. Cross.

7. Pave.

8. Tabar.

9. Tsai, "Scoring Errors."

10. Tsai, "Marathon Crosses Finish."

11. Tsai, "Women's Winner."

12. Tsai, "Soaked Success."

13. Tsai, "Winner Disqualified."

14. Tsai, "Marathon Feels Chicago's Heat."

15. Takano's story overshadowed the death of a volunteer during the same race. Despite the portable defibrillators stationed along the course, medical

personnel could not save fifty-five-year-old Kāneʻohe resident Jonah Pak, who was stricken with chest pains while manning an aid station in Waikīkī. He was transported to an area hospital, where he later died.

16. Tsai, "Second Wind."

Chapter 11: An Economic Engine

1. Tsai, "Honolulu Marathon Generated."
2. "Hawaiʻi Tourism Strategic Plan."
3. Hernandez.
4. Glauberman.
5. Agrusa, Interview.
6. Agrusa, Interview.
7. Nearly 97 percent of Japanese visitors answered that they intended to spend more money in Hawaiʻi, due to the strength of the yen. Average daily spending by Japanese runners and their companions was $6 higher than the previous year.
8. Agrusa, Interview.
9. Lee.
10. "New Study."
11. "Marine Corps Marathon Has Economic Impact."
12. "2014 Boston Marathon Will Mean 175.8 Million."
13. "Lt. Gov. Tsutsui to Lead."

Chapter 12: Behind the Scenes

1. Watanabe.
2. Lawson.
3. Lawson.
4. Lawson.
5. Kono.
6. Lawson.
7. Lawson.
8. Tsai, "Behind the Scenes."
9. Kitamura.
10. Volunteer labor by Hawaiʻi Stevedores, the HMA's neighbors on the pier, made the latest move possible. They used their crane to move the containers, and trucked the contents to the site themselves. Chun calls it another example of "local kōkua."
11. Chun, Ronald.
12. Chun, Ronald.
13. Branson.
14. Monti, Interview.

15. Cross.
16. Branson.
17. Cross.
18. Cross.
19. Bigold, Interview.
20. Taniguchi.
21. Chapman.
22. The Honolulu Marathon Association website states there are sixteen aid stations.
23. Taniguchi.
24. Chapman.
25. Bigold, Interview.
26. Bigold, Interview.

Chapter 13: The Road Ahead

1. The term "ekiden" is a composite of the Japanese words for "station" and "between," and refers to an early system in which runners would relay messages from station to station. Following the first ekiden race in 1917, the team relay format was adopted at the high school, collegiate, and professional levels, and has become an immensely popular spectator sport in Japan. The All-Japan Corporate Ekiden Championships consist of a series of regional qualifiers, followed by men's and women's championships in the winter.
2. Cross.
3. Bigold, Interview.
4. Branson.
5. Monti, Interview.
6. Krieger.
7. Kitamura.
8. Kitamura.
9. Tsai, "Behind the Scenes."
10. Kono.
11. Lawson.
12. Kono.
13. Cross.
14. Grube.
15. Scaff, Interview.
16. Scaff, Interview.
17. Scaff, Interview.

Bibliography

"1984 Honolulu Marathon Brought State $12.3 Million." *Honolulu Advertiser,* October 12, 1985, C-5.

"2012 Boston Marathon Weekend Will Mean $137.5 Million." *Boston Athletic Association,* Boston Athletic Association, April 11, 2012, http://www.baa.org /news-and-press/news-listing/2012/april/boston-marathon-weekend-economic -impact.aspx.

"2014 Boston Marathon Will Mean $175.8 Million for Greater Boston Economy." *Boston Athletic Association,* Boston Athletic Association, April 14, 2014, http://www.baa.org/news-and-press/news-listing/2014/april/2014-boston -marathon-will-mean-175-8-million-for-greater-boston-economy.aspx.

"About Us." *Great Aloha Run,* accessed February 5, 2015, http://greataloharun .com/about-great-aloha-run/.

Abramo, Nick. "Fast Friends," *Honolulu Star-Bulletin,* December 11, 2004.

Agrusa, Jerome. *2007 Honolulu Marathon & Race Day Walk Statistics and Economic Impact.* Report to the Honolulu Marathon Association, 2007.

———. *2012 Honolulu Marathon & Race Day Walk Statistics and Economic Impact.* Report to the Honolulu Marathon Association, 2012.

———. Personal interview, January 9, 2015.

Agrusa, Jerome, Joseph Lema, Todd Botto, and Yoon Choy. "When Sports Equal Big Bucks for a Tourist Destination: A Three-Year Comparative Study of the Honolulu Marathon." *The Consortium Journal of Tourism and Hospitality* 13, no. 1 (2008): 5–12.

Agrusa, Jerome, John Tanner, and Dan Lema. "Japanese Runners in the Honolulu Marathon and Their Economic Benefits to Hawaii." *Tourism Review International* 9 (2005): 261–270.

Alameida, Roy. "Moʻolelo o na Aliʻi." *Northwest Hawaiʻi Times,* April 2008.

Altonn, Helen. "Runners Gird for the Long Trek." *Honolulu Star-Bulletin,* December 15, 1973, A-6.

———. "Still Making House Calls." *Honolulu Star-Bulletin,* March 28, 2000.

"American Airlines Joins Japan Airlines in Sponsoring Honolulu Marathon." *American Airlines,* December 2011.

"Anton Kaoo's Large Grouch." *Hawaiian Star,* November 16, 1911.

"Are Kenyan Runners Stoking Violence?" *Foreign Policy,* February 22, 2008.

"Australian Wins the First Hawaiian Marathon." *San Francisco Call,* March 30, 1909. *Chroniclingamerica.*

Avrasin, Maya. "Setting the Stage for a Special Event: Coordinating Special Fitness Events Is a Complicated Task for Park and Recreation Departments, but Can Reap Huge Benefits." *Parks & Recreation* 40 (2005).

Ayers, H. M. "Who'll Offer Cup for Kalakaua Avenue Walking Competition?" *Hawaiian Star,* November 16, 1911.

Banowetz, Jeff. "Bruce Cleland: The First Charity Runner." *Competitor,* January 2013.

Barrett, Greg. "Marathon's a Long-Distance Lure." *Honolulu Advertiser,* December 11, 1995, D7.

———. "Record Heat Fells Runners." *Honolulu Advertiser,* December 11, 1995, D1.

Bass, Clarence. "Lifting Wisdom from Tommy Kono." *Ripped,* December 18, 2014.

Baumann, Robert, Victor Matheson, and Chihiro Muroi. "Bowling in Hawaii: Examining the Effectiveness of Sports-Based Tourism Strategies." *College of the Holy Cross, Department of Economics, Faculty Research Series, Paper No. 08–06,* July 2008.

Beckwith, Martha. *Hawaiian Mythology.* Honolulu: University of Hawai'i Press, 1970.

"Big Bucks." *Honolulu Advertiser,* November 25, 1986, D-1.

"Bigger and Better Future." *Honolulu Advertiser,* December 19, 1973, F-4.

Bigold, Pat. "Agent Claims He Also Was Fooled." *Honolulu Star-Bulletin,* December 21, 1988, C-1.

———. "Barahal Is Looking for More Aloha." *Honolulu Star-Bulletin,* March 27, 1997.

———. "Barahal Says Mystery Runner Was 'Terrified.' " *Honolulu Star-Bulletin,* December 17, 1988, B-1.

———. "Doctors Operate for Free on Former Runner from Tanzania." *Honolulu Star-Bulletin,* December 14, 1993, D-5.

———. "Formal Probe Underway." *Honolulu Star-Bulletin,* December 19, 1988, D-1.

———. "The Gold has been Tarnished by Success." *Honolulu Star-Bulletin,* December 5, 1996.

———. "Hall of Fame to Induct Frank Shorter." *Honolulu Marathon 2008 Press Packet,* 2008.

———. "Honolulu Paid Price for Fast Finishes." *Honolulu Star-Bulletin,* December 9, 1985, C-3.

———. "Marathon Marches to Millennium." *Honolulu Star-Advertiser,* December 8, 1999.

———. "Marathon's Mystery Man Almost Won It." *Honolulu Star-Bulletin,* December 12, 1988, D-1.

———. "Marathon Threatened by Infighting." *Honolulu Star-Bulletin,* January 3, 1986, C1.

———. "Marathon Turns 25, Still a Shorter Race." *Honolulu Star-Bulletin,* December 14, 1997.

———. "Memories of the Honolulu Marathon." *Honolulu Star-Bulletin,* December 10, 1998.

———. Personal interview, March 31, 2014.

———. "Plans for Hawaii's Largest Race in the Making." *Honolulu Star-Bulletin,* May 14, 1996.

———."A Problem for Every Mile." *Honolulu Star-Bulletin,* December 15, 1987, C-1.

———. "Race Too Japanese for Japanese?" *Honolulu Star-Bulletin,* December 14, 1987.

———. "Record 3,553 Japanese Fill Out Marathon Field." *Honolulu Star-Bulletin,* December 8, 1986, C-5.

———. "Record Run Likely with Strong Field." *Honolulu Star-Bulletin,* December 7, 1985, B-4.

———. "TAC Official: 'Conspiracy' Is Uncovered." *Honolulu Star-Bulletin,* December 20, 1988, D-1.

Blauvelt, Harry. "Kenyan Runner Sets Honolulu Marathon Record." *Honolulu Star-Bulletin,* December 9, 1985, C-1.

Branson, Zane. Personal interview, December 3, 2013.

Bronstein, Stanley F. *A.IQ: Achievement IQ Moments.* Virginia Beach: Cereb, 2008.

Browning, Robert. "Pheidippides." In *Browning's Shorter Poems.* Ed. Roy L. French. New York: Heath, 1929.

Bryant, John. *The London Marathon: The History of the Greatest Race on Earth.* London: Hutchinson, 2005.

Bryant, Mark. "Marathon Now a Goal for Everyday Runners." *Arizona Republic,* December 1, 2003.

Bull, Andy. "The Forgotten Story of Sohn Kee-Chung, Korea's Olympic Hero." *The Guardian,* August 27, 2011.

Burnton, Simon. "How Dorando Pietri Lost the Race but Won the Hearts of Millions." *The Guardian,* February 29, 2012.

Burris, Joe. "Hussein's Brother Following in Footsteps." *Boston Globe,* April 9, 2002.

Carroll, Dink. "Playing the Field." *Montreal Gazette,* December 5, 1956.

Cart, Julie. "Smuggling a Banned Commodity." *Los Angeles Times,* May 8, 1990.

Chapman, E. Walker. Personal interview, July 19, 2014.

Christensen, John. "On Running the Marathon and Running It Well." *Honolulu Star-Bulletin,* December 4, 1985, B-1.

Chun, Jeanette. Personal interview, October 17, 2013.

Chun, Ronald. Personal interview, October 17, 2013.

Cisco, Dan. *Hawaii Sports: History, Facts & Statistics.* Honolulu: University of Hawai'i Press, 1999.

Clark, Michael. "The Real Story of the Marathon." *Runner's World,* March 24, 2003, http://www.runnersworld.co.uk/event-editorial/the-real-story-of-the -marathon/877.html.

Cobb, Steven, and Douglas Olberding. "The Importance of Import Substitution in Marathon Economic Impact Analysis." *International Journal of Sport Finance* 2 (2007): 108–118.

Collings, Timothy, and Stuart Sykes. *Marathon: The Story of the Greatest Race on Earth.* London: Virgin Books, 2004.

Connelly, Michael. *26 Miles to Boston.* New York: Lyons, 2003.

"Contributor: Dr. Jack H. Scaff Jr." *Hawaii Sports Hall of Fame and Cybermuseum,* Hawaii Sports Hall of Fame, accessed March 22, 2015, http://www.hawaiisportshalloffame.com/wp/dr-jack-h-scaff-jr/.

Corkill, Edan. "Better Late than Never for Japan's First, 'Slowest' Olympian." *The Japan Times,* July 15, 2012.

Creamer, Beverly. "Macdonald, Youngsters Make Marathon Magic." *Honolulu Star-Bulletin,* December 17, 1973, C-3.

Crosbie, Karol. "The Marathoners." *Wooster.* College of Wooster, 2011, http:// www.virtualonlinepubs.com/display_article.php?id=715403.

Cross, Jonathan. Personal interview, May 9, 2014.

Derderian, Tom. *Boston Marathon.* Champaign, IL: Human Kinetics, 1996.

Dicus, Howard. "Van Morrison Ticket Sales Suspended." *Pacific Business News,* May 1, 2003.

Doxsie, Don. "Running Defines a Nation." *Dallas Morning News,* September 12, 2003.

Doyle, Arthur Conan. "Excerpt from Sir Arthur Conan Doyle's *Daily Mail* Article on the 1908 Marathon." *Publicdomainreview,* accessed March 22, 2015, http://publicdomainreview.org/excerpt-from-sir-arthur-conan-doyles -daily-mail-article-on-the-1908-marathon/.

Dunbar, Helene. "Determining Significance: Hawai'i's Ala Kahakai." *Cultural Resource Management: Information for Parks, Federal Agencies, Indian Tribes, States, Local Governments, and the Private Sector* 20 no. 1 (1997): 8–11.

"Entrants from Japan 1973–2007." *2008 Honolulu Marathon Press Packet,* Honolulu Marathon Association, 2008.

"Ever Wondered What It Takes to Conduct a World-Class Marathon?" *2008 Honolulu Marathon Press Packet,* Honolulu Marathon Association, 2008.

Fasi, Charles. "Eulogy for Mayor Frank Francis Fasi." *Fasiphoto.com*, accessed March 22, 2015.

Ferris, Jim. Interview, *1987 Honolulu Marathon,* KHON-2, Honolulu, 1987.

Gallagher, Bill. "Bill Bowerman: The Man, the Legend and the New Biography by Kenny Moore." *Brainstormnw,* n.d.

Gambaccini, Peter. *New York City Marathon: Twenty-Five Years.* New York: Rizzoli, 1994.

Gee, Bill. "How about That." *Honolulu Star-Bulletin,* December 18, 1973, C-1.

Glauberman, Stu. "A Run for the Money ($140 million)." *Honolulu Advertiser,* December 6, 1995, A1.

Goldstein, Richard. "Bill Bowerman, 88, Nike Co-Founder, Dies." *New York Times,* December 27, 1999.

Gomes, Andrew. "Organizers Pumping Up May Trans Koolau Race." *Pacific Business News,* July 19, 1996.

Grube, Nick. "Running a Business: Inside the Honolulu Marathon." *Civil Beat,* December 11, 2013.

"Hall of Famer Patti Dillon: Former Queen of the Roads." *The Honolulu Marathon,* The Honolulu Marathon Association, 2002, accessed December 6, 2002.

Hamilton, Scott. "Hawaii's 'Mr. Long Distance Running.'" *U.S. Masters International Track Team,* June 1973, 8.

———. "MPRRC Celebrates 40 Years with Highlights from Its Long-Running Memory Banks." *The Mid-Pacific Road Runner,* 2004, 3, 10.

Hawai'i Tourism Strategic Plan, 2005–2015. *Hawaii Tourism Authority,* Hawaii Tourism Authority, 2005, http://www.hawaiitourismauthority.org/default /assets/File/about/tsp2005_2015_final.pdf.

Hernandez, Stacy Yuen. "The Business of Sports in Hawaii." *Hawaii Business,* June 2012.

"Herodotus." *The Histories.* New York: Penguin, 2001.

Hersh, Phillip. "Running Is the Easy Part." *Chicago Tribune,* October 3, 2001.

"Honolulu Marathon Hall of Fame." *Honolulu Marathon,* Honolulu Marathon Association, accessed March 22, 2015.

Hogan, Carol. "It All Began with a Simple Suggestion." *Honolulu Advertiser,* December 11, 1983, Special Section, 2.

Hooper, Susan. "Frank Fasi Crazy Like a Fox." *Hawaii Business,* March 1, 1992.

Hunter, Pat. "Canadian Heart Expert Here to Tell How Running Helps Patients." *Honolulu Advertiser,* December 14, 1973, D-4.

———. "They'll Put Their Hearts into It." *Honolulu Advertiser,* December 10, 1973, D-1.

"Inseparable! Jimmy Muindi and the Honolulu Marathon." *Race Results Weekly,* International Association of Athletics Federations, December 12, 2008.

Jacob, Steve. "Kenneth Cooper Marks 45th Anniversary of *Aerobics.*" *Dallas Fort Worth Healthcare Daily,* March 19, 2013.

Judah, Tim. "Abebe Bikila: The Glory Trail." *The Guardian,* June 26, 2008.

Kalb, Ben. "Hawaii's 'Boston Marathon' Tomorrow." *Honolulu Advertiser,* December 15, 1973, C-1.

———. "Honolulu Marathon: 151 of 167 Finish." *Honolulu Advertiser,* December 17, 1973, D-2.

Kaneshiro, Jason. "Fasi's 'Initiative and Clout' Brought Marathon to Honolulu." *Honolulu Star-Advertiser,* December 8, 2010.

"Kaoo Running Well 'Under Wraps' and Pleases Touts." *The Evening Bulletin,* October 27, 1910: 10. *Chroniclingamerica.*

Kardong, Don. "Another View of How Money Came into Running." *Runner's World,* September 7, 2011.

Kato, Gerald. "Heart Cases in Marathon." *Honolulu Advertiser,* December 14, 1974, D-3.

"King Cops Fifteen-Mile Championship of Hawaii." *The Hawaiian Gazette,* November 1, 1910, 5.

Kitamura, Jiro. Personal interview, December 10, 2013.

Kono, Tommy. Personal interview, February 27, 2014.

Krauss, Bob. "Remembering Statehood Drive and Buchwach." *Honolulu Advertiser,* February 25, 2004.

Kreifels, Susan. "Officer Resigns, Pleads Guilty in Prisoner Beating." *Honolulu Star-Bulletin,* July 22, 1999.

Krieger, Daniel. "Everyone's an Athlete in Tokyo Marathon." *New York Times,* February 25, 2011.

Kurtis, Doug. "Crim Legends." *RunMichigan,* August 24, 2006.

———. "Ex-Michiganders Make Hawaii Marathon Go." *Michigan Runner,* December 30, 2002.

Laskow, Sarah. "The Man Who Made Jogging a Thing." *The Atlantic,* September 30, 2014.

Lawhead, Terry. "Salmonella Named Marathon Culprit." *Honolulu Advertiser,* December 17, 1987, A-5.

Lawson, Valerie. Personal interview, April 30, 2014.

"League Defers to Ten-Mile Race." *Pacific Commercial Advertiser,* September 9, 1909, 3.

Leavy, Jane. "N.Y. Marathoners Offered Cash Prizes." *Washington Post,* April 7, 1980.

Lee, Soonhwan. "A Review of Economic Impact Studies on Sporting Events." *The Sport Journal* 4, no. 4 (2008).

Longman, Jere. "In Kenya, Violence Shakes Running Community." *New York Times,* May 13, 2008.

Louie, Elaine. "At Work With: Dr. Kenneth H. Cooper; The Fit Commandment." *New York Times,* July 12, 1995.

"Lt. Gov. Tsutsui to Lead New Sports Development Initiative." Hawaii.gov. October 15, 2013, accessed September 20, 2014, http://ltgov.hawaii.gov/blog/lt-gov-tsutsui-to-lead-new-sports-development-initiative.

Luis, Cindy. "Running the Marathon an Expensive Business." *Honolulu Star-Bulletin,* December 11, 1981, E-1.

Mak, James. *Developing a Dream Destination: Tourism and Tourism Planning Policy in Hawaii.* Honolulu: University of Hawai'i Press, 2008.

Malo, David. *Hawaiian Antiquities.* Honolulu: Hawaiian Gazette, 1903.

"Marathon History." *AIMS WorldRunning,* Association of International Marathons and Distance Races, accessed March 30, 2015, http://aimsworldrunning.org/marathon_history.htm.

"Marathon Men Are Matches and Running Game Makes Fresh Sport." *Hawaiian Star,* October 10, 1911, 3.

"Marine Corps Marathon Has Economic Impact of $88 Million." *VirginiaBusiness.com,* January 27, 2014.

Martin, David E., and Roger W. H. Gynn. *The Olympic Marathon: The History and Drama of Sport's Most Challenging Event.* Champaign, IL: Human Kinetics, 2000.

Martin, Douglas. "Frank F. Fasi, 89, Mayor of Honolulu for 22 Years, Is Dead." *New York Times,* February 13, 2010.

McClelland, Edward. "How Oprah Ruined the Marathon." *Salon,* November 3, 2007.

Meyer, John. "1981 Cascade Run Off: The Race that Changed the Sport." *Runner's World,* May 6, 2011.

———. "The TAC Trust and the End of Shamateurism: The Rest of the Story." *Denver Post,* June 1, 2010.

Millar, Dewar. Letter, *Honolulu Star-Bulletin,* December 17, 1986, A-15.

———. Personal interview, April 23, 2014.

Miller, Ann. "The Race that Won't Sell Out." *Honolulu Advertiser,* December 10, 1982, D-1.

"Mini-Rebellion in Road Racing." *Sports Illustrated,* October 6, 1980.

Monti, David. "Biktimirova Ready for Title Defense in Honolulu." *Race Results Weekly,* International Association of Athletics Federations, December 11, 2008.

———. "Inseparable! Jimmy Muindi and the Honolulu Marathon." *Race Results Weekly,* International Association of Athletics Federations, December 12, 2008.

———. Personal interview, December 4, 2014.

Moore, Kenny. "Dawn of a New ARRA." *Sports Illustrated,* July 6, 1981.

———. "Dormant No More, Duncan Is Erupting." *Sports Illustrated,* February 14, 1977.

————. "Hawaii Five Double O." *Sports Illustrated,* October 8, 1979.

————. "The Rules of the Road." *Sports Illustrated,* February 27, 1978.

————. "Sons of the Wind." *Sports Illustrated,* February 26, 1990.

————. "Tears of Aberash: The Ordeal of Mamo Wolde." *The Honolulu Marathon,* Honolulu Marathon Association, n.d.

Murfin, Gary. Personal interview, February 25, 2014.

Nakaso, Dan. "H-3 Trek Grueling for Organizer." *Honolulu Advertiser,* May 9, 1997, A-1.

————. "Marathon Runs on Big Numbers." *Honolulu Advertiser,* December 14, 1997, A-1.

"Native Wins Marathon." *Hawaiian Star,* November 8, 1909.

Neff, Craig. "A Bleak Run in Boston." *Sports Illustrated,* April 22, 1985.

"New Study Finds Bank of America Chicago Marathon Delivers More than $253 Million in Business Activity." Bank of America Newsroom, Bank of America, August 21, 2014, http://newsroom.bankofamerica.com/press -releases/community/new-study-finds-bank-america-chicago-marathon -delivers-more-253-million-bus.

Nichols, Katherine. "Room Shortage Limits Marathon Roster." *Honolulu Star-Bulletin,* December 2, 2006.

————. "Physician Paces for Success." *Honolulu Advertiser,* May 27, 2002.

"Nigel Jackson Would Run Kaoo Before King Arrives." *Evening Bulletin,* September 21, 1910, 4.

Osmun, Mark. "Foster Makes Good on Pre-Race Tests." *Honolulu Advertiser,* December 15, 1975, D-1.

————. *The Honolulu Marathon.* New York: Lippincott, 1979.

Pacheco, Bill. Letter, *Honolulu Star-Bulletin,* January 18, 1986, A-30.

"Past Years: Race History." *Maui Marathon,* Valley Isle Road Runners, April 3, 2003.

Pave, Martin. "Personal Best for Runner: DVD Records Journey." *Boston Globe,* April 16, 2014.

Peace, William. "26.2 Miles of Trouble." *Ragged Edge Online,* October 18, 2004.

Plutarch. "Whether Military or Intellectual Exploits Have Brought Athens More Fame." In *Essays.* New York: Penguin, 1992.

"Race over Real Marathon Distance Is Arranged." *Pacific Commercial Advertiser,* March 23, 1909.

"Race's First Top Kenyan Woman Further Deepens Sunday's Field." *Honolulu Marathon Press Release,* Honolulu Marathon Association, 2002.

Rader, Benjamin. *Sports: From the Age of Folk Games to the Age of Televised Sports.* New Jersey: Prentice Hall, 2004.

Reardon, Dave. "Lifestyle and Illness Felled Honolulu Marathon Winner." *Honolulu Star-Bulletin,* December 4, 2006.

Reavis, Toni. "The Road to Go Pro: A New ARRA." *ToniReavis.co,* last modified September 9, 2013, accessed March 30, 2015, https://tonireavis.com/2013 /09/09/the-road-to-go-pro-a-new-arra/.

Reese, Robert James. "The Most Popular Marathons in the U.S. Over Time." *Runner's World,* March 11, 2013.

Rishe, Patrick. "Inflated Economic Impact Projections Complicated New York City Marathon Decision." *Forbes,* November 2, 2012.

Robb, Sharon. "Kenyan, Briton Love N.Y. Marathon." *The Sun-Sentinel,* November 2, 1987.

Robbins, Liz. "Running for Charity Fuels a Boom in Marathoning." *New York Times,* October 21, 2010.

Robinson, Roger. "Roger on Running: When Money Came into Running." *Runner's World,* August 17, 2011.

Rodgers. Ted. "150–200 Runners Poisoned." *Honolulu Star-Bulletin,* December 14, 1987, A-1.

Running USA. *2013 State of the Sport—Part III: US Race Trends,* Running USA, July 28, 2013, accessed March 21, 2015, http://www.runningusa.org/state-of -sport-2013-part-III.

———. *2014 State of the Sport—Part III: US Race Trend.,* Running USA, July 9, 2014, accessed March 21, 2015, http://www.runningusa.org/2014-state-of -the-sport-part-III-us-race-trends.

———. *2014 Annual Marathon Report.* Running USA, May 15, 2014, accessed March 21, 2015, http://www.runningusa.org/marathon-report-2015.

———. *Largest Races.* Running USA, 2014, accessed March 21, 2015, http:// www.runningusa.org/largest-races.

Scaff, Jack. "The H-3 Run; or the Trans-Koolau Trek; or Hei Hei o Halawa Ekolu; or a Large Footrace on H-3." *The Mid-Pacific Road Runner* 9, no. 2 (2010): 6–7, 15.

———. Personal interview, August 17, 2013.

———. "A True Fairy Tale: How John and I Invented Running." Unpublished essay, 1979.

———. *Your First Marathon: The Last World in Long-Distance Running.* Honolulu: Belknap, 2011.

Schroeder, Jo Ann, and John O. Wagner. Letter. *The Western Journal of Medicine* 129, no. 3 (1978): 241.

Skinny. "Drama on School Street." *Honolulu Record,* March 21, 1957, 4.

Sokei, Debbie. "Run Brought $86.8M to State." *Honolulu Advertiser,* April 6, 2004.

"Soldier King Will Run Forward in Tomorrow's Great Marathon." *Hawaiian Star,* December 9, 2011.

"Statistics 1973–2009." *Honolulu Marathon Association Press Packet 2009,* Honolulu Marathon Association, n.d.

Stewart, Phil. "The First Professional Road Race of the Modern Era." *Runner's World,* December 1, 1980.

"Surge in 2012 Honolulu Marathon Entries." *HawaiiNewsNow,* November 14, 2012.

Sylvester, James. "Marathon Boon to Isle Economy." *Honolulu Star-Bulletin,* November 8, 1984, D-1.

Tabar, Jerome. "Honolulu Marathon DVD Company Sues Rival." *Pacific Business News,* February 12, 2014.

"Tamanaha Favored in Marathon." *Honolulu Advertiser,* March 29, 1953, 2–1.

"Tamanaha Wins AAU Marathon Run." *Honolulu Advertiser,* March 30, 1953, 2–1.

Taniguchi, Rick. Personal interview, April 25, 2014.

Thielke, Thilo. "Running for Their Lives." *Salon,* February 14, 2008.

Ting, Yu Shing. "Barahal's 25th Honolulu Marathon." *MidWeek,* December 7, 2011.

"Tommy Kono." *Sports-Reference,* n.d.

"Travens Upset Winner in 151/2 Run; O'Brien Sheds Shoes, Finishes Fourth." *Honolulu Record,* February 13, 1958, 6.

Tsai, Michael. "Every Marathon Time Might Be Off." *Honolulu Advertiser,* December 14, 2007.

———. "Honolulu Marathon Feels Chicago's Heat." *Honolulu Advertiser,* October 10, 2007.

———. "Honolulu Marathon Generated More than $100M." *Honolulu Advertiser,* February 21, 2009.

———. "Honolulu Marathon Will Test for Drugs." *Honolulu Advertiser,* May 9, 2007.

———. "Honolulu Marathon Winner Disqualified." *Honolulu Advertiser,* June 25, 2008.

———. "Honolulu Marathon Women's Champion Suspended." *Honolulu Advertiser,* May 14, 2001.

———. "Honolulu Marathon Women's Winner Tests Positive." *Honolulu Advertiser* May 8, 2007.

———. "JAL Expected to Remain Marathon Sponsor." *Honolulu Advertiser,* January 26, 2010.

———. "Marathon Crosses Finish Line with Corrected Race Results." *Honolulu Advertiser,* February 28, 2007.

———. "The Marathon Man." *Island Scene Online,* October 1, 2003.

———. "Regulations Seen as Crushing Burden on Hawaii Businesses." *Honolulu Advertiser,* August 23, 2009.

———. "Runner Gets More than Second Wind." *Honolulu Advertiser,* December 13, 2006.

———. "Running the Marathon from behind the Scenes." *Honolulu Advertiser,* December 4, 2002.

———. "Scoring Errors Mar Hawaii Marathon." *Honolulu Advertiser,* December 11, 2007.

———. "Screw-up Causes Some Marathon Timing Errors." *Honolulu Advertiser,* February 28, 2008.

———. "Soaked Success." *Honolulu Advertiser,* December 10, 2007.

———. "Tourism Leads Economy." *Honolulu Advertiser,* August 16, 2009.

Tymn, Mike. "20 Years Old, Born to Run." *Honolulu Advertiser,* December 8, 1992, C-1.

———. "African Runners Might Surprise." *Honolulu Advertiser,* December 7, 1984, C-1.

———. "Aloha Run Could Exceed 12,000." *Honolulu Advertiser,* January 13, 1985, H-4.

———. "Barahal and Cross Team Together to Bring Out the Best." *Honolulu Advertiser,* December 2, 1986, C-3.

———. "Boss of the Honolulu Marathon." *Honolulu Advertiser,* December 5, 1982, D-14.

———. "Conversion Tables Help in Race against Time," *Honolulu Advertiser,* December 6, 2000.

———. "Déjà Vu: Hussein Triumphs in Record-Breaking Fashion." *Honolulu Advertiser,* December 8, 1986, C-1.

———. "Expectations Are Running Higher." *Honolulu Advertiser,* December 2, 1986, C-3.

———. "Great Strides." *The Honolulu Advertise,* December 12, 1997, D-1.

———. "Hussein Is First African to Win Honolulu Marathon." *Honolulu Advertiser,* December 9, 1985, C-1.

———. "Local Interest Declining in Honolulu Marathon." *Honolulu Advertiser,* December 16, 1986, F-3.

———. "Marathon Faces Many Challenges." *Honolulu Advertiser,* November 28, 1984, E-6.

———. "The Marathon Has Come a Long Way." *Honolulu Advertiser,* December 8, 1988, D-1.

———. "Marathon Has Come a Long Way Since Pheidippides." *Honolulu Advertiser,* December 9, 1999.

———. "Marathon Has Record Field, New Course." *Honolulu Advertiser,* December 12, 1992, D-1.

———. "Marathoners Ran for Keeps—and for $2,500 1st Prize." *Honolulu Advertiser,* December 18, 1985, C-3.

————. "Musyoki, Springs Win 10Ks, but Good Times Had by Many."
    Honolulu Advertiser, November 4, 1984, I-1.

————. "On Dec. 8, Marathoners Can't Take Money and Run." *Honolulu
    Advertiser,* November 6, 1985, D-3.

————. "Sore-Legged Postal Clerk Delivers Win." *Honolulu Advertiser,*
    December 14, 1992, C-1.

————. "What Started as a Jog Turned into a Full Sprint." *Honolulu Advertiser,*
    December 14, 1997, C-3.

————. "What the Marathon Lacks Is Marketing, Promotion." *Honolulu
    Advertiser,* January 1, 1987, F-3.

————. "World Class Field Here to Make a Run at $100,000." *Honolulu
    Advertiser,* November 2, 1984, D-6.

United States Census. *Honolulu Population by Decade.* Washington, DC: GPO,
    2013.

United States Department of Treasury, Internal Revenue Service. "2008 Return
    of Organization Exempt from Income Tax (Form 990): Honolulu Marathon
    Association." *990 Finder.* Foundation Center, 2008.

United States Department of Treasury, Internal Revenue Service. "2010 Return
    of Organization Exempt from Income Tax (Form 990): Honolulu Marathon
    Association." *990 Finder.* Foundation Center, 2010.

Viner, Brian. "There's a Good Reason Why Our Leaders Don't Jog." *The Indepen-
    dent,* August 3, 2000.

"Waialua Horse Wins Race in Heart-Breaking Sprint." *Pacific Commercial
    Advertiser,* November 8, 1909, 3. *Chroniclingamerica.*

Watanabe, June. "Finding Their Niche." *Honolulu Star-Bulletin,* April 24, 1996.

Watson, Nick, Stuart Weir, and Stephen Friend. "The Development of Muscular
    Christianity in Victorian Britain and Beyond." *Journal of Religion and
    Society* 7 (2005): 1–21.

"What a Difference a Year Can Make." *Spartanburg Herald-Journal,* June 26,
    1983, A-13.

"Wheelchair Race Is Called off; Tomorrow's Marathon in Doubt." *Honolulu
    Star-Bulletin,* December 12, 1987, A-1.

Wood, Hal. "The Rim Run." *Honolulu Advertiser,* December 14, 1974, D-2.

Wright, Walter. "Marathon Runner's Death Saddening, Puzzling." *Honolulu
    Advertiser,* December 10, 2002.

Wyatt, Jack. "Big Names Don't Run for Nothing." *Honolulu Star-Bulletin,*
    November 22, 1984, G-4.

————. "Chairborne Marathoners to Wheel It on Saturday." *Honolulu Star-
    Bulletin,* December 5, 1984, E-4.

————. "Fast Men's Field in Honolulu Marathon." *Honolulu Star-Bulletin,*
    November 29, 1985, C-3.

————. "Honolulu Marathon: Running Strong." *Honolulu Star-Bulletin,* April 14, 1988, D-1.

————. "Meet the Marathon's 'First Family.'" *Honolulu Star-Bulletin,* December 9, 1987, D-2.

————. "Numbers Down for Marathon." *Honolulu Star-Bulletin,* November 21, 1985, D-5.

————. "Run Festival's Pace: Slow, Fun." *Honolulu Star-Bulletin,* May 27, 1985, C-1.

————. "Running's the Only Thing for This Jack of Hearts." *Honolulu Star-Bulletin,* March 2, 1984, C-2.

————. "Runningest State in the Nation, Per Capita." *Honolulu Star-Bulletin,* February 17, 1987, Special Section, 8.

Yamanouchi, Kelly. "Skyrocketing Marathon Entries to Boost Tourism." *Honolulu Advertiser,* November 14, 2002.

Index

Page numbers for illustrations are in boldface.

ABOUT THE AUTHOR

Michael S. K. N. Tsai is an award-winning reporter and columnist for the *Honolulu Star-Advertiser* and an instructor of English at Kapiʻolani Community College. He has completed seventeen marathons and ultra-marathons, including eight Honolulu Marathons.